Preface & Contents

As the Luftwaffe's circumstances changed during the course of the Second World War, so too did its requirements for new aircraft. At the beginning of the war it needed close-support aircraft that could back up Germany's advancing ground troops. During the Battle of Britain it needed high-performance fighters and strategic bombers.

The invasion of the Soviet Union saw a renewed need for close-support aircraft and as British and American air raids over occupied Europe grew in frequency and potency, there was a need for heavily armed fast interceptors to combat them.

As each new need arose, the Reichsluftfahrtministerium (RLM – the German air ministry) attempted to meet it by issuing requirements and specifications to Germany's aircraft manufacturers – some of them private companies and others wholly owned by the state – who would then produce designs for aircraft intended to meet the specifications.

The competing designs were rigorously tested using mathematical formulas and existing performance data to work out whether they were likely to do what the manufacturers claimed. One or more might then be ordered as mock-ups which, if approved, might be followed by prototypes. Without the aid of computers it was a slow and laborious process but it was well understood that rushing it would likely result in potentially fatal errors.

The war spanned seven years for Germany and during that time the needs of the Luftwaffe regularly shifted and evolved – leaving the RLM struggling to keep up. The average development time for a new aircraft was five years, which meant that much of the war had to be fought with aircraft designed and built, or at least in development, before it started.

Many design competitions were held during those seven years and many competing designs were drafted. The aviation companies also carried out their own technical studies to anticipate requirements – producing still more designs. And Germany's multitude of aviation research centres contributed designs to solve particular problems.

Some of these potential aircraft went forward into development and then became prototypes but many more never did. Some of these have been written about over the last 75 years or so and some have not. Those who have written about these designs have often found it difficult to make sense of them and such was the case when I first happened upon them during the late 1990s.

There were so many strange designs with weird features and the information presented to accompany them was often contradictory. When I was in a position to carry out my own research I therefore resolved to go back to the original period documents to uncover the truth as far as it could be determined. The result has been the Luftwaffe: Secret series, of which this is the sixth volume. Once again, searching through captured German documents and Allied intelligence reports of the immediate postwar period has revealed many previously unknown designs and known designs about which previously unknown details can now be provided.

The reason why Gotha began to study rammers has become apparent, Nazi Germany's three-step process of investigating supersonic flight has been chronicled, the origin of the mysterious Bf 109 S has been uncovered and further insight can now be offered on the unfortunate story of the Me 210.

Within this publication you will find these and many other snippets based on original documents which, I hope, will interest you as much as they have me. ●

Author: Dan Sharp
Design and reprographics: atg-media.com
Publisher: Steve O'Hara
Advertising manager: Sue Keily, skeily@mortons.co.uk
Publishing director Dan Savage
Marketing manager: Charlotte Park
Commercial director: Nigel Hole

Published by: Mortons Media Group Ltd, Media Centre, Morton Way, Horncastle, Lincolnshire LN9 6JR. Tel. 01507 529529

Thanks to: Jens Baganz, Steven Coates, Zoltán Csombó, Calum Douglas, Carlos Alberto Henriques, Luca Landino, Paul Martell-Mead, Ronnie Olsthoorn, Alexander Power, J. Richard Smith, Greg Twiner, Stephen Walton and Tony Wilson

Printed by: William Gibbons and Sons, Wolverhampton

ISBN: 978-1-911639-06-0

OPPOSITE: Me 163 designer Alexander Lippisch's penultimate wartime project – the turbojet-powered delta-winged P 14.
IOWA STATE UNIVERSITY LIBRARY SPECIAL COLLECTIONS AND UNIVERSITY ARCHIVE

The German Gladiator

Arado E 216

Arado's Ar 68 was the Luftwaffe's first standard fighter, next to the Heinkel He 51, and the firm had big plans to improve it even as development was fast progressing on the aircraft that would soon supplant it – the Messerschmitt Bf 109.

The enforced nationalisation of Arado in 1935-36 came about even as the company was enjoying its greatest successes. Clean designs such as the E 208 monoplane trainer – soon to become the Ar 96 – showed what the firm was capable of while its aggressive-looking Ar 68 was becoming a symbol of Germany's reborn air force.

But the Ar 68 was never quite as capable as Arado's designers had hoped. Once the machine was in production, the company set about planning a series of subtle but substantial tweaks that would make the aircraft faster, more compact and above all far more versatile. These were embodied in the E 216 design.

The February 1936 brochure, which shows what looks like an Ar 68 carrying four bombs under its wings on the front cover, is entitled 'Mehrzwecke Einsitzer Weiterentwicklung der Ar 68' or 'Multipurpose single seater development of the Ar 68'.

The introduction says: "E 216 as improved Ar 68 is to be used as land and seaplane. For the latter purpose, the machine is built for catapult launch. The use is for day and night flight.

"The E 216 and Ar 68 have outwardly barely visible differences. The entire airframe has remained almost the same in its external dimensions. The fuselage front part is taken over unchanged from the Ar 68,

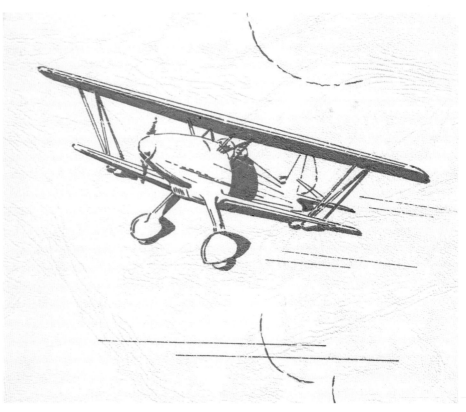

ABOVE: An artistic view of the E 216 from the front cover of the project brochure.

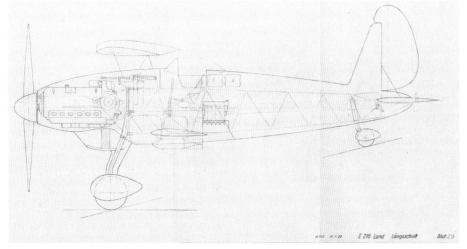

ABOVE: Side view of the E 216 in wheeled undercarriage configuration. The most noticeable differences between this design and the Ar 68 are the cockpit canopy and DB 600 C engine.

including the proven arrangement of control and fuselage equipment; the good visibility is thus maintained. However, the fuselage length of the E 216 is about 70cm shorter."

The E 216 measured 9m long and 3.5m tall in land plane configuration and 9.8m/4.5m as a floatplane. It had a wingspan of 11m and an overall wing area of 27.3m². By comparison, the Ar 68 in F configuration was 9.5m long, 3.3m tall and had the same wingspan.

The brochure continues: "The improvements sought relate essentially to the performance of the machine and, in connection therewith, to an aerodynamically more perfect design. For power, the engine DB 600 A or C engine.

"Fuselage: In the fuselage smoothness and the cleanest execution of all parts lying in the airstream is particularly valuable. Contributing to this are a reduction in fabric

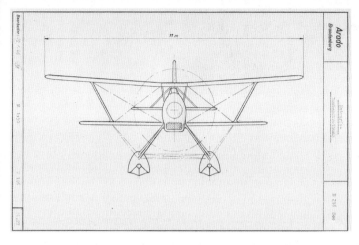

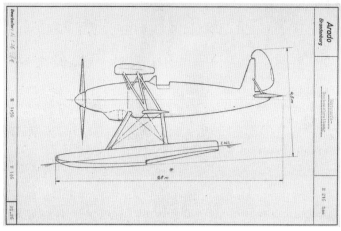

ABOVE & RIGHT: The floatplane version of the E 216. It would never be built but Arado would go on to produce a successful series of floatplanes in the Ar 196.

seams on the fuselage rear section and a closed streamlined cockpit cover for the land machine, or an aerodynamically favourable open seat covering for night and sea use.

"The aim is to use the same cockpit panelling whether the hinged hood is fitted or removed, so that the panelling remains unchanged. The fuselage frame is welded from steel tubes like a truss. It is designed either as a pure land fuselage with fittings only for suspension connection, or as a fuselage with connection fittings for the float struts, in which, however, the attachment of a chassis is possible. The double execution has a favourable effect on the weight of the land machine.

"The steel tube fuselage is surrounded by a wooden forming frame, over which the fabric skin is stretched. Where the fuselage panelling is with sheet metal, as on the fuselage front portion, the panels are made as large as possible, i.e. as little as possible subdivided in order to preserve the outermost shape of the hull.

"Landing gear: The chassis has internal compression rubber suspension and oil drainage on the front fuselage frame. The wheels, constructed from electron-metal, are braked and provided with low-pressure tyres 690-200. The spur is executed as a one-leg spur with internal compression rubber suspension. The tail wheel size is 350 x 135, also of electron-metal. The wheel covers are streamlined.

"Floats: The float gear consists of two single-stage floats in full metal design. They are hinged to the hull with 4 support struts. The plane between the struts is crossed with strands. The floats are connected by a rail with intermediate wire outcrossing.

"Tail unit: All-metal with one strut on each side towards the fin. The tailplane has a metal skeleton with torsion nose and fabric cover. Construction of the vertical stabiliser analogous to the same as the tailplane. Rudder with ground adjustable trim. The ailerons are attached to the upper wing. Frame with metal torsion nose, outer skin fabric covering."

For an aircraft that Arado presumably hoped would go into production during late 1936 or 1937 the E 216 seems to have had a lot of fabric-covered components at a time when most companies were in the process of switching to all-metal construction. Even the wings, while they had metal skins on their upper surfaces,

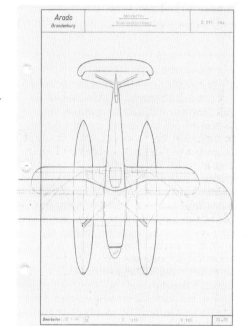

had fabric covered ends and undersides.

The land version of the aircraft was to be powered by the Daimler-Benz DB 600 C, with 770hp at sea level and 880hp at 4000m, while the floatplane version was to have the DB 600 A with 880hp at sea level. These were excellent choices at the time although the DB 600, which powered a number of Bf 109 prototypes, would be quickly superseded by the DB 601.

Armament consisted of two MG 17s built into the upper part of the front fuselage and firing through the propeller – similar to the arrangement envisioned by Messerschmitt for the Bf 109 A – and two more MG 17s in the wings which the Bf 109 at this time was actually unable to accommodate. It is unclear from the drawings appended to the brochure just whereabouts these would be fitted however.

A small bomb bay was to be installed in the centre of the fuselage behind the cockpit, capable of housing five 10kg bombs, and a further four 50kg bombs could be attached to the underside of the lower wings beneath the struts.

Unlike the E 208, the E 216 appears to have gone nowhere. Although the very last version of the Ar 68, the Ar 68 H, did get an enclosed cockpit, there never was a floatplane Ar 68. Had it been built, the E 216 would have ranked among the most sophisticated biplane fighters of its time – a sort of German Gloster Gladiator. ●

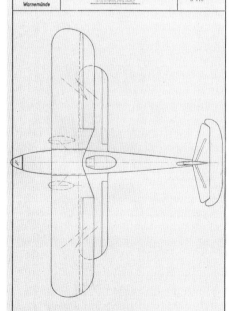

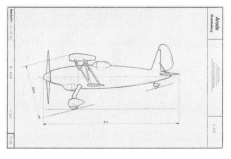

ABOVE & LEFT: Three views of the E 216 land version – one of the last non-maritime biplanes designed for service with the Luftwaffe.

Covering every angle

Arado E 500

The twin-turret twin-boom heavy fighter developed by Arado as the E 500 is relatively well known – but what's not so well known is just how close it came to being built.

What little has previously been published on the Arado E 500 comes primarily from a report compiled between late 1941 and early 1942 by company director Walter Blume. Entitled Arbeiten und Gedanken über die bewegliche Bewaffnung der Flugzeuge or 'Work and thoughts on the mobile armament of aircraft', this explains the company's efforts to develop effective defensive armament for aircraft starting in 1925.

Blume runs through various turret and gun position arrangements before discussing efforts to develop turrets for a flying wing aircraft design in 1935. In order to get the best defensive field of fire there would need to be two turrets each housing two 20mm Ikaria cannon - one on top of the wing in the centre and the other below, each with 360° visibility. Blume described these two turrets as effectively the upper and lower halves of a single ball turret. In each case, the cannon were side-by-side next to the gunner.

Unfortunately, a wing surface area of 165m² would have been needed to provide sufficient space for the turrets and the aircraft would weigh 22 tons – far too much even for a heavy fighter. The wings could have been made smaller by extending the wing centre section but it was still deemed too risky.

It was decided instead, therefore, to adopt a design where a central gondola was positioned between two tail booms. The basic arrangement was worked out by Dipl. Ing. Jürgensmann before work focused on how best to set up the turrets within the gondola.

According to Blume, one of the original guiding principles of the project was to make life

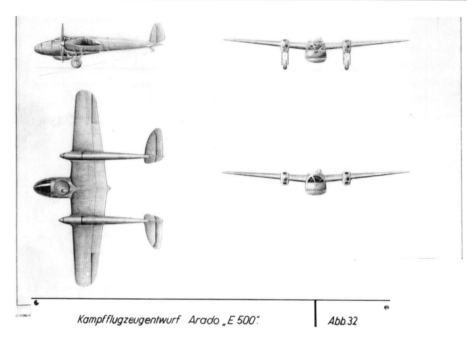

Kampfflugzeugentwurf Arado „E 500".   Abb.32

ABOVE: The completed design for the Arado E 500 heavy fighter.

as easy as possible for the gunners. With this in mind, a system was arranged which would automatically offer the gunner fresh magazines via a rotating drum. However, Blume wrote: "This system has to be considered very complicated according to today's terms. However, since 1000 rounds of ammunition were provided per mission, one could not be satisfied with manual operation."

Empty magazines would be disposed of using another complicated system involving

a chute and conveyor belt. But "before the completion of the overall design, the gun calibre size was reconsidered once again. The Rh.C 30-Automat [this may refer to the 3.7cm SK C/30 anti-aircraft gun] was, as already explained, apparently too big. The space- and weight-saving Ikaria cannon was doubted because of the ballistic properties in that they did not give the prospect of destroying the opponent before entering his own effective firing range."

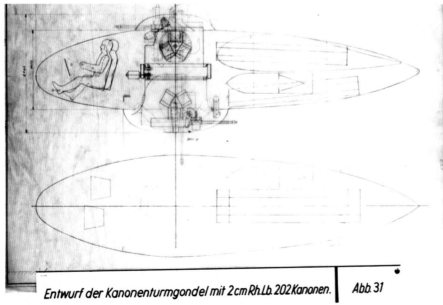

Entwurf der Kanonenturmgondel mit 2cm Rh.Lb.202 Kanonen.   Abb. 31

ABOVE: The interior of the E 500 showing all four crew positions.

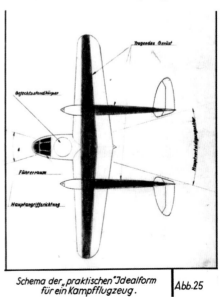

Schema der „praktischen" Jdealform
für ein Kampfflugzeug .   Abb.25

ABOVE: Arado's basic concept for the twin boom E 500.

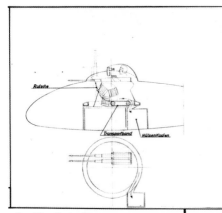

Vorschlag für den Abtransport der
Leerhülsen.   Abb. 30

ABOVE: Design for how the upper turret's guns might be fed automatically using cartridge drums.

As a result, the Ikaria cannon were replaced with 2cm Rh. Lb 202 cannon and the design, by Jürgensmann with Dipl. Ing. Wilhelm van Nes and Obering. Franz Meyer, was finally completed towards the end of 1935. Blume wrote: "Subsequently, the quietly drafted proposals were made public and an implementation was suggested. The RLM considered the novel ideas to be of great value in the long run and ordered the initiation of a development of the experimental aircraft."

Now Rheinmetall-Borsig gave direct input on the project, leading to a rearrangement of the cannon so that one was positioned on either side of the gunner. A turret mock-up was built by Rheinmetall-Borsig and then installed within a full scale mock-up of the E 500 built by Arado.

The first mention of the Arado E 500 in the RLM's Flugzeugentwicklungsprogramm is on July 1, 1936: "Arado Proj. E. 500" appears listed as a "Bomber-Zerstörer". The only note says: "There are no dates yet." The same listing appears on October 1, 1936, with the note "Eigenentwicklung Arado" or 'Arado in-house development' and again no dates are set.

On April 1, 1937, the E 500 appears once again with the note: "The aircraft will be released for construction after the mock-up has been inspected."

However, Blume wrote of the E 500's

ABOVE: The E 500 turret mock-up fitted to the full scale mock-up of the aircraft itself.

ongoing development: "While this was going on and during the period that followed, the discussion about whether to develop lightly armed fast bombers and heavily armed fighter planes reached its heights in wide circles of aircraft development and the Luftwaffe.

"Due to the comparison of excellent high speed aircraft of the time with not yet fully developed heavy fighters the pendulum swung in favour of the lightly armed fast bombers. Unfortunately, the work in the direction of the heavily armed combat aircraft came to a standstill. The development was stopped."

It was by no means the end of the road for Arado's work on turret defences however – with refined systems appearing on both the E 340 design, a contender for the Bomber B competition, and the Ar 240. ●

ABOVE: Mock-up of the E 500's upper turret with Rheinmetall Lb. 202 cannon.

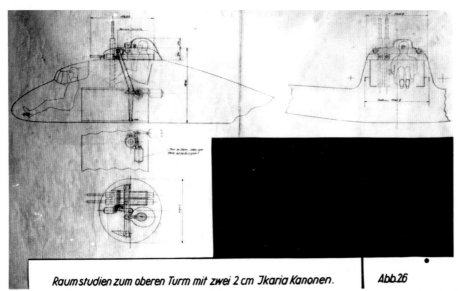

Raumstudien zum oberen Turm mit zwei 2 cm Jkaria Kanonen.   Abb.26

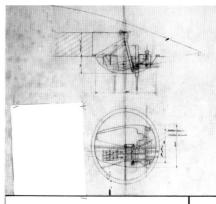

Raumstudien zum unteren Turm mit zwei 2cm Jkaria Kanonen.   Abb 27

ABOVE & LEFT: Upper and lower turret designs for the central gondola. On a number of the images included with Blume's original report, a section has been deliberately obscured for reasons unknown.

'The Ar 196 on steroids'

Arado E 380

The Ar 196 floatplane became the standard aircraft of the Kriegsmarine in 1939 but by 1942 it was obsolete. It naturally fell to Arado to design a potential replacement fitted with the latest engines, weaponry and armour protection...

The main problem facing the German navy in operating the Ar 196 by 1942 was its increasing vulnerability to attack. Its 947hp BMW 132 K engine gave it a top speed of 320km/h, it lacked armour and its armament consisted of two outdated MG FF 20mm cannon and a single MG 17 firing forward plus a single MG 15 to the rear.

In seeking to address each of these problems, Arado came up with a total of seven different designs – the Argus As 402 powered E 380-1 and E 380-1a, the BMW 323 R-2 powered E 380-2 and E 380-2a, and the BMW 801 A powered E 380-3, E 380-3a and E 380-3b.

The difference between each of the pairs was that the 'a' models only had the same equipment as the standard Ar 196, making them smaller and lighter with better range. The others had extra armour and improved equipment, with the exception of the E 380-3b, also powered by a BMW 801 A, which was a separate design.

The essential features of these designs were outlined in a relatively brief and undated brochure – although the date can be approximated to mid-November 1942 since the appended drawings are dated between October 6 and November 14, 1942.

The introduction cuts straight to the chase: "Due to the obsolescence of the engine BMW 132 K, the MG FF and the swivel arm mount a replacement of the Ar 196 is necessary. The present designs are a further

development of the Ar 196 and show the motors: As 402 with 950 PS starting power, BMW 323 R2 with 1000 PS starting power and BMW 801 A with 1560 PS starting power.

"The redesign sought to improve the speed, range, armament and wingline stability of the Ar 196. Furthermore, armour and fuel tank protection should be provided. In order to clarify the impact of these improvements on the weight and performance of the aircraft, two designs were developed for each engine, which are valid with and without reinforced equipment, thus giving the upper and lower limits in weight. In order to allow a perfect comparison, wings and tail units are adapted to the resulting different flight weights.

"In the lighter aircraft, therefore, only the outgoing weapons are replaced and wing strength increased for the seemingly necessary mass. Between the two weight limits the final form may be found, with weight-altering changes and the resulting loss of performance carefully weighed.

"In addition to the above designs, a proposal was made with the engine BMW 801 A, which fulfils all wishes regarding armament, armour and fuel tank protection, but the flight distance was limited to 800km and the surface load is higher than that of the other designs. This results in a relatively small, handy aircraft, as it is necessary for on-board use."

This latter design was the Arado E 380-3b. A handful of further points are made by the brochure, including the fact that the old gun mounting used for the open rear cockpit of the Ar 196 was no longer being manufactured – so "the designs show in contrast to the Ar 196 a rear closed hood with lens mount.

"The floats are each connected with a single leg to the wing and contain as before the fuel tanks. The fuselage is made of light-alloy sheet metal, which will make the compass more accurate than what was possible in the steel tube fuselage of the Ar 196. The dimensions of the designs with folded structure are included in the list."

All of the E 380s had the same basic armament – two forward-firing MG 151/20 cannon and a rear-firing MG 131 J. The 'heavy' E 380-1, -2, -3 and -3b had 60mm armour at the front and a 15mm armoured bulkhead to the rear, which the others lacked. The 'heavy' designs could also carry either two 140kg depth charges, one 250kg bomb or four 50kg bombs. Bomb load for the 'light' designs was restricted to just two

BELOW: The Arado E 380-1 with As 402, dated October 25, 1942, from drawing number 380-13. Though its inline engine, single-strut floats, enclosed rear cockpit and gullwings made it look quite different it was actually the closest of the E 380s to the Ar 196 in performance.

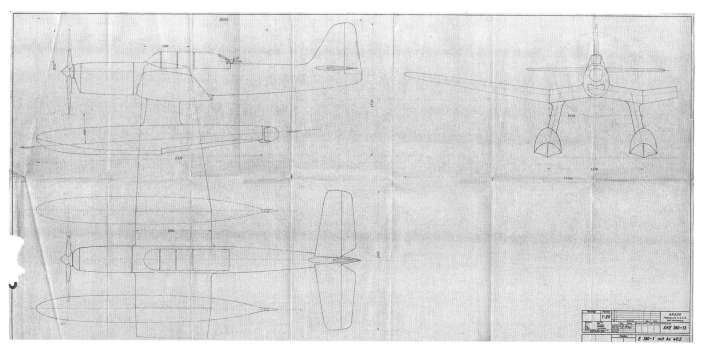

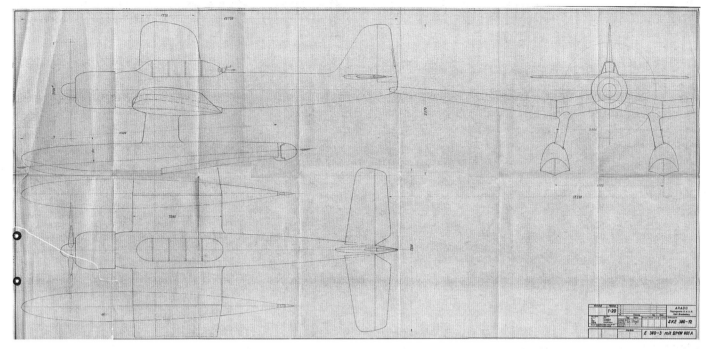

ABOVE: Big and beefy, the E 380-3 was a large aircraft at 13.73m long and with a wingspan of 16.2m as shown here (the text report gives the figures as 13.75m and 16m respectively). That would make it nearly 3m longer than the Ar 196 and with a span 3.6m wider. Even the high-altitude Ta 152 H-1 only had a wingspan of 14.44m. Dated October 6, 1942, this is the earliest known E 380 design.

50kg bombs. Range for every design except the 800km E 380-3b was 1000km.

The rest of the brochure is all stats. The Ar 196 A-3 measured 10.96m long with a wingspan of 12.44m and a wing area of 28.3m². All of the other designs, even the 'light' types, were bigger – some much more so.

E 380-1, -2 and -3 had wingspans of 14.1m, 14.4m and 16m respectively and were 12.5m, 12.3m and 13.75m long. The E 380-1a, -2a and -3a's wingspans were 13.55m, 13.85m and 15.3m, while their lengths were 12.2m, 12.05m and 13.4m. The E 380-3b had a 14.5m wingspan and was 12.2m long. Oddly, some of these numbers differed slightly from what appears on the drawings appended to the report.

Top speeds were 337km/h for the E 380-1, 328km/h for the E 380-2 and a respectable 386km/h in the E 380-3. The 'light' types were even better with 346km/h, 340km/h and 402km/h respectively. Best of all was the E 380-3b with 404km/h.

Unfortunately for Arado, by the end of 1942 the needs of the German navy were coming a distant second to those of the Luftwaffe and the E 380 was not taken forward, though it's clear that the E 380-3b was the company's preferred choice. The Ar 196 was left to soldier on. ●

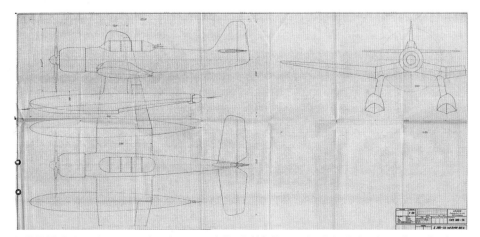

ABOVE: An also-ran design, the E 380-2 with BMW 323 R-2 was unusual only in having vertical struts for its floats. The drawing is dated November 4, 1942.

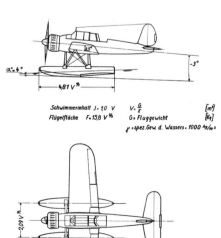

ABOVE: The Ar 196 from an Arado report on floats for comparison.

ABOVE: Well-armed, armoured and compact, the E 380-3b was Arado's choice to replace the Ar 196, even though its range was consequently inferior to that of the other E 380s. The drawing date is November 14, 1942, making it the last E 380 design.

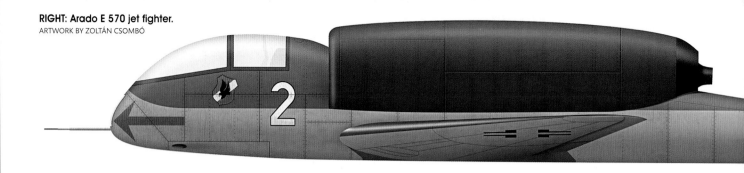

RIGHT: Arado E 570 jet fighter.
ARTWORK BY ZOLTÁN CSOMBÓ

From Stuka to jet fighter

Arado E 570

Serious efforts to build a direct replacement for the Junkers Ju 87 dive-bomber began towards the end of 1942 but it was soon suggested that the Focke-Wulf Fw 190 might fulfil the same role without the need for a new aircraft. Nevertheless, Arado began work on its 'Jabo' – the E 570.

The RLM sent Arado a set of fairly exacting specifications for a single seat 'Nahkampfflugzeug' or 'close support bomber' on February 18, 1943. This would appear to be the specification for a single-seat Junkers Ju 87 replacement – similar to what Blohm & Voss was already working on in the form of the P 171 (see p14-15).

The aircraft in question had to have "engine power about 2000hp and because of toughness and armour weight-saving air-cooled engines are preferable". The pilot had to have at least the same visibility as that available from the pilot's seat of the Ju 87, plus a cockpit floor sighting window similar to that of the Ju 87.

Standard weaponry was to be two fixed forward-firing MG 151/20s and two fixed rearward-firing MG 131s with options to fit either two or three MK 103s, two 3.7cm Flak 18s or a single 7.5cm Pak 40 as equipment packs.

Bomb load was to be a single 500kg or 1000kg or three to four 250kg bombs or the equivalent load in other munitions. The attachment of the bombs "must be carried out in the most aerodynamic possible for to give maximum speed". Cockpit armour was to protect against 2cm rounds from the front, rear and underneath, plus protection of the engine's "sensitive parts (oil sump, pipes etc.)".

Top speed was to be "not below 500km/h"

and the aircraft had to be capable of flying from "field aerodromes". Dive speed with extended brakes was to be 550km/h. Range was 1000km with the option to fit drop tanks for a further 400km. The aircraft had to have the "best flight characteristics and rudder effects. Good control rudders in a dive, without automatic systems. The aircraft must also be suitable for night flight."

And on top of all that, the aircraft had to offer "low maintenance, best wear resistance, best accessibility although access to electrical and hydraulic system is to be limited to the unavoidable degree. The simplest structure of all actuation

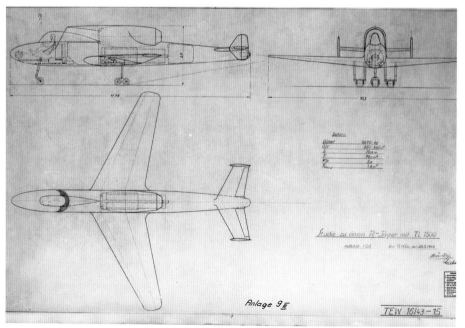

ABOVE: Arado's K-Jäger fighter design of March 20, 1943, bears a remarkable resemblance to the E 570 sketch of 10 days earlier.

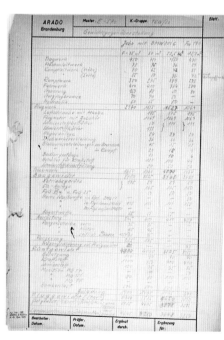

ABOVE: Table of weights for Arado's BMW 801 C powered version of its fighter-bomber design.

mechanisms. The production effort in mass production must not exceed 3000 hours under any circumstances".

After studying the Ju 87, the Hs 123, the Douglas DB 19 (apparently the Douglas SBD Dauntless, based on the stats Arado gives for it) and the Fw 190, Arado began project E 570 for a 'Jabo mit BMW 801 C'. Three different sizes were projected for this aircraft, a wing area of either 35m², 30m² or 22.5m² and each had two MG 151s, one in each inner wing.

But on April 15, 1943, Arado sent the RLM a letter which said: "The work for a single-seat close support aircraft according to the guidelines mentioned in the above letter of February 18 was started in our design office and we searched for favourable versions. However, this had to be cancelled because the capacity in the design office is not sufficient to carry on this work in addition to the project of the multirole transporter and the Ar 234 B, as well as the design of the Ar 396 and Ar 432. So, to our great regret, we need to refrain from further work, but we do not want to offer nothing. In short, here are the lines of thought that we consider appropriate to solve the problem.

"Since the visual demand in a single-engine normal form with air-cooled radial engine results in very high fuselage superstructures, which contradicts the wishes for great speed, the following routes were investigated: a) Retractable cockpit. As a result, good forward visibility is created in the dive down and at the same time an increased drag, while in the retracted state the fuselage cross-section can be kept small.

"b) Engine behind the pilot's cockpit. As a result, very good visibility was achieved for small fuselage cross-sections. The disadvantage of this arrangement is that probably only one liquid-cooled motor can be installed. c) Jet engine. The engine is a jet-unit, which is mounted in aerodynamically good shape to the fuselage, whereby the pilot's space can be formed as full vision cockpit. Unfortunately, with these preliminary studies, we had to conclude the work for reasons mentioned above."

The letter states that three sketches are appended showing the three designs but these are missing. However, all the information known about the E 570 is contained in a single folder marked 'Jabo' and among the various notes is rough sketch showing what appears to be the 'c) Jet engine' design. It is a low-wing tail-sitter aircraft with twin-fin tail and the turbojet positioned on its back – allowing the inclusion of a 'full vision cockpit' similar to

that of the Ar 240 at the front.

Beneath this drawing is an even sketchier outline showing an aircraft with an air-cooled radial piston engine on its nose and a very low cockpit canopy – presumably the 'a)' design.

On the other side of the same sheet of Arado notepaper, written in pencil, is a list of weights for a Jäger mit Heinkel TL or 'fighter with Heinkel jet'. The list is dated March 10, 1943. Just 10 days later, Arado would produce a drawing of a mixed propulsion jet and rocket fighter it called the K-Jäger or Kombinations-Jäger which bore a striking similarity to the design produced for the E 570 project (see Luftwaffe: Secret Bombers of the Third

Reich p72-73 for more information on the K-Jäger).

It would seem that Arado's designers got diverted into drawing jet fighters when they were supposed to be working on a ground-attack aircraft – before a lack of capacity forced them to stop doing either. The K-Jäger of March 20 is one of three single seat fighter designs included in a report of August 11, 1943, concerning the development of fast two-seaters. One of the others, the pure rocket-propelled R-Jäger, was drawn up on March 18 but the third, a pure turbojet design, was not committed to paper until June 3, 1943 – suggesting that there was indeed a genuine gap in the designers' work between March and June. ●

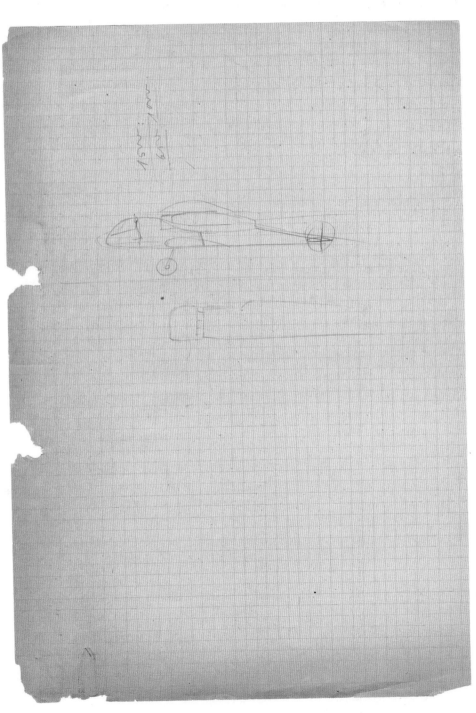

ABOVE: The tail-sitter jet aircraft sketch included in the Arado E 570 file of papers. Its appearance seems to match a description given in a letter to the RLM of a single-jet single-seat dive-bomber designed as a potential replacement for the Junkers Ju 87. A table of weights for a 'fighter with Heinkel jet' dated March 10, 1943, appears on the opposite side of the sheet.

Follow the leader

AVA Air-Train

One of the more unusual concepts worked on by the Aerodynamische Versuchsanstalt (AVA) at Göttingen during the war involved a single aircraft carrying nothing but powerful regeneration gas turbine engines and its crew, hauling a chain of enormous flying wing gliders behind it. This remarkable idea was dubbed the 'air-train' by its creator K. Mende.

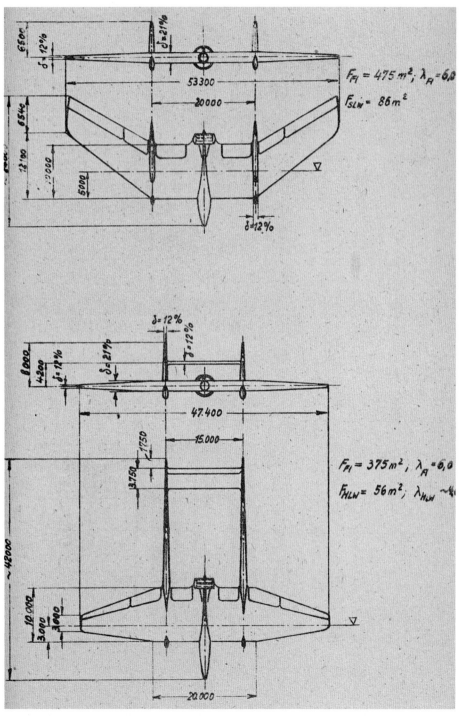

ABOVE: The regenerator gas turbine-powered flying wing (top) and 'normal' aircraft designs developed by K. Mende at the AVA, Göttingen. Each is driven by a pusher prop within a circular duct. Mende worked on these for potential use by the Luftwaffe.

Mende's work focused specifically on what was possible with a regeneration gas turbine (RGT) turboprop – a jet engine driving a propeller where a heat exchanger is used to extract the heat from exhaust gas, which is then used to pre-heat the compressed air entering the engine's combustion chamber, improving combustion efficiency and thereby saving fuel.

He initially worked on military designs for a large twin boom RGT-powered aeroplane, which he referred to as the 'normal aircraft', and a similarly powered flying wing. In both cases, he believed that a pusher prop layout was best, and that the propeller itself should be shrouded in a duct which would allow the necessary blade length to be reduced. He then moved on to the air-train.

His ideas might have been lost to history had it not been for British efforts immediately after the war's end in Europe collectively known as Operation Surgeon. According to a paper entitled 'Ludwig Prandtl and His Kaiser-Wilhelm-Institut' by Austrian physicist Klaus Oswatitsch, who worked at the institute from 1938 to 1942: "Early in April 1945 American troops came to Göttingen, and some weeks later we belonged to the British occupation zone, about 10km off the Russian zone.

"For almost two years the British Ministry of Supply employed many KWI and AVA scientists for a special task. With Betz as editor, a review of all work done in Germany during the war in the field of aero- and hydrodynamics was written down on 7000 typed pages in German English. These were known as the Göttingen monographs of 1945/46. A similar shorter review was done at the same time for the FIAT review of German sciences in the years 1939-46. These reviews were useful and enlightening – at least for the writers. Otherwise, a response did not seem to be forthcoming."

The incredibly long-winded title of Mende's report was 'The Influence of the Mutual Relations Between Structure and Power Plant on the Design of the Structure; the Flying Performance and the Layout of the Regeneration Gas-turbine Power Plant' and it appears as part of AVA Monographs Reports and Translations No. 1019.

Critical to his proposals was the fuel efficiency of the RGT. A reduction in the fuel load required for a given mission would also result in less weight being required for fuel containers and armour protection for those containers – freeing up more weight for other purposes.

It would appear that Mende was not available to transcribe his own work, since he is written about in the third person and the past tense when the monograph notes: "First in principle a military aeroplane is presupposed, since the highest weight savings are to be expected as well as a practically interesting maximum flight range with its limiting conditions with respect to constant load, cruising speed etc.

"The author determined this upper limit by aid of a constructed Longest Distance Reconnaissance Aeroplane provided with piston engines considering in detail the alteration of the structure e.g. for the case of employing regenerator gas turbine power plants at equal wing loading in landing as that of the piston engine aeroplane.

"He found fuel savings of 55% and a reduction of landing weight of 27%."

Mende further theorised that the RGT would actually only weigh about 46% as much as a piston engine, resulting in yet more structural savings. Next he looked at the application of the RGT to "large aeroplanes" – dividing these up into his 'normal aircraft' and flying wings.

The monograph says: "Up to now this flying wing was little fit as a multi-engined large aeroplane owing to its insufficient directional stability, which is particularly disadvantageous in single-engined flight, unless the designer puts up with output from the engine to the propeller via a shaft or the like.

"It must be added as an aggravation that with faster engines the necessary position of the centre of gravity in consequence of the large proportion of the power plant in the total weight can be chosen satisfactorily only with greater or smaller aerodynamic deficiencies.

"Here the turbine power plant, which offers the possibility of concentrating large energies in one unit, seems fit to fill a considerable gap." Mende worked out the minimum size of an aircraft needed to accommodate passengers in the wing – for both the flying wing and the twin boom type – and presumed that a turboprop powerplant producing 10,000 to 20,000hp would be available to propel them which was "the upper limit of a power plant unit that may be reached which is practically reasonable for the time being".

The monograph goes on: "Nevertheless the possibility of uniting such large outputs in one power plant, which makes possible the design of flying wings as large aeroplanes in a simple way, suggests a further design which is likewise discussed in the above paper, i.e. the so-called 'air-train'.

"This means a chain of aeroplanes where the whole propulsive power plant is accommodated in one 'tractor plane'. This so-called 'tractor plane' is only a power plant carrier apart from the crew. Disposable load and fuel are accommodated in one or several trailer planes. Each trailer is designed like the wing of a normal aeroplane and connected with the tractor or the preceding trailer by two poles.

"Considering the large output, extraordinary with respect to the size of the tractor plane and with respect to the single-engined flight, the central arrangement of the power plant is absolutely necessary. Therefore

the result is a double fuselage aeroplane. Since a propeller in consequence of its extremely large diameter, the aircraft would require an extremely high undercarriage, perhaps moreover a cranked wing or the like. The only possibility left is to use a ducted propeller whose diameter is only about 60% of that of the ordinary propeller and whose duct allows a reasonable aerodynamic and static mounting of the power plant to the wing unit.

"The ducted propeller is favourable for all large aeroplanes with a central propulsion, since its advantages are a smaller diameter, normal number of revolutions, smaller moving masses, possibility of control without reduction of static thrust."

The monograph outlines the advantages that Mende's wartime research might now have for civil aviation: "The economic heights of flight [10km or 32,808ft] and therefore of the layout of the turbine power plant which are of special interest in peace-time aviation result in a mean range of about 3000 miles."

Mende's work must have been more than usually academic in nature, particularly if he wasn't writing it himself, since the monograph is rather rambling and unfocused. It does eventually get around to discussing the air-train's RGT powerplant though.

"In the development of power plants it seems quite useful to subdivide the power plant into two groups: compressor + heat exchanger + compression turbine on the one side and power turbine + propeller on the other side. This subdivision guarantees the best aerodynamic arrangement of the power plant at the airframe since then an undisturbed inflow at the compressor and the application of pusher propeller will be possible. Moreover the subdivision alone may in many cases of aeroplane design be a desirable expedient to govern the position of the centre of gravity."

The engines would have a maximum diameter of 2m or 2.5m at the most, and while the normal and flying wing type aircraft would be best fitted with a ducted propeller, this was absolutely essential for the air-train.

Mende had also studied the possibilities for powering the RGT using solid fuel and the potential of small RGT units for powering "unmanned mail-planes" but it would appear that none of his ideas were adopted for production. It is unknown whether he actually worked with any of the large aircraft manufacturers – although a 'Dipl.-Ing. Mende' is believed to have worked on the P 1079, later known as the Me 328, at Messerschmitt during the early years of the war. ●

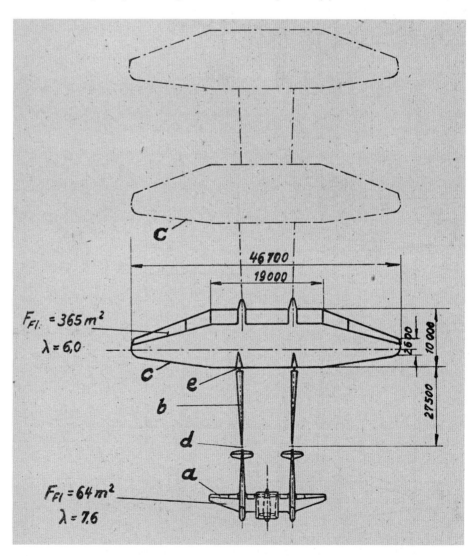

ABOVE: The bizarre air-train concept worked on by Mende. The twin boom 'tractor' aircraft at the bottom of the picture would have carried nothing but crew and engines – its fuel being drawn from its huge flying wing 'trailers', which could also carry passengers and cargo. Its entire centre section appears to be a huge ducted propeller with the engines and crew presumably being housed in the booms.

Asymmetrical attacker

Blohm & Voss P 171

Having had a radical three-engined fast bomber dismissed from the Schnellstbomber competition before it even reached the final round, Blohm & Voss reimagined the design as a dive-bomber with just two engines – making it look even more bizarre.

Outlined in a brochure dated circa September 23, 1942, the Blohm & Voss P 170 was designed for the Schnellstbomber competition (see pages 84-87 for more detail on this pivotal design contest which would eventually produce the Dornier Do 335).

The Schnellstbomber concept was to create a bomber so fast it could not be intercepted by high-performance enemy fighters and to this end the P 170 was to be built like an outlandish racing machine. Its long slender fuselage had a single BMW 801 D or E piston engine at the front and the aircraft's cockpit, housing two crew, right at the back. Streamlined nacelles, each containing another BMW 801, were attached to the ends of its straight wings.

Its tailplanes were attached to the sides of the cockpit and rather than a single central fin it had a small fin on the end of each wingtip nacelle. The aircraft's bomb payload was to be carried externally under its wings.

Unfortunately for Blohm & Voss it was decided at a meeting on November 13, 1942, that a two-engine, single seater configuration was preferred – effectively killing the P 170 outright. Undeterred, the company simply amended the design to create a two-engine single seater which it called the P 171. In a letter to the RLM on December 5, 1942, Blohm & Voss chief designer Richard Vogt wrote: "We deliver in triplicate details of the fast bomber project P 171, each with a weight list and a performance sheet. Following a request of your development department, we limited ourselves to the use of two BMW 801 engines in this project.

"In the battle for every last square metre of surface, the solution to a single fuselage looks particularly advantageous. This will then immediately impact also in the sense of a manufacturing pre-simplification and reduce the otherwise inevitable difficulties of the two fuselage construction. In order to save further surface and reduce drag we have placed the cockpit back in front of the tail unit.

"Wind tunnel testing has shown that this decreases the amount of drag generated. In conjunction with a so-housed pilot, we have designed the project as an extremely high-wing aircraft and, as the overview drawing shows, the improved visibility in flight and landing was still quite useful. An extreme high-winger,

however, is known to be the easiest way of reducing drag with the fuselage (for example, it is used for the engine installation of the de Havilland Mosquito). The combined result of all these attacks on the overall drag resistance is a maximum speed of 780km/h at 5km with full bomb load. The fuel is stored in the wing mid-section between the two engines."

The P 171 was to have a steel skin about 4mm thick and its outer wings would eventually be made of wood. Vogt also pointed out that the new fuselage and nacelle arrangement had "brought a new, in our opinion crucial benefit. We are now able to carry two 500kg bombs internally without additional drag resistance and structural complications, doubling the relevant efficiency".

Between December 5 and December 30, the P 171's role was changed from fast bomber to dive-bomber. A note 'concerning project P 171' from the latter date indicates that Blohm & Voss had been urged to fit a pair of MK 103 cannon to the aircraft with 200 rounds of ammunition if possible

R L M		Flugzeugtypenblatt		Baumuster:
Bildskizze				Maßstab: 1:200

Bauwaise: Stahl - Leichtmetall	Leergewicht:	4360 kg	Motoranlage	3 BMW 801E
Bespannung: 2 Mann	Fluggewicht:	13300 kg	Nennleistung	3×2100 PS
Verwendungszweck: Schnellbomber	Fläche m²:	44 m²	Luftschraube	6 Bl.
Entwurf: P 170.01	Flugzeugname:		Stammfirma: Blohm & Voss
	Spricht: 4k	Insgesamt:		

ABOVE: The three-engined P 170 of late September 1942, from which the P 171 of December 1942 was derived. The requirements of the Schnellstbomber competition called for just two engines and a single seat.

and was now attempting "to obtain the latest documents about the 103 from Rheinmetall-Borsig".

A letter of January 5, 1943, sent from Blohm & Voss's Hamburg headquarters to the company's Berlin office, and headed 'Subject: Stuka P 171', states: "Enclosed I send you the draft of the new guidelines for a single-seat dive bomber of 21.12.42, which today Czolbe handed over to me in advance. The draft is not yet signed, but is based on the recent discussions and our draft P 171.

"Two MG 131 with 400 rounds are fitted instead of an MG 151 as defence weapons. The number of shots for the two equipped MK 103 cannon is given as 150. Henschel will have sent you the construction documents for the installation of a MK 103 with 90 rounds. At Henschel the Hs 129 C has the installation of 2 MK 103, each with 120 rounds. As soon as the work is completed, Mr Nicolaus will also make it available to us.

"Since it will be difficult to accommodate 120 rounds per cannon, the value should be used as a guide. The installation of the MK 103 has to be done parallel to the aircraft axis, because in the attack against armoured vehicles they are targeted by the aircraft. For the attack on marching columns, there is a ready-to-install aggregate of 5 MG 181, which can be attached to the bomb rack at 10° inclination. This unit has long been used at the front in various fighter aircraft.

"An important point that has not yet been put up for discussion is the loading on the railway. I have pointed this out to Mr Czolbe because there is nothing in the directives. The Ju 87 and the fighter can be transported by rail. I cannot imagine that one renounces this requirement, not even with regard to the repair. This will probably mean a significant interference with the design.

"Mr Czolbe would like to have the performance, with and without bombs, of the aircraft as soon as possible, because they should be compared to the Fw 190 before the project is submitted to the Secretary of State.

"After the performance has been increased to 500km/h on the ground, it has now been put over apparently for discussion, whether the fighters can take over the tasks of this new Stuka yet. The biggest disadvantage of the fighter, which would be heavily overloaded for the Stuka

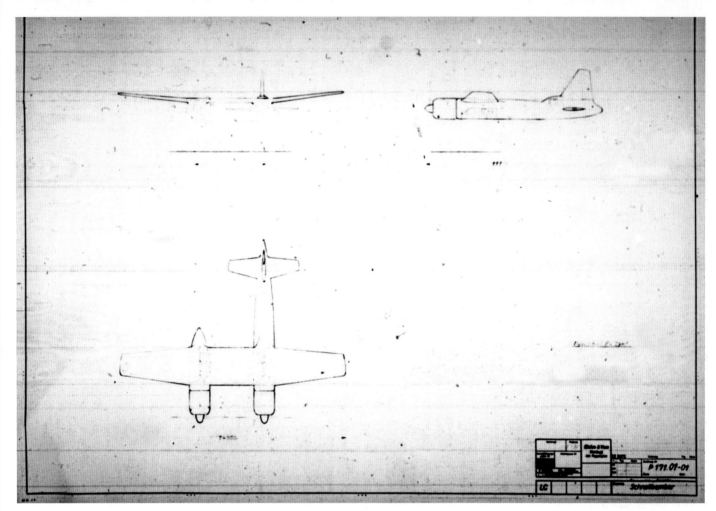

purpose, is the bad take-off characteristics. After speed, the second and most important point is the start and landing characteristics of the type, because the Stuka should be able to be used on airfields of all kinds.

"Mr Malz had reservations about the narrowness of the crew compartment, based on that of the Fw 190; this is described as too narrow by almost all front-line units. This question can only be clarified definitively on the mock-up."

A memo sent to Vogt by Walter at the B&V Berlin office on January 12, 1943, states: "P 171. The mock-up inspection cannot take place this week because the gentlemen from Rechlin cannot come and E 2 [the RLM's E-2 development office] does not want to undertake the sightseeing without Rechlin. A new date is now scheduled for Wednesday 20.1.1943. Coming from the RLM: Malz, Czolbe and Wahl. From Rechlin: Boetcher, Tonnes and Hildenbrandt. From the Luftwaffe: the new general of the bomber pilots Oberstleutnant Pelz, Captain Blasig and Captain Hermann. Oberstleutnant Siegel is not yet back, but the inspector comes by himself."

A meeting of the RLM's development committee was held on April 6, 1943, to discuss the two projects competing to

ABOVE: This badly faded drawing is the only known image of the asymmetrical Blohm & Voss P 171 Stuka.

replace the Junkers Ju 87 – the original piston-engined Junkers Ju 287 presented by Heinrich Hertel and a Blohm & Voss project presented by Richard Vogt. However, the B&V project is described as an asymmetrical single engine two-seater – presumably the P 176 or P 177. The P 171 had already fallen by the wayside because it did not meet the requirements of the 'Nahkampfflugzeug' specifications sent out to aircraft companies in February 1943 (see Arado E 570 on p10-11). ●

BLOHM & VOSS P 175

The tiny P 175 Bordjäger or parasite aircraft was a near contemporary of the P 171. It had a wingspan of just 6.2m, compared for example to the Me 163 B's 9.3m, a wing area of only 6m² and no undercarriage. Its single Jumo turbojet was mounted ventrally, it had a twin-fin tail, a cockpit canopy that slid rearwards, rather than opening outwards, and a highly unusual split spike device on its nose – presumably for hooking onto its host aircraft.

The only known drawing of it is dated March 22, 1943 – which coincides with a series of meetings to discuss whether or not to build the Luftwaffe a new long-range maritime reconnaissance aircraft. Blohm & Voss had four aircraft designs involved in this process. Under the heading of 'Atlantik-Aufklärer', a meeting on March 22 itself

discussed and compared the Fw 200, Ju 290, BV 222 and 238, Me 264 and Ju 390.

By the meeting on April 27, 1943, the heading had changed to 'Atlantik-Aufklärer / Fernkampfflugzeug' and the only Blohm & Voss project in contention was the BV 250 – the wheeled undercarriage version of the BV 238 flying boat. B&V documents from this period show that a small-fuselage version of the BV 250, the P 173, was also being heavily worked on during this time.

No direct evidence is known to exist linking the P 175 to any of these projects, yet the timing fits. It would appear that the P 175 was intended to be carried on the back of or underneath a BV 238 or BV 250. But like many B&V projects it was short-lived and went no further.

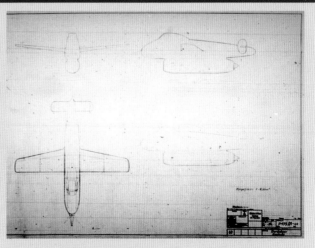

Blohm & Voss P 175

March 1943

Artwork by Luca Landino

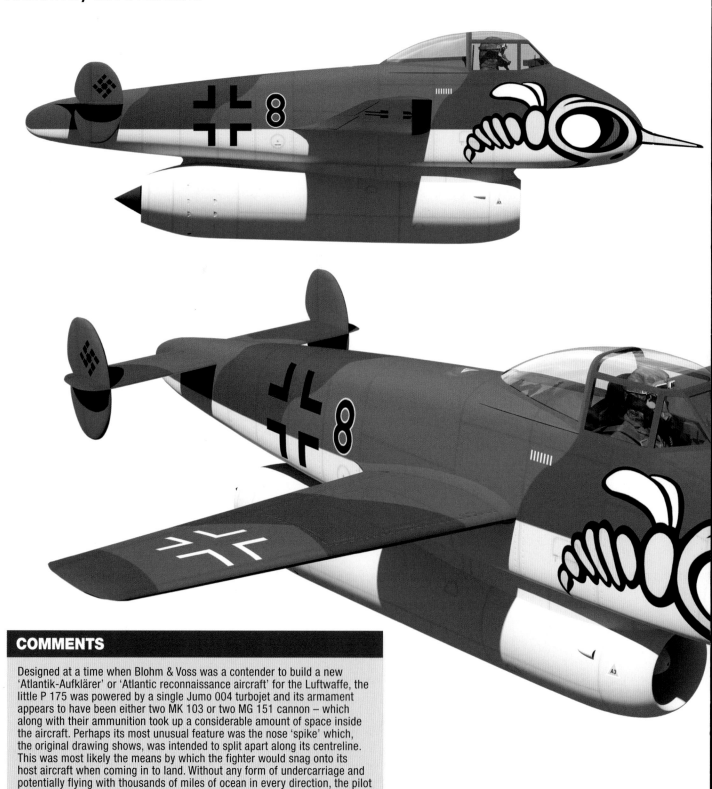

COMMENTS

Designed at a time when Blohm & Voss was a contender to build a new 'Atlantik-Aufklärer' or 'Atlantic reconnaissance aircraft' for the Luftwaffe, the little P 175 was powered by a single Jumo 004 turbojet and its armament appears to have been either two MK 103 or two MG 151 cannon – which along with their ammunition took up a considerable amount of space inside the aircraft. Perhaps its most unusual feature was the nose 'spike' which, the original drawing shows, was intended to split apart along its centreline. This was most likely the means by which the fighter would snag onto its host aircraft when coming in to land. Without any form of undercarriage and potentially flying with thousands of miles of ocean in every direction, the pilot would have needed an easy and reliable way of reattaching his aircraft to its only means of getting back home safely. Exactly what form of hook the spike was intended to snag is unknown, however, as is precisely how the host aircraft would have carried the P 175.

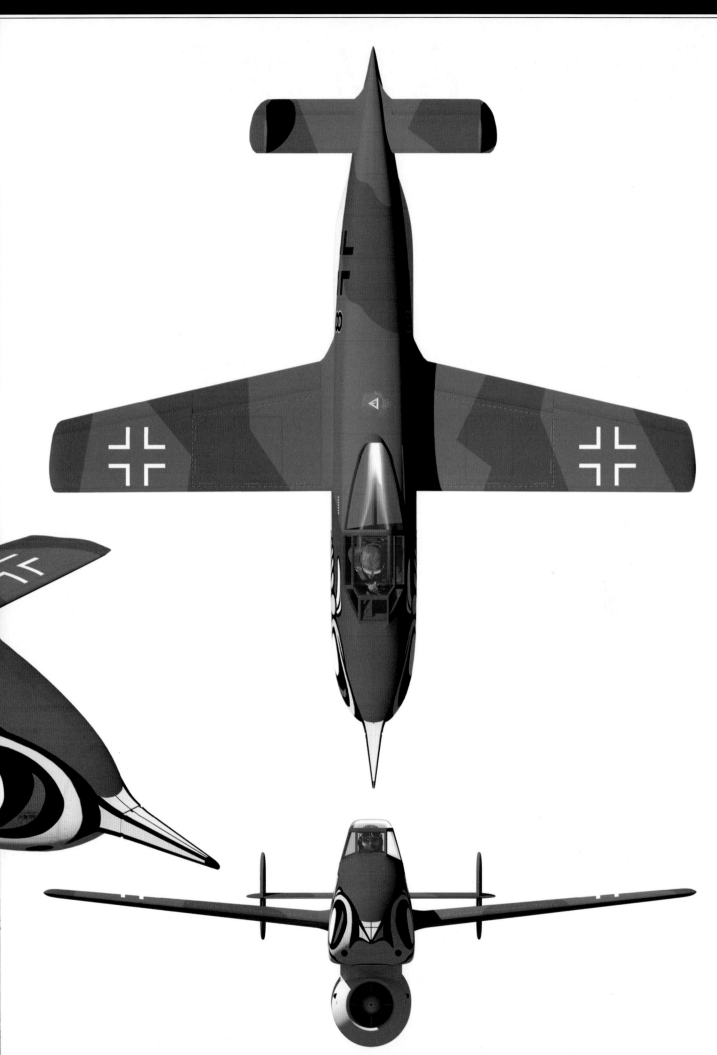

Prop propaganda

BMW PTL bombers

When it came to designing jet engines BMW, like its rivals Junkers and Daimler-Benz, agonised over how they would be fitted to aircraft in practice. But unlike Junkers and Daimler-Benz it often went as far as designing whole aircraft to show just how its engines might best be installed. During the summer of 1944 it showcased two such potential designs for bombers...

BMW spent most of the Second World War working on its P 3303 jet engine, redesignated BMW 018 by April 1943. This 2.5 ton 12-stage axial compressor device was intended for aircraft flying up to an altitude of 16km (52,500ft) and measured an enormous 5m from end to end with a diameter of 1.25m.

The company foresaw great potential for the 018 but even greater potential for the Propeller Turbinen Luftstrahltriebwerk (PTL) or turboprop version of it – the BMW 028, formerly known as the P 3320. In its most basic form, the 028 consisted of an 018 with its turbines driving a pair of contra-rotating propellers positioned directly over its intake, with air having to flow around the spinning hub and blades to enter the engine.

However, it was soon determined that this arrangement was far from ideal and that better performance would result from moving the propellers away from the intake opening if possible. Another tricky problem was how to actually install PTL engines in or on an aircraft. After a great deal of research and experimentation, BMW produced a report on June 6, 1944, EZS Bericht Nr. 48 EZV Nr. 592/44, entitled Der Einbau des PTL-Geräts

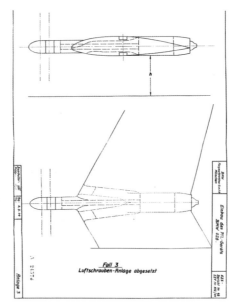

ABOVE: 'Case three' for the 028. The jet part of the engine is built into the wing's trailing edge, connected to the contra-rotating propellers by a long shaft. The engine's intakes are either side of the prop shaft though still within the circumference of the spinning blades.

BMW 028 or 'the installation of the PTL device BMW 028'.

This followed on immediately after a report of May 25, 1944, EZS Bericht Nr. 47 EZV Nr. 536/44 – Flugleistungen von TL-Bombern or 'flight performance of jet bombers', which had detailed a pair of tailless bomber designs powered by the BMW 003 and 018.

The June 6 report examined different ways in which the 028 could be fitted and tried to reach a conclusion on which was best. In the introduction it stated that the engine would probably always be installed in or on the aircraft's wing and underpinning this arrangement was the realisation that "in order not to affect the propeller efficiency too much and to avoid damaging vibrations, the propeller must be a certain distance from the wing leading edge. In spite of this, the length of the PTL device is probably in all practical cases shorter than the wing depth".

If keeping the prop away from the wing was the only essential requirement, there were four main options available. Firstly, the 028 could be fitted as originally designed with the props right over the engine intake and the whole arrangement slung below and forward of the wing leading edge. The advantages of this were easy accessibility to the engine for maintenance or to change the unit and no alterations necessary to the aircraft's existing wing structure. However, the disadvantages were huge drag, a reduction in useful thrust, a congested intake, the need to break the flaps around the engine exhaust and the need for high ground clearance resulting in either a long undercarriage or a shoulder-wing arrangement for the aircraft.

In the second case, the original props-over-intake arrangement would again be retained but with the whole engine built into the wing's structure. This reduced drag, kept the undercarriage to a normal length and allowed continuous flaps. It also resulted in a long exhaust nozzle and interference with the aircraft's wing structure, not to mention the usual congested intake.

Thirdly, the engine could be built into the trailing edge of the wing and connected to props protruding from the wing's leading edge by a long shaft and gearbox. In this case, the engine would be fed by intakes on either side of the rotor hub but still behind the propeller's sweeping blades. Advantages were low drag, normal undercarriage height and

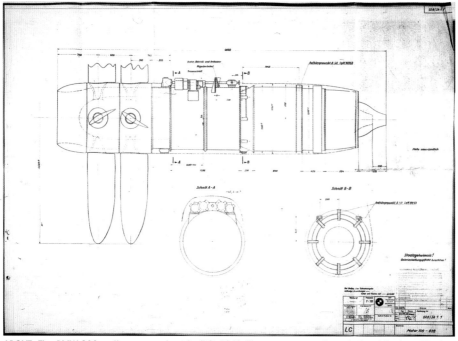

ABOVE: The BMW 028 as it appeared on April 9, 1943. The company acknowledged that positioning the propeller hub directly over the engine's air intake was less than ideal.

clearer intakes. Disadvantages were the need to keep the connecting shaft steady and the lesser disturbance to the intakes still caused by the spinning prop blades.

The fourth and final arrangement was similar to the third but with the intakes positioned outside the diameter of the propeller's blades and the gearbox offset to the rear. This resulted in low drag, "no disturbance of the laminar flow at the wing, thus the possibility of using laminar profiles over the entire span", no intake congestion, normal landing gear height and continuous landing flaps. Disadvantages were, again, the connecting shaft, "strong disturbance of the wing structure" and "complicated exhaust gas routing with two special nozzles".

Having evaluated these four designs, BMW concluded that the first was simplest and most favourable from a maintenance perspective, and was "suitable for heavy high-altitude long-ranged aircraft with not too high speeds" but "it is less suitable for the fast bomber". The second would be "well-suited for high-speed flight design, the disadvantages are not too serious" and the third "is probably the highest quality of the compared designs, but requires a departure from the previous overall structure, which is perhaps worthwhile, especially because of the achievable reduction of intake congestion". Finally, "case four is well suited for very high speeds, when the advantages of laminar flow are so great that it pays off the very significant change and installation costs. However, it is believed that all in all, the pure turbojet propulsion is preferable for the desired high speeds. This installation case would probably always be a special case and as such unsuitable for large series".

The second and third designs – prop over intake but built into the wing and prop separated from intakes – were "shortlisted" and "case three should be the preferred and generally the best solution. However, this arrangement requires a substantial change of the previously pursued design. It is therefore proposed to first examine the structural possibilities of this arrangement,

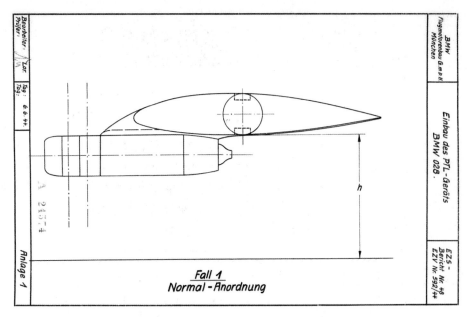

ABOVE: In a report of June 6, BMW outlined four potential installation arrangements for the BMW 028 turboprop. This is 'case one' with the engine suspended below and in front of the wing's leading edge.

in particular from the construction side, and to continue to seek the opinion of the RLM and the airframe companies for this type".

After discussing the possibilities for rearranging the 028's external fixtures and fittings to best suit the third installation case, the report then states: "Of course, in addition to the installation cases discussed above, other possibilities are conceivable which, however, lead to aircraft designs which would deviate considerably from the previous ones and which, for concerning the centre of gravity could lead to difficulties. As an example, in appendix five, the free-running installation of the device on a stem is shown, which could also be so modified as a kind of canard with the engine-bearing wing set forward.

"With a similar arrangement to the design shown, it might be easier to exploit the laminar effect in a large part of the wing than with propeller arrangements with PTL drive. There are also other, more or less unusual

arrangements which have not been discussed here and which can not be considered a normal case for installation. In summary, it can be said that the incorporation of PTL devices into suitable airframes raises questions that require quite urgent clarification with the RLM and airframe companies. The arrangement according to case three could be of interest."

THE COMBO BOMBER
Just over six weeks later, on July 21, 1944, BMW produced another report, EZS Bericht Nr. 50 EZV Nr. 681/44, which showed an evolution of the company's earlier line of reasoning. Entitled Der Schnellbomber mit kombiniertem PTL-TL-Antrieb or 'The fast bomber with combined turboprop-turbojet drive', it was much more specific about the use of PTL engines as part of a fast bomber's design and operation in practice and argued that it would be best to use them in combination with turbojets rather than as the aircraft's sole form of propulsion.

It states: "For the required purpose, the allocation of the entire drive system in 2 TL and 2 PTL engines proves to be expedient. In a calculated example project with two BMW 028 devices and two BMW 018 devices the maximum speed after the bombing is about 800km/h, and at five tons bomb loading the penetration range is about 2000km if all four engines are running at full throttle. The range can be increased if one shuts off the two TL devices after the dropping of the bombs and undertakes the return flight with the two PTL devices under full load.

"With this mode of operation, the maximum range can increase by about a third. The possible ranges at partial load could not be determined due to a lack of documentation, nor can anything be said about whether partial load operation of all four engines or switching off of the TL devices is preferable.

"If even higher ranges are needed, then the transition to pure PTL drive is required. For the large area between the jet bomber

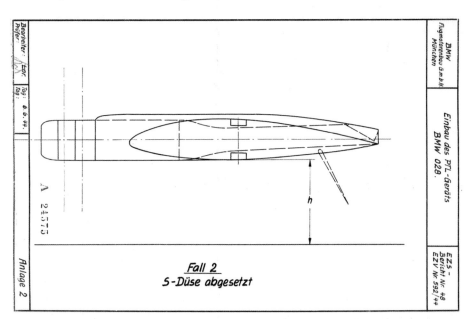

ABOVE: BMW's 'case two' for the 028. Now the engine is built into and projected forwards from the wing's leading edge. The exhaust runs through a long channel within the wing's structure.

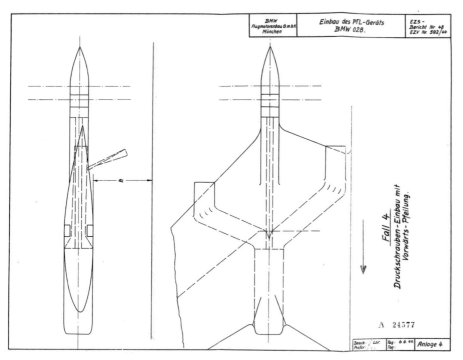

ABOVE: The fourth for the 028's installation. This involved a dramatic shifting of the engine's air intakes away from the props.

and the long-range fighter aircraft thus the combined drive with PTL and TL devices represents a promising solution. It may therefore be appropriate to build a specific airframe initially as a four-jet bomber, with lower takeoff weight or use starting aids for a higher weight, and then replace two of the four jets with PTL equipment as the development progresses."

Backtracking slightly, the report then sets out its terms more generally: "The development of engines and airframes in recent years has enabled an ever-increasing maximum speed for bombers and fighters; with the speed superiority of the fighters, the effectiveness of the fast bomber has been significantly reduced, especially at high altitudes. However, a strong increase in the defensive power of the slower heavy bomber units has made it increasingly difficult for fighters to combat them effectively.

"The use of jet fighters is expected to result in a sudden increase in speed, giving them new opportunities to fight the much slower bombers. For the fast bomber, it will now be decisive whether it will be able to get back on a par with the jet fighter in the race for speed and altitude. It is obvious that this is only possible by using corresponding engines suitable for high speeds. It is clear that the Mach number sensitivity of the airframe is also crucial for the fast bomber.

"The engines to be selected should thus offer first and foremost favourable possibilities for high-speed installation and, moreover, as a result of their fuel consumption characteristics, allow penetration depths as required for the bomber deployments in question. One may well assume a theoretical range of 4000km to 5000km as the upper limit of what is required for a fast bomber to outrun the jet fighters, and one can therefore expect the highest attainable velocities and flight speeds at these ranges to be essential for the usability of fast bombers.

"In addition, it would be very desirable if this fast bomber, as it is the case today with the bombers with piston engines, was able to achieve a higher range when used over a less well defended area, for example, over the sea, when speed can be allowed to drop. As we know, the piston engine offers quite good opportunities due to its fuel consumption characteristics, whereas this is not the case with the jet drive.

"Which engine arrangement is the right one for the intended fast bomber? At first, no doubt, just as the fighter-bomber was developed from the piston engine fighter, it would be possible to derive a fighter-bomber with quite high speed from a high-speed jet fighter. Depending on the reserves that the original fighter had with regard to surface load and undercarriage, one could increase the payload and thus the bomb load more or less. But ranges that are significantly above the jet fighter's range you will not achieve this way, if one assumes significant bomb loadings.

"However, the fast bomber described here is to be understood as being an aircraft that is far superior to a jet fighter, so one will have to assume a design quite different from the fighter. Here the PTL drive comes to the fore, because for the high required range it ensures better efficiency and because it supplies much more thrust at takeoff – which will certainly be critical due to the large payload compared to the jet fighter.

"For the dedicated high-altitude long-range bomber, if at the same time the demand for high speeds is made, the pure PTL drive is the right thing. The question now arises as to whether the combined use of PTL and jet devices is the right choice for the fast bomber required here, which is to maintain a parity to the fighter-bomber produced from the jet fighter in terms of speed.

"As appendix one shows, jet units do not deliver much less thrust at the targeted high speeds, but they are undoubtedly easier to install for high speed, so the combined propulsion of TL and PTL equipment does not appear to be unfavourable. The question arises as to whether the benefits expected from the use of PTL devices are still sufficient."

The report argues that a fast bomber with both jets and turboprops would benefit from fighter-like speed, extended range and high load-carrying capacity. It then turns its attention to detailing a specific design – labelled simply 'Schellbomber mit kombiniertem PTL + TL-Antrieb'. This was to have two BMW 018s and two BMW 028s, each of the latter with two four-bladed

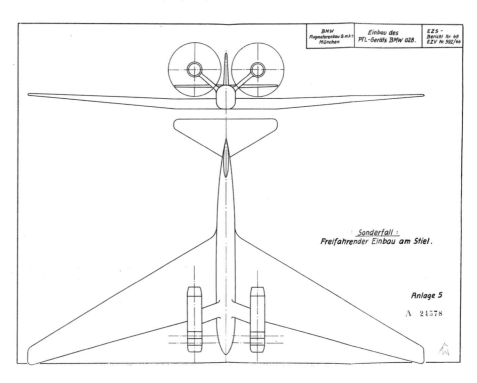

ABOVE: BMW claimed to have studied numerous alternative installations of its BMW 028 and offered this one as an example. The engines would be relatively easy to maintain and would be kept well away from the wings but the unusual 'canard' arrangement would no doubt have created its own problems.

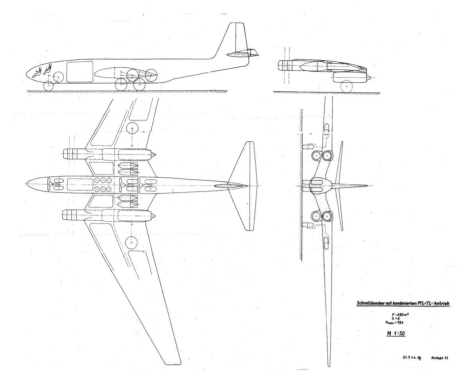

Schnellbomber mit kombiniertem PTL+TL-Antrieb

F = 250 m²
λ = 8
G_max = 75 t

M 1:50

21.7.44. By   Anlage 13

ABOVE: The only illustration from BMW's July 21, 1944, shows a large fast bomber designed using what the company believed to be the optimal combination of two turbojets and two turboprops.

contra-rotating propellers spinning at 1130rpm which, according to the report "corresponds approximately to the suggestions of VDM". It is interesting that BMW chose the supposedly less attractive 'case two' from its report of six weeks earlier for this new design, rather than the preferred option of 'case three'.

Maximum takeoff weight is given as 75 tons, maximum total load 30 tons, maximum fuel load 29.5 tons, maximum bomb load 15 tons, wing area 250m and wing length 8m. At maximum takeoff weight, the runway takeoff distance would be 1000m – about the same as that needed by a Me 262.

According to the report: "With these assumptions, it was initially attempted to design the closest possible approach to a flying wing aircraft. It would take too long if one wanted to mention all the reasons and thoughts that led to the suggestion of the normal layout plane shown in appendix 13.

"Ultimately the decisive factor for this type was the double wing angle sweep associated with the use of twin-propeller PTL devices, the undercarriage question and the control of the centre of gravity migration due to fuel consumption and discharge of loads".

The report's author says that a tailless version of the design might be possible "but existing documents at EZS were not sufficient to justify this type". But in any case "the space in the wing was used extensively for the absorption of bombs and fuel, resulting in smaller centre of gravity shifts and thus tail moments as if the fuselage would serve to absorb the total consumption and discharge loads. Thus, a small tail appears admissible.

"The chosen undercarriage arrangement is particularly worthy of note. With such large land planes, the landing gear question is always particularly difficult to solve. Finally, an arrangement was chosen that reminds one of the circumstances of a flying boat. The lateral support wheels are only

slightly loaded and perform the function of support floats, while the main landing shock is absorbed by double wheels stored in the fuselage, whose number could be increased by a couple if necessary.

"The V-position of the inner wing ensures that the height of the undercarriage due to the ground clearance of the propeller is possible without too much weight expenditure on the main landing gear. It should also be noted that the chosen overall arrangement also offers the following: the lower development time of the jet engines means that they are available in series earlier than the PTL devices. It is now possible to bring out an aircraft of the type considered without difficulty initially with a pure jet drive, whereby the take-off weight must be kept down so that the rolling distance is sufficient. In practice this means a reduction in bomb load and range". Once turboprop engines became available, the

aircraft could be switched to the two jet and two PTL arrangement originally intended. After another brief run-down of the aircraft's calculated performance, the report concludes: "In summary, a fast bomber development series with the engine arrangement under investigation may allow fairly good flight performance and, above all, greater attention needs to be paid to the combined use of TL and PTL equipment."

It has been suggested that the German aircraft manufacturers sometimes produced reports and brochures on aircraft designs as 'marketing hype' and while this appears to have very little basis in truth for the likes of Focke-Wulf and Messerschmitt, reports such as these from BMW do seem to be less-than-subtle advertisements for the company's products presented in the form of helpful suggestions for the aircraft builders and the RLM. Nevertheless, reports illustrated with practical examples of how engines might be used are undeniably easier to read that those presenting cold scientific data on engine arrangements in the form of graphs and tables alone.

Incidentally, both the odd 'canard' PTL bomber and the four-engined combination bomber were included in the British report of January 1946: German Aircraft: New and Projected Types. On the former, it says only "a BMW drawing shows a proposal for carrying two 028 propeller/turbine units on outriggers from the fuselage of what appears to be a large bomber. The outriggers are inclined at about 45 degrees". On the latter, it outlines the engine arrangement then says: "The fuselage is very small in relation to the wing root thickness and is upswept to a surprisingly conventional empennage.

"On the other hand the undercarriage is anything but conventional. There are two pairs of main wheels under the fuselage, each pair being carried by a common oleo leg. In addition there is a wheel under each wing outboard of the propulsion units and retracting outwards, and a twin nose wheel." It also gives some performance data gleaned from the graphs appended to the original BMW report. The combination bomber appears to have been BMW's last known aircraft design of the war. ●

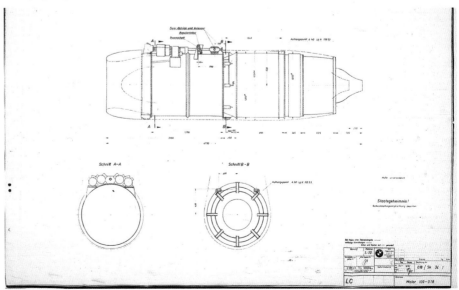

ABOVE: The propeller-less BMW 018 turbojet on which the 028 was based, as it appeared on March 12, 1943. By November 1944 it had grown in length by 250mm but the diameter remained the same.

Mr Übelacker's plan for self-destruction

Daimler-Benz P101/006 SV-Flugzeug

At the end of 1944 two of Daimler-Benz's top men came up with a novel carrier aircraft concept and commissioned Focke-Wulf to carry out the detail work on it – resulting in what are commonly known today as the 'Daimler-Benz projects'. But just how much of their design came from Daimler-Benz and how much from Focke-Wulf?

Towards the end of 1944 Germany's situation was becoming increasingly desperate. Relentless Allied bombing was taking a devastating toll on the German economy – restricting fuel supplies, curtailing manufacturing output and making it that much harder to fight back.

Among the many potential solutions involving everything from rocket interceptors to storm weapons was a concept put forward by Daimler-Benz director Fritz Nallinger and his colleague Erich Übelacker.

Their idea, they thought, would put a stop to the bombing raids without the need to directly engage the Allied bomber fleets or their deadly fighter escorts. It was outlined in a document entitled 'Reflections on the development of a

fast bomber' which was evidently composed by Nallinger in the first person. He wrote: "My colleague, Mr Übelacker, and I have especially thought about how the bases of the enemy bombers, the airfields, hangars and supplies can be effectively combated.

"It is reasonable and extremely effective to launch the largest possible surprise attack and bombard these airfields and hangars. If it were possible to destroy these bases in one day or over several consecutive days, including the aircraft located there, then it would at least for a time, allow us to recover from the bombing of the enemy that is paralysing us.

"Our industry and our transport network could make a reasonable recovery during this time, which would in turn create the

opportunity for us to build the fighters we need for the defence of our homeland and to make fuel available for them. Such a surprise attack against the enemy could not be carried out by German bombers of the normal type, such as the enemy use themselves, not even a bomber of a more modern design with a speed of 372-434mph. Such an attack, even started with a great company of bombers, would miserably expire when faced with the exceptionally strong opposing fighter force."

A fast jet bomber would be able to bypass any interceptors or flak, flying directly to the Allied bomber bases and annihilating them. But then there was the problem of how to get such a bomber off the ground. A heavily laden jet bomber would need a long concrete

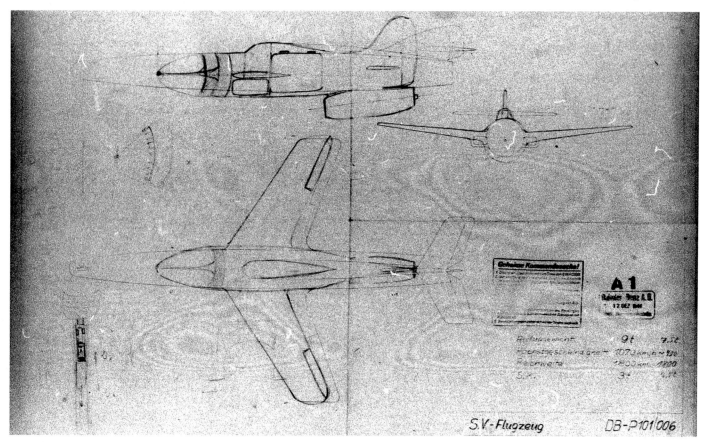

ABOVE: Daimler-Benz drawing DB-P101/006. This shows two designs for an 'S.V.-Flugzeug' or 'Selbstvernichter-Flugzeug' – self-destructive aircraft. The more prominent design has a short fuselage with a turbojet engine positioned beneath its tail. The fainter design is longer and slimmer with a swept tail, an internal jet engine and wing-root intakes. The drawing is stamped December 12, 1944, but it would have been drafted earlier than that.

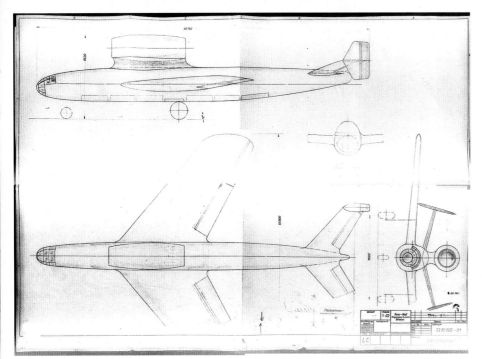

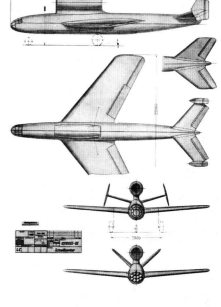

ABOVE: Focke-Wulf's first drawing of a 'Daimler-Benz project'. This shows the fast bomber that would be lifted into the air under a carrier aircraft. It is 30.75m long – slightly longer than the massive Junkers Ju 290 and more than twice the length of an Arado Ar 234. In spite of its size, it only had a crew of two and no defensive weapons. The drawing number is 0310 256-01 and the drawing is dated December 12, 1944, though it is stamped January 8, 1945.

ABOVE: Not quite the final version of the Daimler-Benz fast bomber, drawing 0310 256-05 of February 7, also from Kurzbeschreibung Nr. 28, shows a number of subtle changes when compared to the fast bomber in Focke-Wulf drawing 0310 256-01. The length has been reduced to 30m, the shape of the twin fin plates is different and the engine nacelle is a little slimmer. Wingspan is still 22m, the undercarriage mainwheels are still 7.8m apart and height is still 8.5m.

runway to get airborne but by late 1944 most of Germany's long concrete runways had been wrecked by bombing. However, the Daimler-Benz engineers thought they could get around this by attaching the bomber to a very large but very basic carrier aircraft capable of rough field takeoffs and landings.

Nallinger went on: "Borrowing the large wing area and the strong landing gear of the carrier, the bomber can start on any normal airfield. The take-off run can be very short, less than 500m, so that even small airports can be used. The carrier aircraft makes possible further rapid deployment of the composite from one place to another because it can also be used to some extent as a large van within which the entire entourage can be transported. With the carrier aircraft, it is possible not only to launch fast bombers but also other high wing loading special aircraft."

Effectively, the big cumbersome carrier would take off with the jet bomber attached to its underside, haul it up to the appropriate altitude then release it to fly off on its mission. The carrier would then be able to turn around, land, and do it all over again with the next jet bomber in line.

Focke-Wulf's Kurt Tank had "taken an active interest in our proposal, and he has taken our proposal and had it checked by his company, who have drawn it up in the form of a project. I would like to thank Professor Tank for his responding to this proposal. In cooperation with Professor Tank and his staff we have calculated the proper values for this project. Details I will show later in the summary. More detailed information can be found in the Kurzbeschreibung Nr. 28 brought out by the Focke-Wulf company. From this, it is apparent that the objectives of this proposal can be achieved."

All this – particularly "who have drawn it up in the from of a project" – makes it sound as though the concept belonged to Nallinger and Übelacker but the actual aircraft designs came from Focke-Wulf. So what were the "other high wing loading special aircraft"?

Nallinger continued: "I want to present this complementary proposal by my colleague, Mr Übelacker. He suggests the extension of the fight against the enemy bomber force through the building of manned self-destructing aircraft, each with a 2.5 tonne explosive charge which is housed in the fuselage nose. Such aircraft can of course also be unoccupied and equipped with remote control.

"This aircraft also has the high wing loading of about 500kg per square metre and is as fast as the bomber previously described. It would start from the same carrier aircraft as a team. Here, however, the carrier aircraft can launch anything from a single aircraft up to six of them."

Rather than being launched directly against Allied bomber formations however, this explosives-packed suicide attacker was to be used primarily against ships. The importance that the Germans attached to sinking Allied shipping has seldom been so clearly put: "It is proposed that these aircraft will be used for fighting ships, in this case in particular to combat tankers. The destruction of a tanker of 15,000 tonnes means the loss of fuel for three major attacks on Germany by the enemy.

"The idea here with the sacrifice of a man and an aircraft, or using remote control only an aircraft, to prevent three large attacks is, in my view, significant. Of course, this aircraft can also be used for attacking different shipping targets, i.e. warships.

"The bombing and torpedo bombing of ship targets is generally of poor efficiency and tankers are particularly hard to sink, whereas the correct application of a 2.5 tonne shaped explosive charge is the fastest way to get the

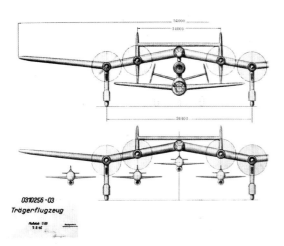

ABOVE: The first of the 'presentation' drawings from Kurzbeschreibung Nr. 28, 0310 256-03, shows the fast bomber beneath the six-engined carrier aircraft which would have got it airborne. The drawing is dated February 7, 1945.

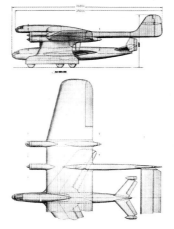

ABOVE: The other part of 0310 256-03 showing top and side views of the fast bomber beneath the carrier aircraft.

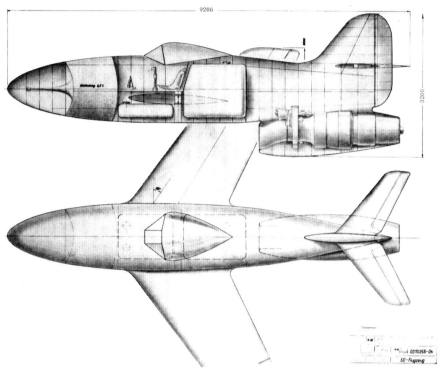

ABOVE: The last known version of Daimler-Benz's 'S.V.-Flugzeug', labelled the 'SO Flugzeug' by Focke-Wulf. Drawing 0310 256-04 is dated February 7, 1945, and is the second of the drawings from Kurzbeschreibung Nr. 28.

job done. Besides the carrier aircraft, which can be used here in the same design as for the fast bomber, also the fast bomber itself can now be used as reconnaissance for this self-destructing aircraft. Thanks to its high range as a scout it will be able to locate ships early enough before they dock. As a result of its high speed, the fast bomber cannot be attacked as a single machine.

"Furthermore, the self-destructors can optionally be guided to their target under the leadership of the fast bomber. Work on the self-destructor aircraft has also been commissioned from Professor Tank by my staff."

In Kurzbeschreibung Nr. 28, Focke-Wulf describes the suicide attacker as the 'SO Flugzeug', with the 'SO' standing for 'Selbstopferung' or 'self-sacrifice aircraft'. But did Focke-Wulf actually come up with the designs for the jet bomber, the carrier and

the suicide attacker? It would appear that Übelacker himself or his staff certainly did design the suicide attacker but called it the 'SV Flugzeug' instead, with 'SV' standing for 'Selbstvernichter', making it the 'Self-destructive aircraft'.

A Daimler-Benz drawing numbered DB-P101/006, stamp-dated December 12, 1944, shows a small single seater aircraft with a turbojet slung underneath the tail section. A large fuel tank is positioned just behind the pilot and another sits beneath his feet. In the nose is a huge cylindrical lump of explosives with a long slender detonator stretching forward to meet the tip of the aircraft's aerodynamic nosecone.

The forward view shows a light dihedral to the wings and the top view shows off the canopy's teardrop form. The information panel to the bottom right shows two versions

– one weighing nine tons with a top speed of 1070km/h, a range of 1800km and an explosives load of three tons. The second version weighed seven and a half tons, had a top speed of 900km/h, a range of 1800km and an explosives load that is nearly indecipherable but which could perhaps be one and a half tons.

Looking closely at the drawing, it is in fact possible to discern two designs, one overlaid on top of the other. The other design is markedly different from the first – characterised by a long slender fuselage, sharply swept fin, internal turbojet and intakes in the wing roots on either side, judging by the forward view. It would appear that the long thin design was the nine ton version, while the shorter design was the seven and a half ton version. It should be noted that although the drawing is stamp-dated December 12, 1944, in practice drawings were typically stamped in this way days or even months after they were actually drawn – the small handwritten date at the bottom usually indicating the drawing's true date. Sadly the Daimler-Benz drawing is so degraded that the handwritten date is illegible.

Pinning down who designed what and when is very difficult where the 'Daimler-Benz projects' are concerned but it may be assumed that the DB-P101/006 came before anything done by Focke-Wulf. The latter's first visual work on the concept is drawing number 0310 256-01, which shows the fast bomber on its own with a single large dorsal turbojet and a twin-tail. This is hand-dated December 11, 1944 – the day before the Daimler-Benz drawing was stamped – but the handwritten project notes it is based on date from as early as December 5, 1944. This would appear to be the date of Focke-Wulf's first involvement with the 'Daimler-Benz projects'. Focke-Wulf drawing 0310 256-02 is unknown.

Drawings 0310 256-03, -04 and -05 were evidently all produced on the same day, February 7, 1945, and it is these that appear as the illustrations for "Kurzbeschreibung Nr. 28 brought out by the Focke-Wulf company". The first one (0310 256-03) shows the big carrier aircraft with the fast jet slung underneath and an alternative load of five SO-Flugzeugs, the second (0310 256-04) shows the short fuselage SO-Flugzeug and the third (0310 256-05) shows the fast bomber on its own with an alternative V-tail.

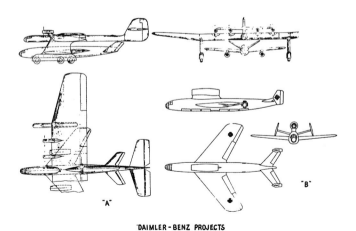

'DAIMLER-BENZ PROJECTS'

ABOVE: Illustrations from the British January 1946 intelligence report German Aircraft: New and Projected Types. This page shows 'A', which is a straight copy of Focke-Wulf drawing 0310 256-07, and a rough-looking version of the fast bomber with Luftwaffe markings applied. This would appear to be an original Daimler-Benz drawing from the autumn of 1944, rather than Focke-Wulf's later version.

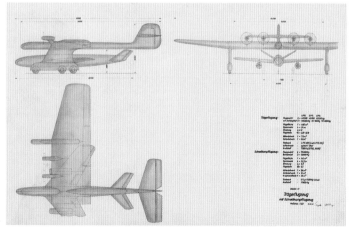

ABOVE: Focke-Wulf drawing 0310 256-07 was the last of the company's 'Daimler-Benz projects' designs. This shows both the bomber and carrier looking substantially different. The carrier is now powered by four turboprops and the bomber has two under-wing turbojets – it's also 25cm longer, wingspan has been increased by 1.2m and the undercarriage is 10cm narrower. The date is March 19, 1945 – about three weeks before Focke-Wulf's offices were overrun by the advancing Allies.

Focke-Wulf drawing 0310 256-06 is also unknown. But 0310 256-07 is dated March 19, nearly six weeks after the initial 'presentation' set, and shows the fast jet and carrier looking slightly different. The carrier is now powered by four turboprops instead of six piston engines and the bomber has the V-tail exclusively and an unnamed turbojet under each wing.

The title 'Daimler-Benz projects', the name by which these designs are collectively most commonly known, actually comes from the British January 1946 report 'German Aircraft: New and Projected Types' – a compilation of drawings and statistics copied directly from original German projects documents. This presents the 0310 256-07 drawing alongside some others which, while they appear to be the familiar 'Daimler-Benz projects', seem less polished and oddly sport German air force markings.

The report arbitrarily assigns the 0310 256-07 drawing the letter 'A', while something that looks very similar to be the earlier 0310 256-05 design is labelled 'B'. The other drawings are labelled 'C', 'D', 'E' and 'F'. It is clear that these letters are not the names of the designs – just markers assigned so that the author of the report can refer to them in the text more easily. 'C', 'D', 'E' and 'F' depict the same six-engined carrier as 0310 256-03 but with a different, long-fuselage version of the SO-Flugzeug. This looks rather like the one shown in the DB-P101/006 drawing but with the turbojet mounted above the cockpit to the rear rather than slung under it or fitted inside it.

The exact wording of the German Aircraft: New and Projected Types text says: "As an alternative to the single bomber the tug can carry up to six S.V. (self-destroying) aircraft or piloted flying bombs (Dwg 'E' & 'F') ... The Daimler Benz project P 100/003 follows on the same general lines as those already described."

Together, the reference to an "S.V." aircraft – Daimler-Benz's term – and the use of the company project number P 100/003 suggest something rather striking about the 'Daimler-Benz projects': that with the exception of the modified March 19 versions they all sprang fully formed from the minds of Daimler-Benz engineers. Focke-Wulf just tidied them up, applied accurate dimensions and crunched some numbers to see whether they would work as real-world aircraft.

The author of German Aircraft: New and Projected Types does not appear to have been aware of Focke-Wulf's involvement in the projects at all – hence why he calls them simply 'Daimler-Benz projects'. During the weeks or perhaps months before Focke-Wulf's earliest known work on the projects, December 5, 1944, Nallinger and Übelacker or their staff must have designed the bomber, carrier and suicide attacker.

The drawings that appear in German Aircraft: New and Projected Types, with the exception of drawing 'A', presumably came from a Daimler-Benz report or brochure and probably therefore represent the original pre-Focke-Wulf designs when they were just 'Daimler-Benz projects' and were known by Daimler-Benz numbers including P 100/003 and P 101/006.

As for what happened to the 'projects', Focke-Wulf's Kurzbeschreibung Nr. 28 was dated February 10, 1945. The designs it showcased were then compared against those of the competitors for the 'Langstreckenbomber' aka 'Grossbomber' competition, which had begun in November 1944 when Willy Messerschmitt offered the Entwicklunghauptskommission a four-engine jet bomber design. These were the Messerschmitt P 1107, the Junkers Ju 287 and the Horten XVIII.

The comparison document, entitled 'Betrachtungen zum Projekt Nallinger-Übelacker' or 'Reflections on the Nallinger-Übelacker project', is undated but was presumably produced some time between February 10 and February 20 when the Langstreckenbomber design conference began. Since the Daimler-Benz projects are not mentioned at all in the Langstreckenbomber post-conference report of February 25, 1945, it must be assumed that they were either too late or were simply not deemed worthy of consideration at that time. ●

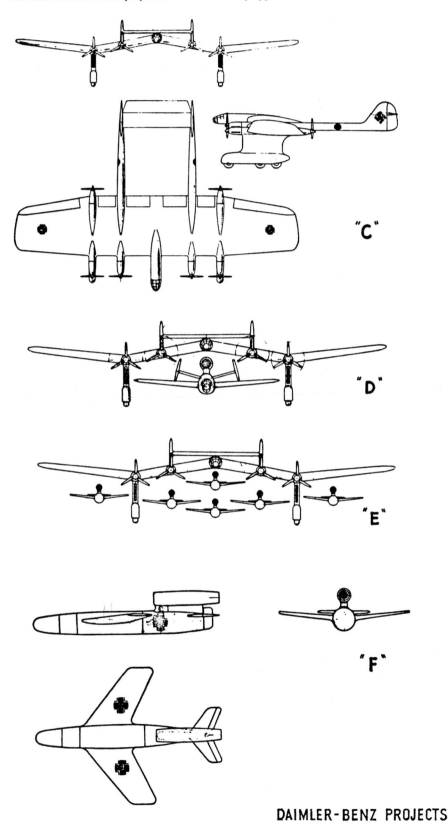

"C"

"D"

"E"

"F"

DAIMLER-BENZ PROJECTS

ABOVE: The second page of Daimler-Benz projects drawings from German Aircraft: New and Projected Types, showing the carrier and what might be an early version of the SV-Flugzeug suicide attacker design. The latter appears to have much in common with the more slender SV-Flugzeug design from Daimler-Benz's P 101/006 drawing, right down to the wing dihedral.

Meet the twins

DFS 203, Wolf Hirth Hi 23 and Jacobs-Schweyer Jas P 5

German engineers harboured a desire for a twin-fuselage wing profile test vehicle for most of the Second World War – starting in August 1940. It was a desire that would ultimately go unfulfilled but not for want of trying.

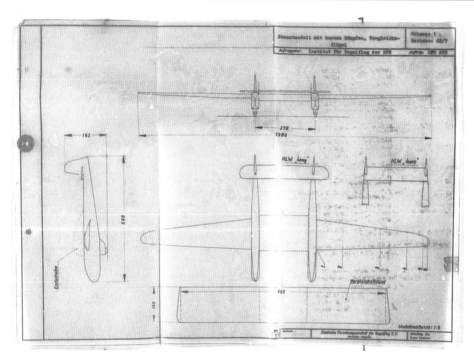

LEFT: The 'long' DFS 203 with extended fuselages.

1941 – Wolf Hirth and Jacobs-Schweyer Flugzeugbau. The former company had enjoyed success with its Göppingen Gö 3 Minimoa glider and in 1941 had built the experimental Gö 9, which had a pusher propeller. The latter was responsible for designing and building the DFS 230 itself, among many other designs.

The aircraft had to have a wing profile measurement depth of 3m, the capability to adjust the wing form being measuring by plus or minus 10°, a measuring speed of 500km/h (311mph) and the strength to withstand speeds of up to 625km/h (388mph).

Both companies submitted tenders – Jacobs-Schweyer's Jas P 5 design dated October 7, 1941, and Hirth's Hi 23 dated October 15, 1941. The former's was entitled 'Vorentwurf für Forschungs-Segelflugzeug Jas P 5' or 'Preliminary draft for research glider Jas P 5' and the first page was headed 'Doppelrumpf-Messflugzeug' or 'Double fuselage measuring aircraft'.

There is no introduction explaining the design, it simply begins with 'performance considerations', stating: "The glider shown in the overview drawing has a maximum flying weight of 2800kg, which is composed of the weight of 1400kg and the payload of

The twin-fuselage aircraft was nothing new by 1940 – the Blackburn TB of 1915 had a twin-fuselage layout and the Savoia-Marchetti S.55 had famously set 14 world records during the 1920s. But the idea of using a twin-fuselage design as a flying laboratory to test different wing profile shapes appears to have originated in Germany during 1940.

The concept was simple and ingenious – link two similar fuselages in the centre with a straight section of wing shaped to the profile you wanted to test. The aircraft would have normal outer wings and tail fins with a single horizontal stabiliser running between the fuselages to the rear. And in order to prevent any interference from a propeller, the aircraft would need to be a glider.

The earliest known design created for this purpose was the DFS 203 – a pair of DFS 230 glider fuselages connected in the centre with a 'messflügel' or 'measuring wing' to create a 'messflugzeug' or 'measuring aircraft'. Wind tunnel tests on two models of the DFS 203 – one with the usual DFS 230 form and one with a lengthened fuselage – were carried out "with interruptions from August 27 to December 16, 1940" according to a retrospective report on the tests issued on October 3, 1942.

Three- and six-component measurements were made of the models in the DFS's 2m

tunnel "as well as pressure measurements on the centre profile itself and shortly after it in the wake of the double-fuselage model DFS 203. Furthermore, paint spraying photographs were made to visualise the pressure conditions in the boundary layer. The purpose of the measurements was the one-sided effect of influencing the pressure ratios at the central measuring wing by the fuselages and outer wings, [and] on the other hand the longitudinal and lateral stability ratios of the aircraft pattern composed of two normal LS (DFS 230)".

The mention of the tests being 'interrupted' may give some indication of the work priority assigned to the DFS 203. Nevertheless, the tests were completed even if the full report on them does not appear to have been completed until nearly two years later.

It seems as though, at some point, it was decided that a normal glider would be too slow to accurately simulate the conditions a powered aircraft's wings were likely to encounter. Therefore, rocket motors would be needed to boost the test vehicle up to the sort of speeds usually reserved for high-performance fighters. And since the DFS 230 was not suitable for rocket propulsion and high-speed flight, a new design was needed.

Specifications for a twin-fuselage research glider were issued to at least two prominent glider manufacturers in

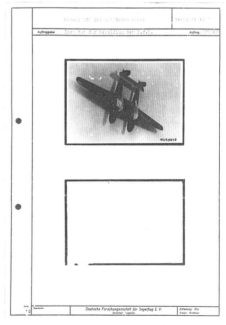

ABOVE: One of the two DFS 203 wind tunnel models tested. The photo of the other is missing from the document.

1400kg. The equipped weight is determined by the required permissible speeds of 500 or 625km/h.

"The payload is composed of: 2 man crew = 200kg, rocket motors with 5kg/100kg thrust at 1600kg thrust = 80kg; fuel: 0.0075kg/sec [this figure is underlined in pencil with a question mark next to it] at 40 sec = 480kg; fuel container, piping etc. = 50kg; course control system = 50kg; measuring instruments: 2 oscillographs = 50kg; converters, Switches, Indicators = 40kg; 100 measuring elements = 30kg; 2 batteries = 50kg; cables, piping, control equipment = 40kg, impulse measuring grid with suspension = 20kg."

The dimensions of the aircraft are given as wingspan 17.8m, wing area 28m², length 12.7m and height 1.8m. The central 'measuring wing' was the required 3m deep but the outer wings were tapering and much more slender, with the rocket motors built into their trailing edges. The document gives the "lowest possible surface load of 100kg/m²" which "results in a lowest speed of 117.5km/h. As a result of the fuel consumption during the measurement fight, however, the surface load decreases to about 80kg/m². This results in a landing speed of 105km/h.

"Since the glider is imagined only to be landed on airfields, the landing speed is not too high according to the experience made with heavily loaded gliders. For the execution of the measurement flight it is necessary to

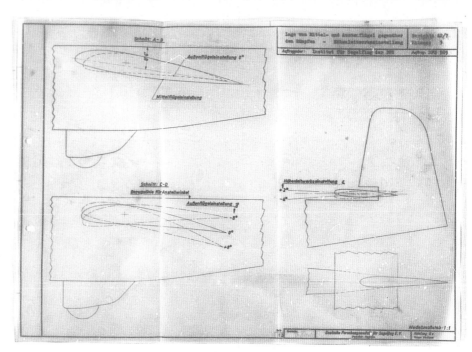

ABOVE: Location of the DFS 203's central and outer wings relative to each other and tailplane adjustment options.

achieve a sufficient initial height.

"Therefore indicated in Fig. 3 are the climbing speeds for 3 different motorised towing aircraft. Ju 52 fails because at the required towing speeds (180 + 200km/h) the power surplus becomes too low. The

specifications for He 111 are only valid for version H-3. The H-6 seems due to the tractor experience with gliders of similar surface load particularly suitable for towing, but accurate performance calculations could not be performed due to lack of necessary

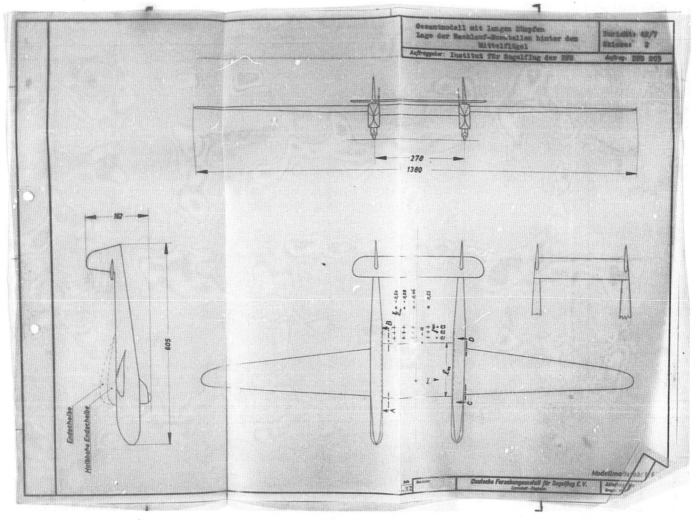

ABOVE: The 'short' version of the DFS 203, which was two standard DFS 230s linked together.

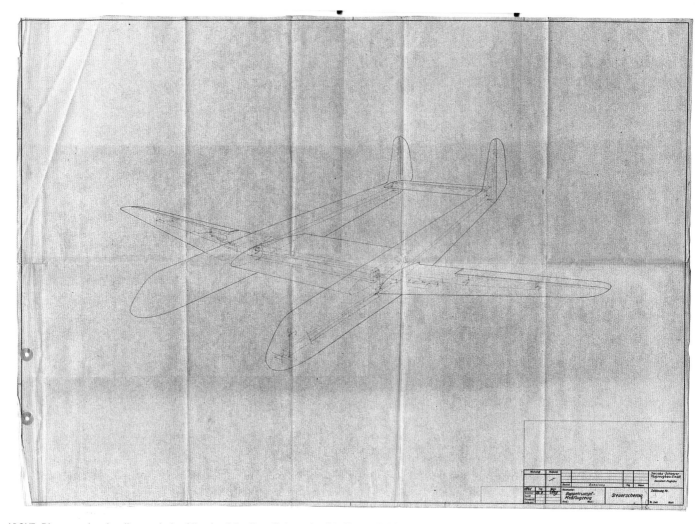

ABOVE: Diagram showing the controls of the Jas P 5 – the pilot was to sit in the port side fuselage. The drawing is dated September 29, 1941.

documents. The flight experience with Me 110 as a towplane, however, is not satisfactory. With He 111 as well as with Me 110 the attainment of a sufficient towing height is to be taken for granted.

"There are two possibilities for achieving the required measuring speeds: 1) Pressing the glider in steep gliding flight to the desired speed with subsequent horizontal flight and simultaneous switching on the rocket units. 2) Turn on the rocket unit at a normal speed until the desired measuring speed is reached."

After some discussion of altitudes and diving angles, it was determined that the option to dive and levelling off before firing the engines would be best for achieving the necessary measuring speed. This was mainly because too much fuel would be needed to reach the measuring speed if the rocket motors were fired without the glider having first gained momentum by diving.

The report states: "A combination of the two specified methods significantly reduces the operating times, as can be seen from graph. The rocket units are switched on only at a higher initial speed, which is achieved by steep gliding flight. Example: The glider is pushed to 400km/h. For this, the height loss is about 900m. Upon reaching level flight the rocket devices are turned on, bringing the glider to 500km/h after 8 seconds burning time.

"There is then still sufficient fuel

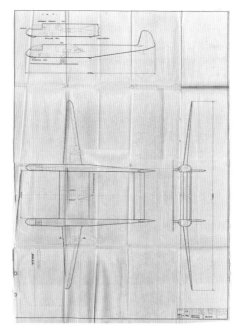

ABOVE: The Jacobs-Schweyer Jas P 5 as it appeared on October 2, 1941. The upper part of the drawing shows all the measuring equipment that was to be installed for monitoring the movements of the central 'measuring wing' at speed. The aircraft's four rocket motors can be seen on its wings – two on each. Note the flattened off inner side of each fuselage – a measure intended to reduce any aerodynamic influence on the measuring surface.

available to maintain this speed during the measurement time of 30 sec. For the achievement of 625km/h a burn time of the rocket units of 33 sec. is required. The required fuel of the rocket units can be accommodated in the aircraft due to the payload reserve. The speed can be regulated by operating the dive brakes."

The dive brakes in question were to be installed in the aircraft's outer wings. As far as landing gear was concerned: "Due to the 4.5m wide measuring wing a central skid is not possible. Landings on two skids are very sensitive due to ground friction and skid resistance irregularities. The aircraft does not keep to the direction of landing and tends to break sideways. For the take-off 2 separate, ejectable chassis must be provided.

"These difficulties are avoided by the design of the retractable and braked wheeled landing gear. In case of failure of the extension mechanism, a spring-loaded auxiliary skid is provided on each side."

And for the controls: "All controls are driven by pushrods for rigidity and ease. The installation of a course control device is planned. On-board communications: The installation of the electrically powered Siemens intercom system is planned, based on the experience in gliders."

The aircraft's tailplane was interchangeable and the fins could be trimmed by plus or minus 10°. The central

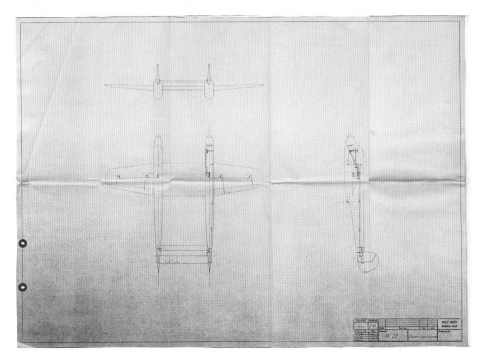

ABOVE: The controls of the Hi 23. The pilot was to sit in the starboard fuselage, rather than the port, because "if you control with the right hand, you have a clearer view to the left". The date is October 20, 1941.

measuring wing was "fixed to the solid continuous spar, the thickness of which is based on the smallest thicknesses of the profiles to be measured. The actual measuring section of about 0.8m width can be specially finished and arranged for profile measurements. The entire wing can be pivoted plus or minus 10° around the spar".

A pressure-measuring device developed by the Flugfunk-Forschungsinstitut Oberpfaffenhofen was to be installed within the measuring wing and could be accessed via a removable flap. And "for momentum loss measurements, a measuring grid swivelling with the centre wing can be attached to two reinforced wing ribs".

The report then notes that: "A final installation drawing for the rocket-equipment could not be made due to lack of necessary documents. The dimensions given by LC 1 for the rocket motors are to be observed in the overview drawing."

Finally, the short report gives two suggestions for "the experiments necessary before the construction: 1) Six-component wind tunnel measurements to determine the performance and behaviour of the glider in the possible settings in mid-air and to determine the air forces. 2) Large-scale wind tunnel tests to clarify the influence of the activated rocket-units on the flow conditions in the measuring level".

As an aside, the ninth, tenth and eleventh graphs included in the report include the note: "(Calculation method: Lippisch)", which presumably shows the ongoing influence of Me 163 designer Alexander Lippisch in glider-designing and aerodynamic testing circles.

The Wolf Hirth entry was designated Hi 23 – probably a company number rather than an official RLM number since 8-23 had been used by the short-lived Dornier Do 23 bomber.

The Hi 23 was substantially heavier than the Jas P 5 at 3700kg compared to

2800kg take-off weight. It measured 12.5m long with a wingspan of 15m – making it smaller in both dimensions than the Jacobs-Schweyer design. While the central measuring wing was of a similar size, its outer wings were much deeper. And unlike the P 5, the rocket motors were built into the fuselages rather than the wings.

Hirth's report also began without introduction, simply restating the requirements. The first mention of the Hi 23's capabilities says: "The fuselage distance and the length of the front part of the fuselage has been designed so that the measurement section in the middle wing will be free of flow influences. This makes it necessary to balance the weight moment

of the tail almost completely by trim weights. The maximum weight is 700kg.

"The cockpit for the aircraft pilot was provided in the starboard fuselage to allow the pilot to keep an eye on the measuring area and the observer. (If you control with the right hand, you have a clearer view to the left.)"

With rocket engines amounting to 800kg of thrust the Hi 23 could manage a horizontal top speed of 507km/h or 570km/h with a thrust of 1000kg. As with the Jas P 5, the Hi 23 would have needed to dive to pick up speed and reach 625km/h. The rocket units were to be installed as close as possible to the aircraft's centre of gravity.

Again like the Jas P 5, the Hi 23 had a retractable wheeled undercarriage but the wheels protruded slightly even when fully retracted so that the glider could be landed with the gear up if necessary. Fuselage width was 0.72m and "due to the ample fuselage mass the internals make no trouble". Brakes were included.

With the measuring wing, "a steel tube is used to hold it, which connects the two joints and transmits the bending moments and transverse forces as well as the asymmetrical torques. On the tube rotatable clamps are arranged, on which the measuring surface is fixed. Since the pipe has an outer diameter corresponding to the smallest outer-flight thickness, the clamps will protrude beyond the measuring surface at 9% thickness and must be clad cleanly." Dive brakes were also to be included as part of the Hi 23's design.

Precisely why neither the Jas P 5 nor the Hi 23 went any further than design studies is unknown. Certainly, resources were badly needed for frontline operations in the Soviet Union during the autumn of 1941, which may have been a factor. However, this was not the end of the twin-fuselage rocket-propelled glider story. ●

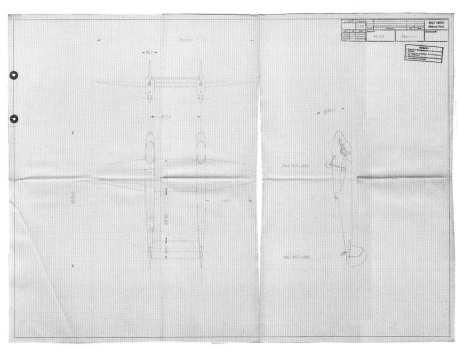

ABOVE: The Wolf Hirth Hi 23 was a slightly smaller aircraft than the Jas 5 and its rocket motors were in its fuselages. This drawing is dated October 20, 1941 – five days later than the date of the report it accompanies.

Jacobs-Schweyer

October 1941

Artwork by Luca Landino

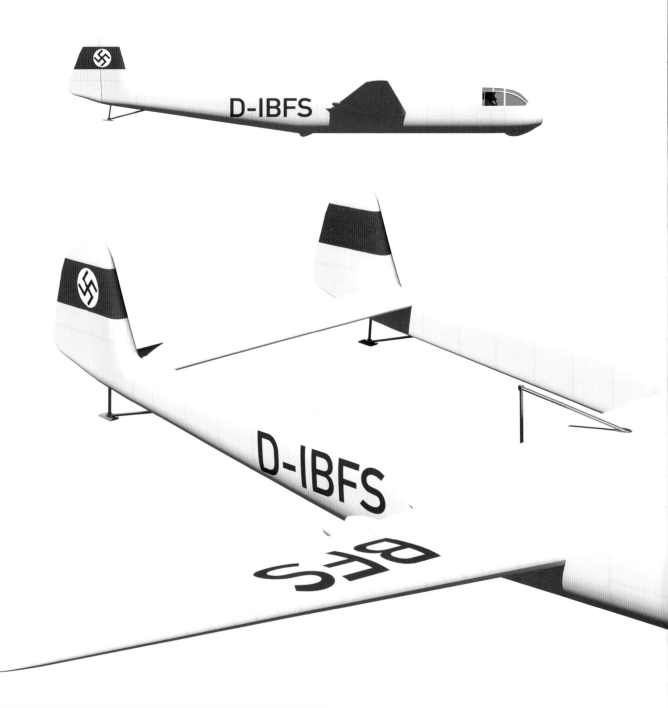

D-IBFS

COMMENTS

The 'measuring aircraft' Jas P 5 featured a clever twin-fuselage layout but little research was available on how the glider would behave when its four wing-mounted rocket motors were fired. The aircraft's highly unusual shape and its requirement to fly at speeds of up to 625km/h (388mph) ought to have necessitated some lengthy wind tunnel studies beforehand too – a point raised in Jacobs-Schweyer's report on the design.

Jas P 5

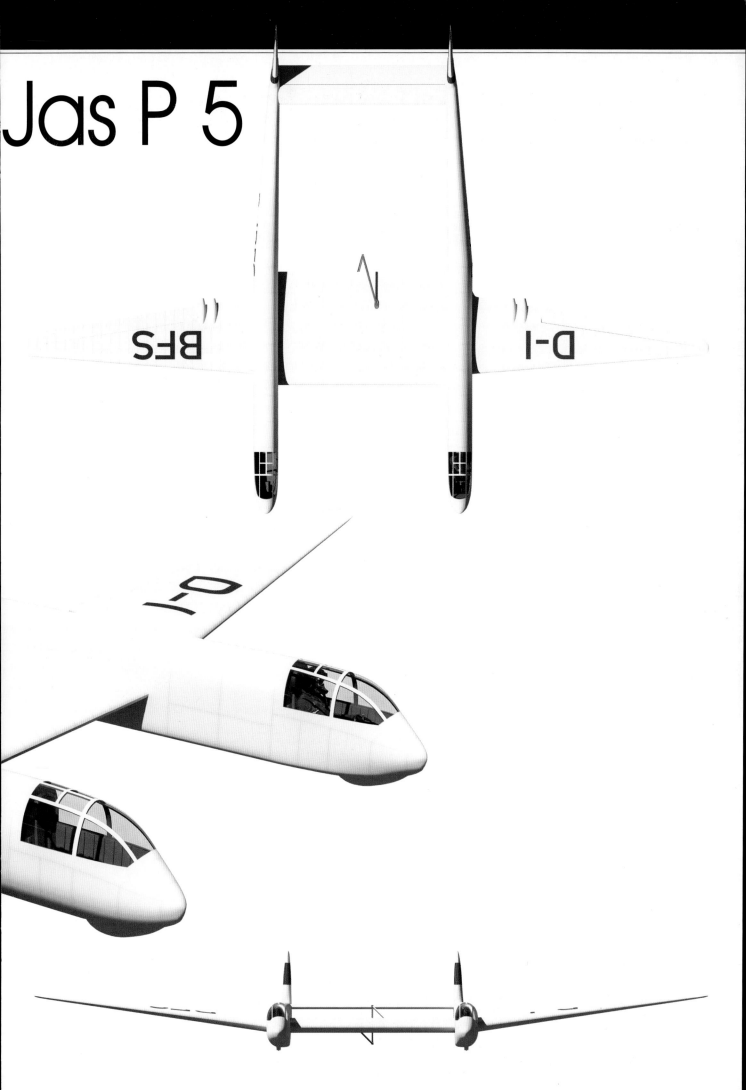

Expect delay

DFS 332

Efforts to create a rocket-powered twin-fuselage wing profile test glider were renewed in 1943 with the DFS 332 and would continue sporadically until the end of the war...

A little more light is shed on the impetus behind the 'Messflugzeug' programme by the major Allied intelligence report on the DFS, CIOS XXXII-66, in which Professor Paul Ruden, director of the DFS institute for aerodynamics, is questioned about his wartime activities.

His part of the report states: "The maximum speed of the DFS 230 [multirole glider] is limited to a little over 200km/h for reasons of stability. A compulsory upper limit resulted for the highest obtainable Reynolds number, which could only be pushed a little over the critical Reynolds-number of the even plate.

"The DFS 230 was not suitable for the examination on the influence of the surface roughness and even less for the examination of laminar profiles.

Construction of a special research glider with greater speed was suggested, which should provide at the same time profile variations by a simple method.

"The suggestion provided for a twin fuselaged aircraft with movable centre wing and was given for construction to the sister institute for glider flight (Dipl. Ing. Kracht, DFS 332). The flight examination on the influence of surface roughness and on laminar profiles were to be continued after completion of the DFS 332 from the institute of the undersigned [i.e. Ruden].

"In order to hasten the work two research gliders were ordered at the same time and one was to be at the disposal for the institute of the undersigned and the other one for the institute for flight mechanics and aerodynamics of the DVL."

'Kracht' was Felix Kracht, head of the DFS institute for glider construction. The DFS was composed of five sub-institutes in all: Ruden's aerodynamics section, glider construction under Kracht, flight experiments under Fritz Stamer, flight equipment under Eduard Fischel and atmospheric physics under Fritz Hohndorf.

The idea for the DFS 332 evidently came from the RLM's Flugbaumeister Scheibe towards the end of 1942. A

BELOW: The DFS 332 twin-fuselage glider as drawn in 1944. It appears to be somewhat more closely related to the Wolf Hirth Hi 23 than the Jacobs-Schweyer Jas P 5 – with its rocket motors in its fuselages and its short, broad, outer wings. The glider had a wheeled undercarriage, rather than the more usual skid, because tests had found that designs with two skids tended to turn sideways on landing.

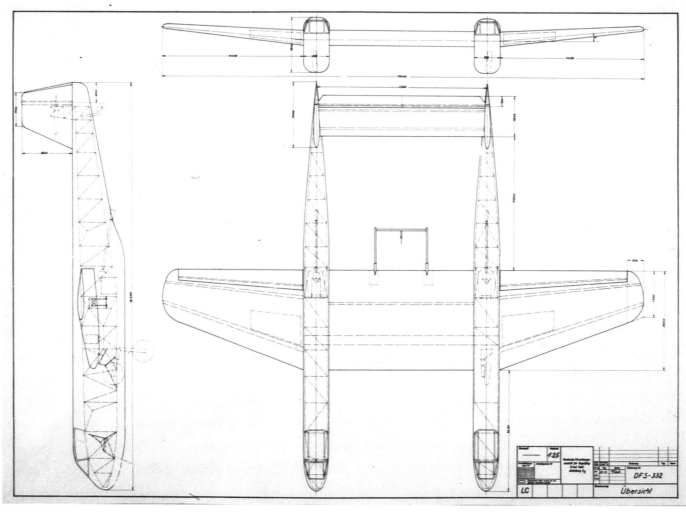

proposal for the aircraft was put together by the DFS and presented to the head of the RLM's C-E department Georg Pasewaldt at the beginning of December 1942. This resulted in a preliminary order for 10 aircraft, according to the minutes of an RLM development committee meeting on January 8, 1943, at which the order was approved by the Generalluftzeugmeister Erhard Milch.

Further explanation of the DFS 332's genesis is offered in an anonymous report of June 18, 1945. Entitled 'Bericht über Aufbau und Arbeiten des Instituts für Flugzeugbau (S) der Deutschen Forschungsanstalt für Segelflug „Ernst Udet" e.V.' or 'Report on the organisation and work of the Institute for Aircraft Construction (S) of the German Institute for Glider Research (DFS) "Ernst Udet",' this report would appear, in fact, to have been written by Kracht based on similarities between the information it contains and other writings directly attributable to him. It says: "The desire of the aviation research office (Luftfahrtforschung) was repeatedly made known, to test the validity of the profile values, established by the wind tunnel, by control measurements in flight in the open atmosphere. These tests were to be extended simultaneously to the Reynolds numbers as they were to be applied to larger airplanes in the near future."

The 'Luftfahrtforschung' referred to here appears to be the Forschungsführung des Reichsluftfahrtministers und Oberbefehlshabers der Luftwaffe at Göttingen – the Luftwaffe's aviation research command, known as 'FoFü' (or sometimes 'Fo-Fü') for short.

The report continues: "For this purpose, the DFS designed a special research airplane, the DFS 332. It was endeavoured to measure approximately the various lifting values in a sphere of ca = 0 to ca = 0.6 with most constant speeds in horizontal flight. Therefore, this measuring wing had to be installed to pivot, in flight, within certain limits – totally about 20° to the other wing.

"In order to eliminate the disturbing influence of the end (wing) conditions and the resulting crosscurrents, the 'measuring profile' was to be situated in the symmetric axis of the wing. These demands necessitated the construction of a twin fuselage airplane, with a fixed outer wing and an easily interchangeable centre wing which was to be adjustable as to its position in flight. It was desired to be able to install profiles of a thickness down to 9%.

"500km/h was provided as a standard measuring speed with a profile chord of 3m, so that measurements with Reynolds numbers of RE = 30.10° could be carried out. The measuring speed in the horizontal flight was obtained and maintained by rocket engines. Cold Walter apparatus with a thrust of 650kg are intended as engines."

According to a brief DFS memo dated March 1, 1945, headed 'Messtechnik' or 'measuring technology': "The aircraft

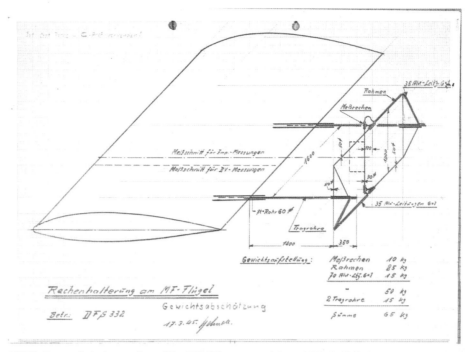

ABOVE: The central wing section of the DFS 332 was movable and fitted with instruments so its reaction to different speeds and angles of attack could be measured. The open frame fitted to the trailing edge was fitted with small measuring devices.

is to be towed to 4000m altitude. After adjusting the measuring angle to the desired angle, the first step is reaching the desired speed with a push [into a dive]. After reaching the measuring airspeed the glider enters a horizontal flight and this is maintained by switching on and regulating the engines for the duration of the measurement.

"The registration of the measured quantities is carried out by four-variable recorder (dynamic pressure, angle of attack, etc.) and multiple pressure gauges (pressure distribution, pulse measurement), which are recorded by robotic cameras. Due to the short duration of the actual measurement flight (1 + 2 min), the turnaround point measurements have to be carried out with an electrical measuring system."

The June 18, 1945, report gives some indication as to why the aircraft took so long to complete: "The difficulties were considerable, especially for the construction, because the complete horizontal tail assembly has to be adjusted along with the measuring wing. The construction, most of which was carried out in the branch of Prien, has been finished for quite a while. All calculation and construction data are in Prien in good condition.

"As a start, two experimental models were to be manufactured, but the workshop capacity of the DFS was not sufficient. Therefore, a great part of the work was given to firms of the aviation industry. Tail assemblies and cowling and fairing of the fuselages were made by the firm Wrede in Freilassing, while the firm Caudron in Paris was commissioned with the construction of the steel tube fuselages and the metal spar for the measuring wing with profiles of 15% thickness.

"However, only the parts for one

aircraft were delivered from there with great delay. For that reason the commission for the manufacture of the second fuselage set and further spars for profiles of 9% and 12% thickness was given in autumn 1944 to the testing station of the GAF [German air force] in Travemünde (Erprobungsstelle der Luftwaffe). The parts were finished there, but could not be sent any more, due to the transport prohibition."

Despite its component parts being mostly completed, the first and only DFS 332 was destined never to be fully assembled. Some postwar accounts of the type have suggested that it flew but the evidence suggests that this is highly unlikely. The report goes on: "The measuring wing, including the measuring equipment installations for the first model are practically finished. The outer wings lack partially the skin as yet. Also finished are all fuselage-build-in parts, whose installation had already begun. All parts for the first model are on the aerodrome Ainring in undamaged condition. Only the ailerons and the fuselage cowling and fairing were destroyed during the fire at the firm Wrede.

"The cold Walter engines provided for the first model were lost in the last few days. Nothing is known yet of their whereabouts. But the engines, delivered for the second model are still in Prien. Therefore, the first experimental model can be completed without great difficulties. Under the present conditions this would require approximately 3 to 4 months."

It would appear that the various component parts of the DFS 332 were scrapped shortly after the war's end – finally concluding a development programme which had begun five years earlier and achieved very little. ●

The zombie bomber

Heinkel P 1068 and DFS P 1068

Having started out as a twin-engine rival for Arado's Ar 234, the Heinkel P 1068 evolved into a six-engine advanced bomber before being scaled back to become the He 343. But the project survived the He 343's cancellation – after a fashion – and ended up being built as a series of DFS flight test aircraft instead...

Heinkel's jet bomber project, the P 1068, appears to have been a direct result of the engine and aircraft layout studies carried out in advance of the Schnellstbomber competition towards the end of 1942 (see p84-87). In trying to work out the best way of building a bomber fast enough to evade any chance of enemy interception, both Heinkel and Junkers had determined that jet engines showed great promise.

A summary of the meeting on January 19, 1943, ends with the note: "For the jet aircraft, a special action is planned anyway; the practical design of the jet bomber is to take place in the form of a joint effort between Heinkel and Junkers."

What happened to this cooperation is unclear but the earliest known mention of the P 1068 comes from a summary of a meeting between RLM GL/C-E 2 representatives Major Hoffmann and Walter Friebel, who was at the January 19 meeting, and Heinkel representatives including Ernst Heinkel himself and company technical director Carl Francke.

The purpose of the meeting, on June 8, 1943, was to "discuss the entire development programme". Item four on the agenda was the P 1068 and the summary states: "EHF [Ernst Heinkel Flugzeugwerke] introduces the 2-motor solution (2 x Hs 11 or Jumo). As a bomb load is provided: 1 x SC 1000. The PC 1400 is very desirable and space as a result of the same dimensions makes this readily possible. The influence of the heavy weight of the bomb on the aircraft's range and takeoff is examined.

"Since the Arado 234 (2-engine) in a similar version as P 1068 already flies in July, a 4-engine

solution was discussed. According to EHF the benefits are not much better. It results in the same speeds and ranges as in P 1068 2-engine with about a double bomb load. The P 1068 2-engine has the advantage over the Arado 234 of internal bombs, which means an estimated speed increase of 80km/h.

"Accurate project comparisons, 2-engine and 4-engine are currently under way at EHF and will soon be submitted to the RLM."

In December 1943, the P 1068 was handed over to the DFS for further development as a 1:2 scale 'model' aircraft. Under a heading of 'Development of a model airplane of the project P 1068', the DFS's monthly progress report for December 1943 states: "The model is intended to clarify the most diverse questions of flight mechanics, in particular slow-flight behaviour with heavily swept wings. The DFS took over the project processing, while construction is to be undertaken by a glider company. The development was started."

Meanwhile, Heinkel still hoped that its P 1068 series would still become a bomber too. On January 14, 1944, the company produced a folder of drawings showing different versions of its P 1068 for the RLM. The introductory note included with this folder, Report No. 1/44, references an earlier report to the RLM, No. 56/43, and states that "compared to the information in report 56, the performance is slightly improved by taking into account the latest profile measurements.

"The aircraft is shown with the same dimensions also with remote controlled rear turret and without rear turret with 6 engines. Furthermore, a data sheet with 2100mm wide

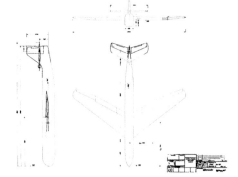

ABOVE: DFS drawing of the P 1068-00.101, which had a wingspan of 9m, dated September 26, 1943. The series of 1:2 scale P 1068 'models' was to be used for investigating different wing sweepback and engine configurations.

hull and 2800mm gauge according to the latest state of construction is attached."

Within two weeks Heinkel had produced a new report entitled 'Strabo 16 to'. This was in response to a request for a rapid availability basic fast jet bomber and Heinkel set out how the 'Strabo' 16 ton bomber – a simplified four-engine version of the P 1068 – could be brought to production in record time using a process which would eventually be put into practice for the He 162.

With some minor changes the 'Strabo' was given the designation He 343, embodied in a report of March 14, 1944, and went on to eventually be defeated by the Ju 287 forward-swept design in July 1944. But work on the P 1068 models continued unabated at the DFS.

A report on DFS activities between December 1, 1943, and March 31, 1944, states: "Model P-1068 – For the 25° swept dynamic-similar model, the construction documents are completed except for the engine nacelles. The parts are under construction. The flight deadline is scheduled for 30.4.44.

"The construction documents for the 35° dynamic-similar model are almost finished, also except for the nacelles. Flight deadline is 10.5.44. For the 0° Mach model currently the construction works, while for the 35° Mach model still basic design questions are to be cleared." What exactly all this meant will be explained in more detail in the next chapter. Suffice to say it clearly indicates that work on four DFS P 1068s was already well under way by the end of March 1944. Hopes of a bomber P 1068 may have died but the project would live on as a sub-scale test aircraft... ●

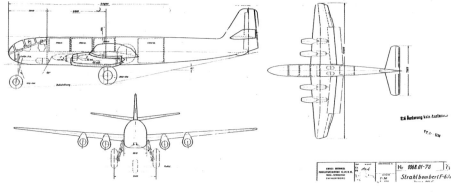

ABOVE: This drawing from the January 14, 1944, report shows P 1068.01-78 – a four-engine 20m long, 19m wingspan, 60m² wing area, design with room for 10,790 litres of fuel and a bomb bay that could take munitions up to the SC2000 bomb. The drawing itself is dated January 7, 1944.

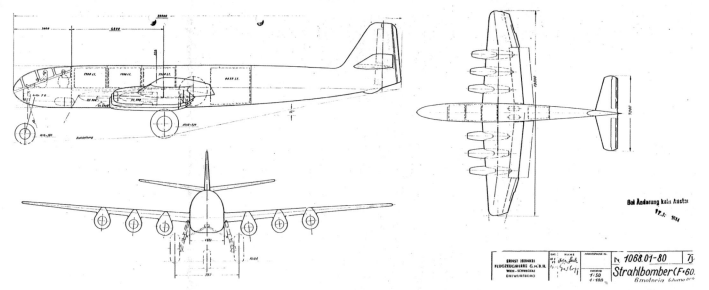

ABOVE: The P 1068.01-80 dated January 10, 1944. The aircraft was the same in every dimension as the -78 but had six engines instead of four.

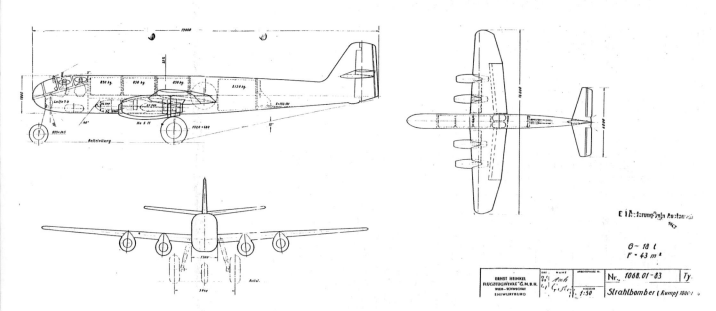

ABOVE: While it may look similar to the -78 and -80, the P 1068.01-83, shown in this drawing dated January 13, 1944, was a very different aircraft. It was much smaller – just 17m long and with a 16m wingspan and 43m² wing area. It carried just 4700kg of fuel for its four engines but had two rear-facing MG 151s in its fuselage for defence.

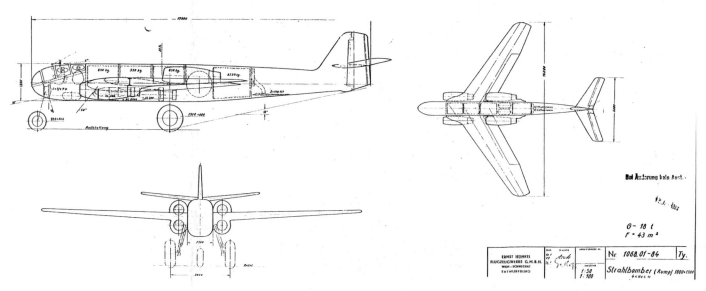

ABOVE: The most extreme P 1068 of all, the .01-84, had the same narrow fuselage dimensions as the -83 and also had a 16m wingspan with 43m² wing area – but it also had sharply swept wings and its four turbojets were attached to its fuselage rather than the wings. Its tailplanes were also swept.

Heinkel P 1068.01-84

January 1944

Artwork by Luca Landino

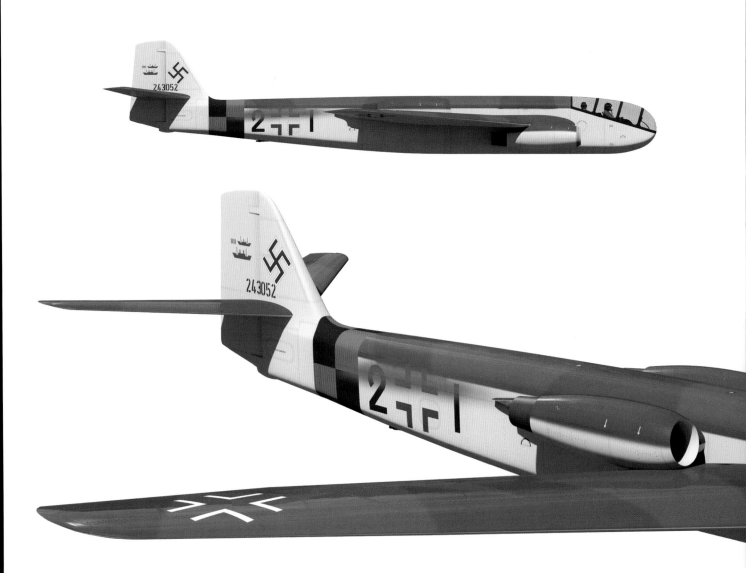

COMMENTS

With its swept wings and turbojets attached to its fuselage, the P 1068.01-84 embodied Heinkel's design philosophy of creating very aerodynamically clean aircraft. As a bomber, it would have been relatively short-ranged, having less than half the fuel capacity of the larger known P 1068 designs. But its swept wings and aerodynamic engine arrangement would probably have given it a useful speed advantage. Dimensionally, it is only slightly smaller than the Junkers Ju 287 which, as built, measured 18.3m long compared to the .01-84's 17m and had a wingspan of 20.11m compared to the .01-84's 16m.

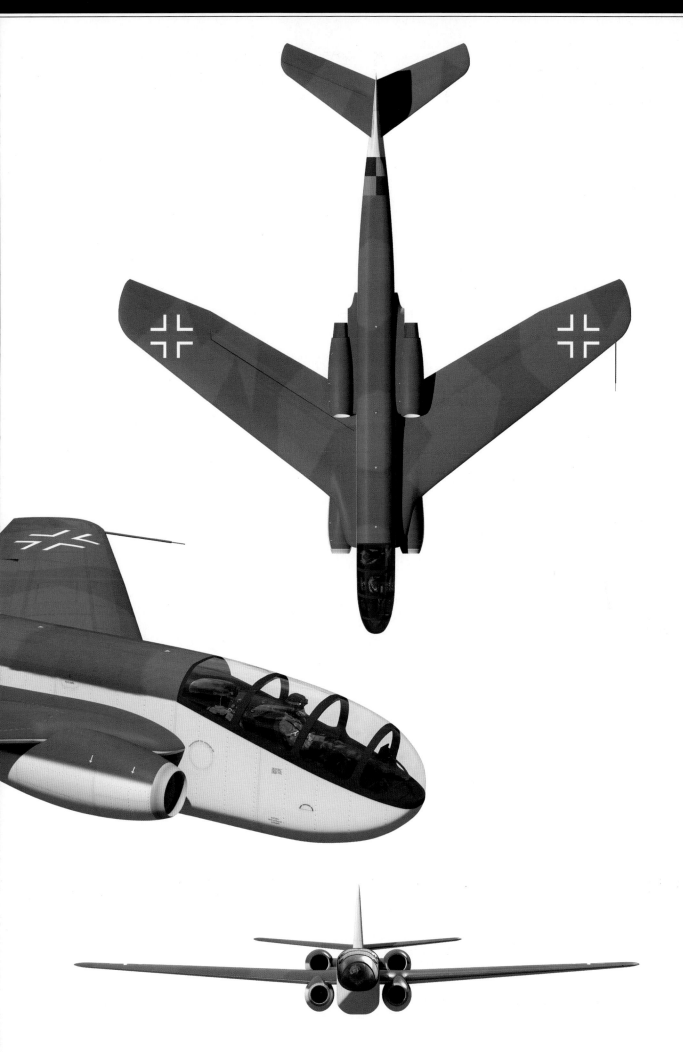

Forward view of the DFS 228 V1. This rare colour image of the aircraft as captured, with its wings still attached, shows just how difficult it must have been for the seated pilot to see out – particularly when landing. A prone pilot position was to have been introduced with the V2.

Feeling supersonic

DFS 228, DFS P 1068 and DFS 346

Even as the war was entering its last desperate stages, the RLM pressed ahead with a three-step programme of research intended to get a rocket-propelled manned aircraft through the sound barrier.

Exactly when the RLM began a programme of research dedicated to studying the effects of high-speed flight up to and through the sound barrier is unclear but it would appear to have been built on the back of a single aircraft design – the DFS 228.

During the 1930s German gliders had been able to achieve ever greater altitudes to the point where they reached the limits of human endurance. Pilots were suffering from oxygen deprivation and severe frostbite and something would need to be done to protect them if still higher altitudes were to be achieved.

The background is explained in a paper prepared by DFS glider construction institute leader Felix Kracht for the Deutschen Akademie der Luftfahrtforschung (DAL), the German Academy for Aeronautical Research in November 1944, entitled Gedanken über

Entwicklung eines Flugzeuges zum Einsatz in extrem grossen Flughöhen or 'Thoughts about developing an aircraft for use in extremely high altitudes'.

He stated that attempts to glide higher "were interrupted shortly after the beginning of the war, as more urgent and immediate tasks came to DFS; but the deeper reason is to be found in the fact that as early as 1940 the limits of the available aircraft were achieved. The ability to substantially exceed 11,600m altitude seems to be within reach according to meteorologists, but requires a flying device that allows the pilot of the aircraft to remain at these heights.

"The normal oxygen system with oxygen mask is no longer sufficient for these heights. So for these research flights a glider would need to be equipped with a pressurised cabin. But that would necessitate the development of a new type of aircraft.

"In spite of the burden of other things, DFS

tackled the solution to this problem, which was a familiar one, and worked on the development constructively. War conditions, however, slowed the execution. Only the pressurised cabin was built, as there was a significant interest in its testing. This was prompted by considerations about the ability of a glider or a plane of comparatively low weight to lift ratio with short-duration engines and to reach heights which are outside the reach of existing warplanes. In the event that such an aircraft still had sufficient performance when it reached its target altitude, it was planned to use it at that height as an unarmed reconnaissance aircraft."

This account of why a high-altitude pressure cabin-equipped glider needed a rocket motor – so it could reach high altitude fast enough to avoid any chance of interference from enemy fighters – skips rather lightly over what was really a lengthy and difficult development process.

ABOVE: The DFS 228 V1, D-IBFQ, as viewed from the side while resting on its landing skid on the back of a low loader.

The unattributed June 18, 1945, document Bericht über Aufbau und Arbeiten des Instituts für Flugzeugbau (S) der Deutschen Forschungsanstalt für Segelflug „Ernst Udet" e.V., probably also written by Kracht, explains that the first of the 'new type of aircraft' in question was the DFS 54 – an unpowered glider fitted with a pressure cabin. Work on this started in the autumn of 1940. The document says: "Development and construction research [for the DFS 54] were finished and the construction of the sample aircraft was about 80 per cent completed. Later, the construction had to be stopped due to the war situation. All constructional parts are in Prien. According to the original plans the completion of the airplane would take about 2 to 3 months, but it has to be considered that the design of the model has been improved by later development research."

The DFS official progress report for September 1942 shows work on the DFS 54 still in progress, stating: "Development of a glider for high altitude. The density tests with the cabin were continued. The breakage test gave a breaking strength of 1.1 atmospheres. Taking into account that the shell was made with 2mm plywood instead of 2.5 and the fibre direction of the planking was unfavourable, the result is very satisfactory, since the operating pressure is 0.6 atmospheres maximum and a safety J = 1.8 has already been achieved in the cabin as built.

"Further, the whole cabin construction was finished. The cable lead-through and the hood locks have already been tested. In addition, investigations were made into whether it is possible to disembark such a special-purpose aircraft."

When the DFS produced Hausbericht Nr. 21 of February 9, 1942, outlining the possibilities for achieving high altitude flight, the RLM requested the development of a high altitude reconnaissance aircraft capable of flying above 10km with a range of 800-1000km. By April, the DFS was working on a new aircraft known as 'A-HS 7' – essentially the DFS 54 fitted with a rocket motor and fuel tanks. This was eventually outlined in a brochure on September 20, 1942, entitled Entwurf eines Segelflugzeuges zum Einsatz als Aufklärer in grossen Höhen or 'Design of a glider for use as reconnaissance aircraft at high altitudes'. Early the following year it received the designation DFS 228. Interviewed by historian David Myhra during the 1980s, Kracht said: "Then came the development of the DFS 54. This had been

ABOVE: Rear view of the DFS 228 V1 with its rocket motor, or perhaps a spare rocket motor, positioned behind it on a wooden crate. The aircraft's tailplanes have already suffered heavy damage.

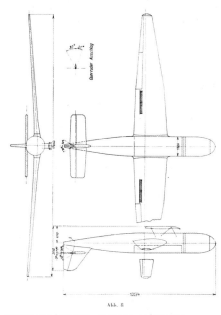

ABOVE: The DFS 228, as shown in Kracht's November 1944 presentation. It was similar to the DFS 54 but with a rocket motor and fuel tanks installed.

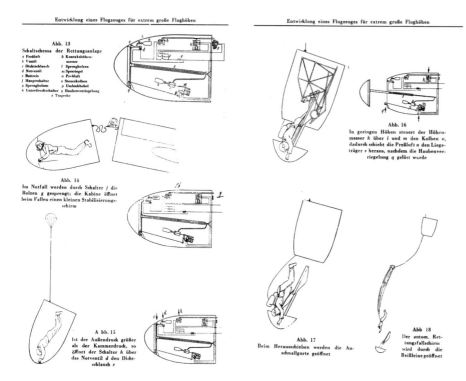

ABOVE: Diagrams showing the innovative escape system developed for the DFS 228 V2. The V2 was mostly destroyed before it could be completed.

finished about 75% but then we shifted over to the DFS 228. This was because in 1943 we didn't have any time any more for pure civil soaring and therefore, we set the DFS 54 aside for more friendly days. I then devoted my full time to the development of the DFS 228."

The August 1943 DFS progress report states: "Development of a glider for high altitude (DFS 54). The construction of the aircraft was completed in the reporting period. The construction of the pressurised cabin is about to be completed. The cabin is then tested in the altitude chamber of the E-Stelle Rechlin.

"Development of a high altitude reconnaissance aircraft (DFS 228). The construction proofs for the fuselage were

largely carried out and the drawings were completed down to the last detail. Individual assemblies are already in workshop processing."

Four months later, the official DFS progress report for December 1943 says: "Development of a glider for high altitude (DFS 54). Construction was completed. The cabin has been completed, it is currently being tested for strength and tightness. Testing in the altitude chamber of E-Stelle Rechlin will follow. The remaining assemblies are expected to be completed by the end of construction.

"Development of a high altitude reconnaissance aircraft (DFS 228). The supporting and tail units are under

construction and will be completed by mid-January. Fuselage, fuel system, engine installation are currently in work. If there are no new difficulties, the V1 will be ready to fly at the beginning of March."

The progress report for March 1944 makes no mention of the DFS 54, only including an entry for the 'high altitude reconnaissance aircraft' which says: "The construction is complete. Wings, tail and fuselage are completed and are currently being assembled; also the cabin with seat carrier and equipment. Delays occurred as a result of procurement difficulties. The aircraft should be ready for flight during the month of May 1944."

SUPERSONICS
But while the pressure cabin tests would have been useful for gliding research, why continue with the programme when the war situation was already going from bad to worse? The June 18, 1945, report next outlines the DFS 228's purpose as part of a wider programme of research into supersonic speeds: "With the increase of flying speeds and their approach to the speed of sound the question of the flight-mechanical behaviour at high Mach numbers grew steadily more important, especially for the reaching and passing beyond the speed of sound. The evaluation of the available wind tunnel measurements on sub and supersonic speeds indicated that exceeding of the speed of sound is possible as far as performance is concerned, with rocket engines, available in Germany, in high altitudes above 20km.

"The execution of these experiments appears especially important to the Luftfahrtforschung (office of air research), because experiments with high Mach numbers above M = 1.1 are not possible in the

BELOW: Side view of the DFS 228 V2 with prone pilot cockpit from Kracht's 1944 presentation.

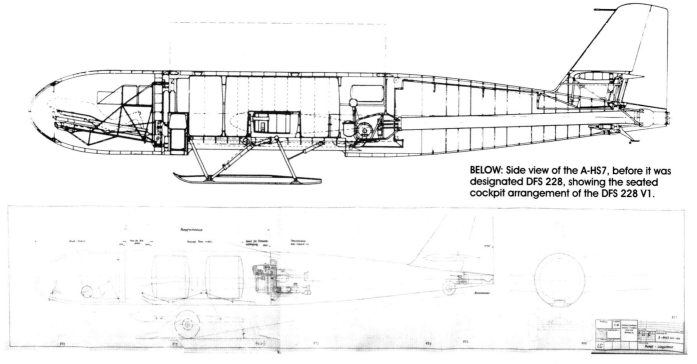

BELOW: Side view of the A-HS7, before it was designated DFS 228, showing the seated cockpit arrangement of the DFS 228 V1.

ABOVE: The DFS 228 V1 coming in to land. The distinctive 'swordfish' graphic painted on the aircraft's port side is just visible.

ABOVE: Rather than being towed aloft, the DFS 228 was launched from the back of a Dornier Do 217 K – only activating its rocket engine at the appropriate altitude.

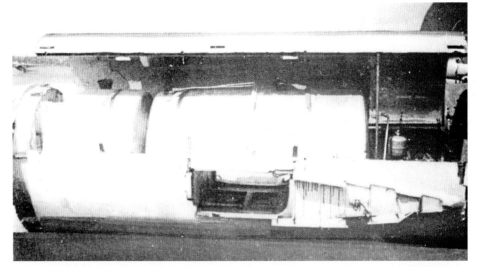

ABOVE: Port view of the DFS 228's fuselage with access hatch open and the aircraft's rocket fuel tanks visible. The central tank was for oxidiser T-Stoff (high-test peroxide) while the tank to the left was for C-Stoff – the fuel itself. The ratio of T-Stoff used to C-Stoff was 3:1.

wind tunnel; and because the influence of the pressure thrust on the flight-mechanical behaviour can be clarified only in free flight. Carrying out the flight in high altitudes has the further advantage, that the stress becomes considerably smaller than on the ground; as the dynamic pressure in the vicinity of the speed of sound, is only about 4% in altitude, of what the pressure would be on the ground.

"Apart from this, the flight in this altitude brings a number of difficulties; especially the air supply for the pressurised cabin. Further, the possibility to use rocket engines in these altitudes remains to be cleared up, and provisions for the rescue of the pilot in case of emergency have to be provided. Independent of that, all possibilities are to be examined, which are apt to move the critical Mach number into the sphere of higher speeds; and to reduce the increased resistance when the speed of sound is exceeded. The greatest gain in this respect is promised by the swept-back wing, but no exact data are available on the optimal sweep back."

In essence, it was thought that four elements were necessary for a supersonic aircraft on which crucial research data was missing: a pressure cabin, a means of pilot escape, rocket motors and swept wings.

The report goes on: "All these problems could not be solved in a single test flight, therefore the DFS proposed a step-by-step solution in three sections. The first section comprises the development and testing of the pressurised cabin and the rescue possibilities for the pilot, in case of emergency. Furthermore, it includes the testing of the engines and the engine installation in great altitudes.

"The second section should determine the best angle of sweep back at which the critical Mach number can be moved back as far as possible, and at the angle the resistance increases when exceeding the speed of sound. Simultaneously this section should determine the flight-mechanical behaviour of swept back wings under high subsonic speeds; especially also in the range of high lifting coefficients, as well as on the efficiency of landing-aid devices. Finally in the third section, it was planned to develop an actual aircraft for flights at and above the speed of sound.

"The first section calls for a test carrier for great altitudes. For this purpose the DFS designed the model DFS 228 which, intentionally, was limited to relatively low Mach numbers (M = 0.75) and to subsonic speeds. On the basis of the submitted data, the RLM was required to construct the aircraft in such a manner that it could be employed for short range reconnaissance purposes at great altitudes over especially dangerous areas."

It would appear that although the DFS 228 was intended as a test aircraft for pressure cabins and rocket engines, whether originally as part of a supersonic research programme or not, the RLM could only get approval to build it on the basis that it would also be able to perform a militarily useful role too – high altitude reconnaissance.

"The flying distance asked for and the

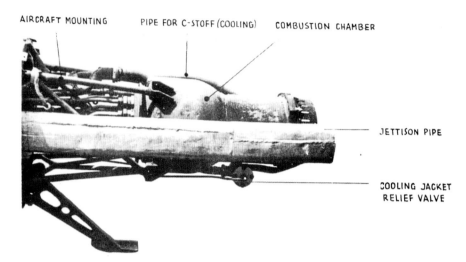

AIRCRAFT MOUNTING   PIPE FOR C-STOFF (COOLING)   COMBUSTION CHAMBER

JETTISON PIPE

COOLING JACKET
RELIEF VALVE

ABOVE: Rear section of the DFS 228's propulsion unit showing combustion chamber and fuel jettison pipe.

fuel capacity required for this, made this task more difficult. However, the aircraft in its present form can still be used for its original purpose. The design was intended for a ceiling of about 25km. The first two prototypes have been completed. Practical experiences with the first model indicated the necessity to modify the pressurised cabin, because the vision was not sufficient and the emergency escape installation as well as the air proofing of the cabin created considerable difficulties, because of the great surfaces involved.

"For this reason the position of the pilot in the second model was chosen to be a prone position, which permits these problems to be solved easily. A part of this cabin could be secured in comparatively good condition in Hörsching. All constructional data are at hand. The wing assemblies and the control assemblies for both X-models were manufactured by the Schmetz firm, Herzogenrath. The fuselages and the cabins were constructed by the DFS. The Wrede firm in Freilassing, who were supposed to have built two further aircraft, did not get started with this work."

British intelligence report A.I.2(g) No. 2/46, on the DFS 228, offers a few more insights on the aircraft and its design: "Performance. Since DFS had built up a greater experience of gliders than any similar institution in the world it was not unnatural that the 228 photo recce aircraft was developed from a glider. The Walter rocket unit is particularly adaptable for powering aircraft of this type since the dry weight of the power installation is only 368lb, thus the gliding weight of the aircraft is low and a wing loading of 15.5lb/sq ft at 75,000ft and 9.4lb/sq ft at 39,400ft permit the extensive glides which make possible the range of 650 miles.

"The maximum speed of 560mph at sea level and 435mph at 75,000ft is limited by the critical Mach number of .66. Since the stalling speed of the aircraft is estimated as being below 500mph it is possible to reach a height of 84,000ft before critical Mach number and stalling speed coincide. Handling of the aircraft would be extremely difficult if not impossible at or near this critical height so the operational height was reduced to 75,000ft.

"In the 228 V1 the pilot sat in the normal

flying attitude with resultant poor visibility. The 228 V2 was to have had a prone position, the pilot then having his head close to the single forward window which gave much improved forward vision.

"Conclusion. The aerodynamic characteristics of this aircraft are of less importance than the design of the pressure cabin. A speed of 435mph claimed at 70,000ft is not great, this being only .66 Mach. High thrust, irrespective of height, makes possible the high rate of climb and the modest wing loading when most of the fuel is used up makes possible the extensive gliding which extends the total range of the aircraft to 650 miles with a full power endurance of only four and a half minutes.

"It is on the reliable operation of the pressure cabin that the success of the aircraft depends. Sudden and absolute failure of pressure at 75,000ft would mean the instant death of the pilot. To build a cabin of light construction that was, at the same time, thoroughly dependable involved a departure from the established practice in pressure cabin design.

"Should it become necessary to abandon the aircraft the pilot must remain within his pressure cabin until a safe altitude is reached at which he could live without additional oxygen. Thus the pressure cabin was to have been jettisoned and the pilot later ejected from the cabin. Planning and design were sound, the difficulties had been faced in a practical manner and although simplification resulted in some discomfort to the pilot this cannot be regarded as serious in view of the short flying time of the aircraft.

"Nevertheless the enormity of the problem of reliable pressurisation, when sudden failure has such dire results, cannot be ignored. The DFS 228 is magnificent in conception, but it had travelled only about a third of the way towards its final development."

DFS P 1068s
Returning to the 'second section' of research on developments necessary for

The DFS 228's Walter
rocket motor.

STEAM
GENERATOR

FORWARD
BULKHEAD

T-STOFF
PUMP

STEAM CONTROL
VALVE

AIR CONTROL
VALVE

ABOVE: Cockpit hatch of the DFS 228 as viewed from the underside.

ABOVE: Emergency ejection valve of the DFS 228.

supersonic flight, the June 18, 1945, report says: "The second section should be solved by the building of the series of P 1068. The following versions were planned: P 1068 with 25° sweep back angle, P 1068 A with 35° sweep back angle, P 1068 B with 0° sweep back angle and additional propulsion, P 1068 C with 35° sweep back angle and additional propulsion, P 1068 D with 35° sweep back angle and laminar wings.

"As landing equipment, all models were furnished with slots and fowler flaps, except that the P 1068 D was to be equipped with leading edge split flaps instead of the standard slots. In all models, engine nacelle and cowling could be built in for the TL propelling units Jumo 004 or HeS 11. The Wrede firm in Freilassing did the construction work.

"The first model survived undamaged and was removed recently from Ainring by American military authorities. Its present location is unknown. The second model was destroyed in the beginning of May in Hörsching. Approximately 40 take-offs were carried out with the first model and flight characteristics of the aircraft body were tested without engines. Then ground tests of the engines and fuel installation were completed. However, due to the flying prohibition flight tests with the engines could not be carried out.

"The data for the construction of the P 1068, P 1068 A and P 1068 B, as well as to a great extent, the data for the model P 1068 D, and also a series of static tests were still necessary to complete the P 1068 C, before the construction of the wings could be started. The construction of all models was planned to be carried out by the Wrede firm in Freilassing. The DFS was limited to supply single complicated parts,

and to install the electric and measuring equipment. The P 1068 was almost finished. The model P 1068 A was completed about 40 to 50%.

"Construction of parts for the P 1068 C had been started. All parts, as well as a small amount of construction data, were completely destroyed by the fire at the Wrede firm."

An interrogation of Walter Georgii on June 10, 1945, reported in Allied CIOS report XXXII-66 Deutsche Forschungsanstalt für Segelflug, Ainring, says: "The 1068 is a series of four aircraft identical except for the angle of sweep-back which was 0, 25, 35 and 45 degrees respectively; the purpose is to check aerodynamic calculations on the effect of sweep-back exchangeable mid-section of

wing mounted in such a way that its angle of incidence can be changed during flight and so that lift, drag and moment can be measured accurately, the purpose is to test high performance air foils at high Reynolds numbers in turbulence-free air.

"The four models of the 1068 were completely designed; drawings are available. The 25° sweep-back model was almost completed and the 35° model was partially constructed at the firm Wrede at Freilassing. They were completely destroyed in a recent raid.

"All four were to be equipped with mountings for four power unit nacelles, whether on the wings or on the fuselage. Either the Ju 004 or the HeS 011 could be used. In addition the 0, 35, and 45 models were

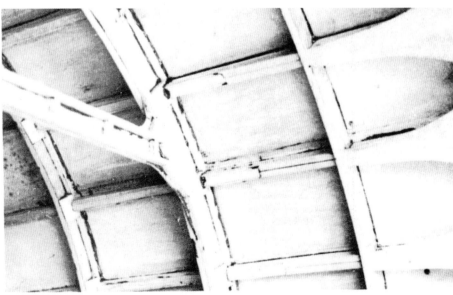

ABOVE: DFS 228 rear fuselage construction as seen from the inside.

ABOVE: Four display models of the DFS P 1068. Each has the same fuselage but a different wing sweepback angle, going from 0° on the model to the bottom left to 25°, centre bottom, 35° on the bottom right model and finally 45° on the model that is fixed to a display stand. Exactly what the full-scale DFS P 1068 looked like is unknown – but sources confirm that it was built.

to have a Walter rocket propulsion unit of 1500kg thrust in order to get excess speed."

The first report states that about 40 take-offs were carried out with the completed but unpowered 25° swept P 1068 1:2 scale 'model', while Georgii states that it was never completed. It is possible Georgii regarded the aircraft as incomplete because it was never equipped with its turbojets.

In any case, the minutes of a meeting held at the FoFü in Berlin on July 18, 1944 suggest that none of the P 1068s were originally intended to include rocket propulsion. Among those in attendance were Walter Georgii, Kracht and Ruden from the DFS, Hans Multhopp from Focke-Wulf, Scheibe and Oberingenieur Malz from the RLM's GL/C-E 2, Adolf Busemann from the LFA, plus two representatives from Heinkel – Motzfeld and Eichler.

The minutes state: "For the airspeed range, in which Mach-influences are not decisive, a manned example of the model P 1068 with Walter drive is to be built. The aim of this model is to measure wing moments and polar. The construction was completed, according to Mr Kracht, in 7-8 weeks. The change of the construction for the above mentioned task will take about 2 months. For the metalwork, the department E 2 will try to free the company Siebel. The reception of the E-Stelle Travemünde for such work is under investigation.

"For woodwork the companies Focke-Wulf and Junkers, the production groups Silesia

and Poznan are to be consulted with the help of the special committee F4. The purpose is to investigate the flight behaviour of low-velocity and high-speed swept wing aircraft and perform profile and roughness surveys. The profile is released by the wind tunnel committee in cooperation with DFS. For measurement purposes, a drive duration of 100 seconds is sufficient.

"The Committee for Aircraft Mechanics will be available to advise on the installation of measuring instruments. The amount of construction hours, wood and metal work is put together and the research management and E 2 announced."

On July 20, 1944, the AVA produced a report entitled 'Stability measurements on the Heinkel overall model P 1068 with special engines'. This states: "Overview: Three- and six-component measurements were made on the overall model P 1068 from Heinkel. In these measurements, special engines were installed partly on the fuselage and partly on the wing. The engines were equipped with electric motors and fans, so that they could be measured without and with exhaust."

The wind tunnel tests carried out by the AVA were intended to determine the effects on stability of attaching the engine nacelles directly to the fuselage, compared to their effect on stability when fitted to the wings. Under model description, the report states: "The planned investigations are for the clarification of fundamental questions.

It therefore seemed necessary to eliminate all parameters which were not absolutely necessary during the measurement.

"For this reason, and to speed up the production of the model, a rectangular wing with a symmetrical profile was provided instead of the swept form designed for the full-scale wing, and a rectangular tailplane was used instead of the swept tailplane. The vertical stabilizer was also rectangular, while the fuselage was modelled to be geometrically similar to that of the full-scale version (P 1068)."

Presumably these tests relate to the Heinkel P 1068, given the scale of the engine nacelles compared to the wings and fuselage, but the test results would also have been applicable to the DFS P 1068 since its fuselage had the same basic shape and Georgii states that each of the four versions was to have turbojet attachment points on its fuselage.

The minutes of a meeting of the Entwicklungshauptkommission, the aircraft chief development commission, on November 21-22, 1944, under the heading 'research

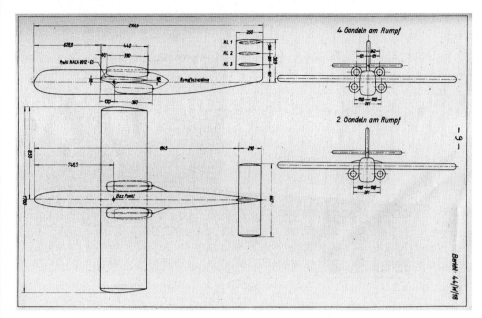

ABOVE: Drawing of a P 1068 wind tunnel model tested by the AVA. The test results were reported in a document dated July 20, 1944. The report makes it clear that the P 1068's wings and tail would not have looked like this – the designs were simplified for the test model because only the positioning of the engines was important.

aircraft' state that: "Work on the '1068' piloted flying model with rocket propulsion was to continue as planned."

And the war diary of Ulrich Diesing, the Chef der Technischen Luftrüstung, head of aircraft development and testing at the RLM, for the period of January 15 to January 21, 1945, says: "After examining the company Wrede-Freilassing, the execution of the order is possible there in addition to the already starting production 1068." But the following week it says: "Study aircraft 1068: FoFü reports that it is unlikely that DFS will be able to build the 35° swept winged area. As requested by Heinkel this wing is to be regarded as a further development of the 162 wing, construction is absolutely necessary. Fa. Wrede cannot take over construction."

No photographs of the completed P 1068 with 25° sweepback are known to have survived and its eventual fate is unknown – but it was undoubtedly built. The P 1068 does not appear on a status report concerning the 'Entwicklungs-Notprogramm' – the emergency development programme – dated circa February 27, 1945, however, suggesting that the project had been abandoned by this point. What does appear on the status report, however, is the 8-346 aka DFS 346.

DFS 346

Regarding the third and final stage of research on developments necessary for supersonic flight, the June 18, 1945, report says: "Based on the above considerations for the third section of this research programme, the DFS developed an aircraft which appeared capable of solving the flight mechanical problems of supersonic speeds. As the institute for aircraft construction was fully occupied with the DFS 228 and P 1068, and in as much as the development of this supersonic aircraft was to be stepped up as fast as possible, the chief research office and the RLM agreed that the DFS would be the chief research office and the RLM agreed that the DFS would be in charge only as far as the project control was concerned; and that

the construction and building would be given to a capable firm of the aviation industry.

"For this purpose the Siebel-Flugzeugbau in Halle was later engaged. All project data, which had been worked out by the DFS survived undamaged. They were sent to the Siebel firm in November 1944, but in March 1945 the construction work on this model did not exceed basic fundamentals. Wind tunnel measurements necessary for the determination of load distribution were carried out in the wind tunnel of the DFS in Darmstadt. A model is being worked on for measurements in the high speed wind tunnel of the DVL in Berlin."

Work on the DFS 346 – the actual supersonic research aircraft itself – appears to have begun relatively late. On May 31, 1944, the RLM's Oberingenieur Malz had sent Messerschmitt, Heinkel, Arado, Focke-Wulf, Siebel and Blohm & Voss, with the DFS and the FoFü copied in, a letter headed 'Subject: Problem of fast flight'. It said: "It is

intended to build a study aircraft at Siebel Flugzeugbau Halle, which is to be used to investigate the problems occurring in the fast-flight and in the wind tunnel.

"This aircraft, which may also be built in some variants, should be provided with TL drive and fuel for an hour of flight time with them. The crew shall consist of an aircraft pilot and a surveyor who will operate the extensive measuring equipment required for the purpose of the aircraft.

"It is a distinct research aircraft, so the equipment can be limited to the aircraft and engine monitoring devices as well as FT system for on-board traffic and the measuring apparatus. For the safety of the crew, special attention must be paid to the fact that the measuring program requires pronounced risks. (Catapult seats or cabin with rescue parachute or the like).

"It is requested to draw up a corresponding draft (only project drawings), which covers the knowledge available to you. Suggestions for a Schnellstflugzeug to be submitted to GL/C-E 2 by July 20, 1944. In a joint discussion with the companies involved, the design of the study aircraft or study aircraft should then be determined. In view of the importance of the task particularly active participation is requested."

In fact, it would appear that the meeting was brought forward two days to July 18 and that this was the same meeting at which it was decided that the DFS P 1068s should be equipped with rocket engines. Evidently Messerschmitt, Heinkel and Arado had all submitted proposals for the design of the Schnellstflugzeug and these were discussed. In the minutes, after the discussion on the P 1068, 'Point 2' says: "For studies in the high speed range of approximately M = 0.9-0.95, a draft to be implemented is based on the Kosin/Arado proposal. The work will be immediately attacked and completed, according to Mr Kracht, in 10 weeks without reinforcement by the company Siebel, or in 7 weeks with reinforcement by 5 men of the company Siebel.

"The developed documents are to be submitted to the company Siebel as demands

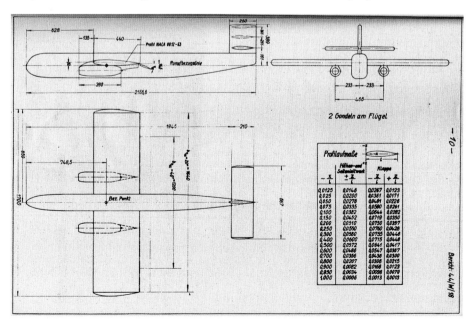

ABOVE: The most basic configuration of the P 1068's engines tested by the AVA.

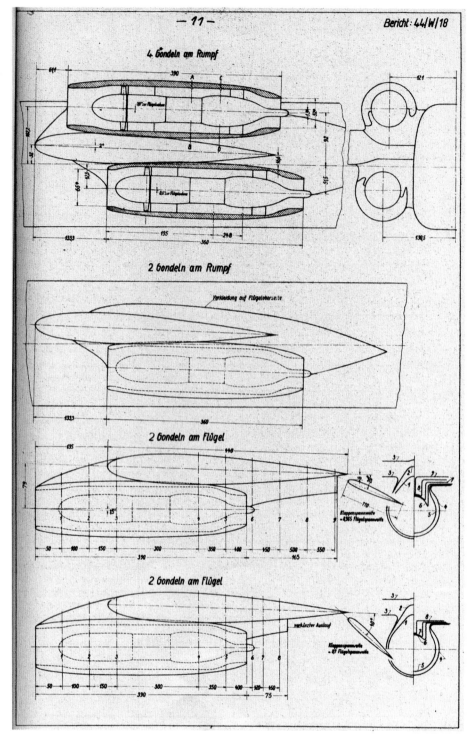

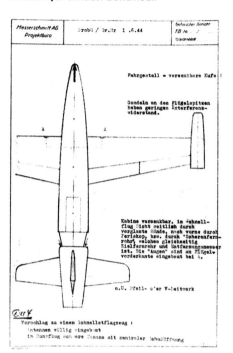

LEFT: Positioning of the P 1068's engines right against the fuselage was controversial because no test data existed to indicate what effect this might have on the aircraft in flight – hence the AVA tests. Unusually, the model's engine nacelles were fitted with small electrically driven fans to simulate the aircraft's jet exhaust behaviour.

ABOVE: The Messerschmitt Schnellstflugzeug of June 12, 1944. This would now appear to have been Messerschmitt's contender for what would eventually become the DFS 346. A design produced by Arado was chosen instead, becoming the HS-8, which in turn became the DFS 346. The design process was unusually collaborative and involved input from Arado, Messerschmitt, Heinkel, Focke-Wulf and the DFS itself before the plans were handed to Siebel, chosen only because it had spare capacity, for construction.

for construction of such an aircraft. The results of the work will be published and reported to the committee on August 10. As design time at the company Siebel 3 months is estimated. The cooperation of Siebel will be negotiated.

"Specifically, the project is based on the following structure: General structure of the aircraft as a mid-wing, the fuselage is held cylindrical in the wing area, the arrangement of the fuselage to reduce drag is clarified by wind tunnel measurements, cylindrical fuselage tip. The final proposal will be examined in the wind tunnel and by dropping tests.

"The wing has 45° sweep angle, chord 1:4, surface load in the final case 100-120kg/m², tapering about 1/3. As control surfaces are provided: a) Rudder with internal compensation – Messerschmitt, b) Split

flaps – Göthert DVL, c) Wing end caps – Kosin/Arado.

"As tail units are provided: a) V-tail – Günter/Heinkel, b) High-altitude tail similar to Me 262 – Messerschmitt. For the aircraft a landing skid is provided. In the construction, 2 expansion stages of the aircraft are to be considered: For the expansion stage 1, an operating height of approx. 10km. It is intended to use the experience gained in the meantime with the DFS 228 pressure cabin for the later measuring flights in great altitudes. For the final version approx. 25km is assigned as working altitude.

"As drive Walter rocket motors. Provided as emergency control will be a small rocket drive. To be investigated: 1) Properties at velocities of M = 0.9 to 1. 2) Power or resistance, 3) Partial resistances. 4) Values for load distribution. For 1) and 2) a proposal

of the DVL flight department after consultation with the Special Committee for Flight Mechanics. From performance measurements arise the requirements: shear measurement, consumption measurement, acceleration measurement, centre of gravity measurement in flight.

"To 3). The measurement of the wing moment is desired; if possible 3-component measurements of the wing. Partial resistors are also measured engine mock-ups. The mock-ups have a corresponding flow and are attached to the wing or the fuselage. For this, the suggestions should be discussed with Dr. Küchemann/AVA. To 4). Pressure distribution measurements on the structure, fuselage and tail are intended to give information about loads and load distribution."

Based on this new evidence, where previously it had been thought that Arado's Überschallflugzeug design was defeated by a DFS design designated 'HS-8' to become the supersonic research aircraft later known as the DFS 346 (see *Luftwaffe: Secret Designs of the Third Reich* p12-13), it would appear that Arado's design actually became the HS-8 and thereby the DFS 346. Similarly, the Messerschmitt Schnellstflugzeug of June 12, 1944 (*Luftwaffe: Secret Designs of* the *Third Reich* p124-125), was presumably Messerschmitt's entry for the competition. Heinkel's V-tail entry remains unknown.

Details of the 8-346 were, as the June 18, 1945, report states, handed over to Siebel at Halle in central eastern Germany for further design and construction work in November 1944. US forces occupied Halle on April 17, 1945, and the following month the technical director of Siebel, Franz Walter, wrote a brief report on the 8-346 for the Americans.

It says: "Purpose. The prototype 8-346 is an airplane with which shall be researched the flying qualities, as there are the stability, the controllability, the manoeuvrability, the values and the distributions of the forces of the directional controls and on the wing and on the tailplanes and all other essential conditions of the flight in the supersonic range and about the most unknown transition point at the velocity of sound. The point where begin the shock waves and therefore the sudden jumping of the centre pressure.

"The aerodynamic qualities of airfoils at very high speeds were determined and in the inland and abroad by model tests in the wind tunnel and in the free air. But the results did not agree satisfactorily, especially for the travelling of the centre of pressure. In order to research all the unknown conditions and to cover a wide range the airplane was designed for a Mach number of 2 (i.e. for a velocity of $V = 2000km/h = 1250mph$) and it should be tested as well with different tailplanes and at a variety of Mach numbers.

"The results of all tests would be of very great importance for the design of all super high-speed airplanes and would make it possible to avoid great errors with probable grave consequences.

"Description. The airplane is of all metal construction (duralumin) and propelled by two liquid-feed rockets. The semi-monocoque wing has an area of 20m and has a span of 9m and has a large sweepback (45). The spindle-shaped fuselage is of semi-monocoque

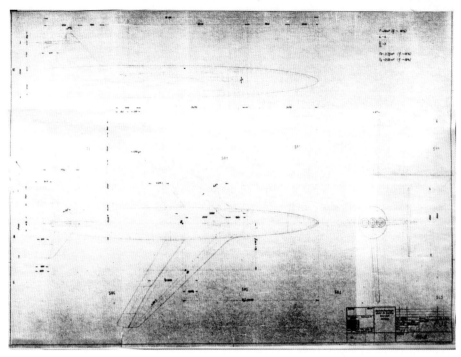

ABOVE: DFS drawing of the HS-8 dated August 6, 1944. Three rocket motors were projected for this early version of what would become the DFS 346. New evidence suggests that the HS-8 was based on an original Arado design submitted for consideration on July 18, 1944.

construction with a maximum diameter of 1.62m. In the nose of it is the pilot's cabin, then comes the pressure cabin for instruments of measuring. In the central part lay the fuel tanks and farther aft the driving gears with the two thrust-jets at the tail.

"Also at the tail are fastened the tailplanes, which have likewise large sweepbacks. In the central part of the fuselage is furthermore built in a retractable skid for landing gear. All control surfaces are divided in two parts, the outer part of each has no aerodynamic balance (no nose part before the hinge) and a great proportion of the airfoil depth, so that in the supersonic range it shall remain efficient (by protruding

from the Mach angle).

"To avoid a too sensitive control the control systems direct therefore alternatively one part or both parts of the control surfaces. The bottom of the pressure cabin upon which the pilot lies can be catapulted and in an arbitrary altitude it will be automatically put off. The whole nose with the pilot's cabin can be blown from the fuselage by means of explosive bolts with which it is fastened. A directional parachute will then reduce the dropping of the cabin.

"The pressure in the cabin will be regulated with an overpressure valve corresponding to an altitude of 8km. A supply of compressed air is stored on board and the pilot gets oxygen for breathing. In every individual control system is built in a meter to register the forces. The wing is fastened on the fuselage by means of measuring columns so that all forces and moments of the wing in and about the three axes can be measured."

In summing up, Walter wrote: "Since the design of the research airplane 8-346 is very far in progress and the materials and the driving gears (from the tailless fighter 8-163) are at disposal and since at this time the men of the engineering staff are still accessible (before they are scattered) the building of this plane would be possible in a reasonably short time."

The Americans left Halle on July 1, 1945, having apparently made only cursory efforts to gather documents on the 346 – although anecdotally it has been stated that they did persuade some former Siebel employees to join them in the American zone. Thereafter the Siebel factory was immediately occupied by Soviet forces, who gathered together all remaining documents on the 346, along with some 500 men who had worked on the project, and transported them back to Russia. Work on the 8-346 then continued as a Soviet project. ●

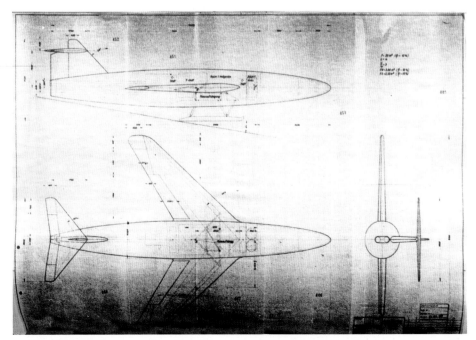

ABOVE: Drawing of what is termed the 'DFS 346 (HS-8) Versuchsflugzeug für Höchstgeschwindigkeiten' from a report dated October 10, 1944. This is relatively close to the design handed to Siebel the following month.

Pole position

DFS Eber

V1

Having spent years studying the use of powered aircraft to get unpowered gliders airborne, the DFS realised that a powered aircraft could also tow aloft a cheap rocket-propelled interceptor – conserving the latter's fuel for the attack itself. The result was Projekt Eber, 'Eber' meaning 'boar' or 'wild boar'.

ABOVE: The original DFS Eber design with split fuselage in experimental yellow.
ARTWORK BY ZOLTÁN CSOMBÓ

Experiments involving close rigid towing had been carried out by the DFS at Ainring throughout the early years of the war, starting in 1939. These involved first a Junkers Ju 52 towing a DFS 230 glider by direct attachment to its tail, then a Dornier Do 17 and Heinkel He 111 performing the same operation.

This work eventually led to a change in the arrangement to incorporate a short shaft or pole between the two aircraft. According to Allied CIOS report XXXII-66 Deutsche Forschungsanstalt für Segelflug, Ainring, "With shaft-towing an auxiliary flying body (small wing surface) was coupled on to a rigid shaft (10m, long steel tube) on one of the fastest aircraft (Me 262) to carry the additional load (fuel, bombs) of the Me 262. Far reaching tests were carried out but not put into use."

This work in mid to late 1944 seems to have led directly to the genesis of Eber – at a time when several vertical launch rocket interceptors, including Erich Bachem's Natter, were already on the drawing board.

The earliest known evidence of Eber comes from a telegram sent to Professor Paul Ruden at the DFS in Ainring on November 9, 1944, by Karl Leist of the FoFü.

Leist says: "According to telex Dr Jennissen, on behalf of Mr Temme I expect to come to Ainring for a week on Monday, November 13, as I am working on the similar Project Bembo. I will bring documents with me and make them available. You will be asked to arrange accommodation for a week."

Joseph Jennissen was a government supervisor for aviation research and Heinrich Temme was another member

of the FoFü who had worked on the Fi 103 flying bomb. Jennissen appears to be putting Leist and Ruden together because they were both working on the same sort of project – although Project Bembo is entirely unknown today. Presumably Ruden hadn't been working on the project for very long at this stage and could therefore benefit from Leist's input.

The following day, November 10, Versuchsingenieur or 'test engineer' Arno Schieferdecker of the DFS sent a telex to the RLM in Berlin requesting "procurement of drawing and installation documents of the machine cannon MK 108 and the rocket R4M, the rocket R4M in 28x tube battery".

Three days after that, Rheinmetall-Borsig wrote to the DFS with drawings showing the MK 108 and two different projects for the installation of R4M rocket tubes, "a drawing showing the arrangement of seven by seven blocks and a second showing a battery of 32. This latter is intended only as a trial execution. For the installation, only the seven by seven block would be eligible".

It goes on to query the request: "We ask, for the sake of order, that you tell us for which installation you need these documents, since we are allowed to issue them basically only by official requirements. It is also appropriate, after the existence of the first project to discuss the internals with the firearm installation subgroup. You should treat the documents of the tubular battery in a particularly confidential manner."

The earliest known mention of the name 'Eber' comes from a drawing dated November 23, 1944 – drawing number 5026-0000. This shows a tiny aircraft just 5.16m long and with a wingspan of 4.16m. Its wing area is 5m^2 and an almost entirely rectangular fin. The pilot sits within an angular box made of armour plates clearly designed to separate from the rest of the aircraft down a dividing line just behind the pilot's seat.

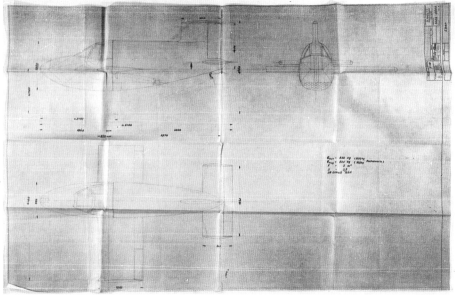

ABOVE: The first DFS Eber drawing dated November 23, 1944. The forward view shows the aircraft's honeycomb shaped R4M rocket launcher and the angular armour plates protecting the pilot. The side view shows the line where the disposable aircraft would split in two, allowing the pilot to escape after making his two attacks.

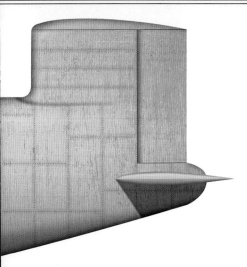

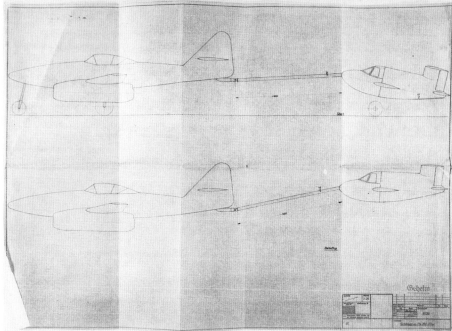

Beneath the pilot is a box containing a honeycomb of 28 R4M missiles and behind him is the aircraft's rocket motor. Just visible below the aircraft is a wheel intended to represent a trolley or other detachable undercarriage for takeoff. The aircraft's starting weight is just 850kg.

Also dated November 23 is a drawing – number '5026' without the zeroes - showing Eber being towed by a Messerschmitt Me 262. The rigid steel pole linking the two is 5m long and rigidly fixed to Eber, only the Me 262 end having flexibility.

Another drawing dated November 28, 1944, number 5026A-0000, shows the aircraft 1cm shorter at 5.15m with the same wings and starting weight. This time, however, the aircraft carries 44 R4M rockets and the fuselage split has been replaced with a more conventional canopy.

A set of handwritten notes and calculations on DFS graph paper headed

ABOVE: Diagrams showing how Eber would take off, fixed to a 5m pole behind a Messerschmitt Me 262.

'Eber I', dated November 30, 1944, show that the anticipated performance of the Eber vehicle was based on data supplied by Henschel relating to the rocket-propelled Hs 295 guided missile.

A meeting was held to discuss Project Eber on December 3 and the summary states: "After a detailed discussion of the project, the following points were noted for the further work: 1. The DFS pursues above all the Eber Project for the shooting approach from behind and above. The aircraft pilot is seated.

"The weapon is R4M device, installed in the direction of a straight line and designed for two attacks. The required number of shots and the probability of hit as a function of distance and scattering are recalculated by the LFA ... as a view finder, a simple reflex sight is provided. The FoFü provides the DFS with documents about the necessary armour of the cabin against 12.7mm projectiles.

"The protection of the aircraft pilot against explosion of the R4M rockets shall be provided by the form of the cabin. At the DVL, the Institute for Aerial Medicine is to provide an estimate of the necessary reaction time for the target, the attack and the flight of the aircraft. The information should be accurate to a few tenths of a second. As an additional drive, the RI 502 device is to be used. Protection of the aircraft against fuel explosions is not provided.

"The landing of the Eber is not planned. The aircraft is to be designed as a disposable device. In order to rescue the pilot by a parachute, the DFS designs the cockpit to break off or installs an ejection seat. For the parachute selection FGZ is to be consulted.

"2. Regardless of the examination of the firing range, the work for the rammer project continues. DFS continues the started model measurements on the destruction work of shell constructions. DVL will begin large-scale trials with a V1 slingshot in Adlershof as soon as the requested equipment and operator's attendant have arrived. The design for DFS completed rammer is built at the DVL. In the DVL flight medical institute, medical officer Dr Henschke will provide the measurements on tolerable acceleration."

Eber was to have an armoured cockpit with a conventional seat for the pilot. His mission would be to make two attacks on enemy aircraft using rocket projectiles before escaping from the vehicle and parachuting to safety. At this point it seems that although ramming was being considered it wasn't yet a definite part of the design.

ABOVE: During the early war years the DFS experimented with a wide range of glider towing combinations – such as this Heinkel He 111 towing a DFS 230.

ABOVE: Another DFS experimental towing combination – a Heinkel He 177 bomber bar-towing a Gotha Go 242 glider.

▶

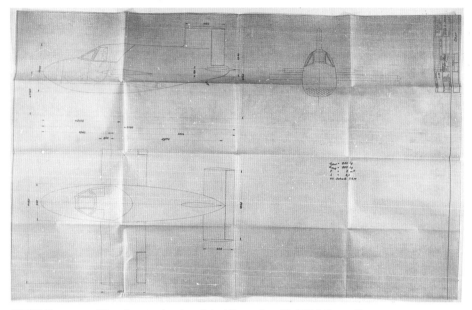

ABOVE: The second Eber from a drawing dated November 28, 1944. The split fuselage concept has been replaced by a primitive drag-chute ejection seat and the number of rockets carried has been nearly doubled.

A new version of Eber appears in a drawing dated December 13, 1944. The earlier square fin has been replaced with a twin-fin arrangement though the aircraft's length and wingspan remain unchanged from the previous design. Now the rocket weapon contains '2 x 20' R4Ms and the original single rocket motor has been replaced with a pair of motors installed at different angles. Overall weight has increased to 870kg and the aircraft is depicted with two large landing gear wheels and legs which presumably would have been jettisoned at takeoff. Another drawing from the same date, number '5026B' shows this version of Eber on tow – the arrangement unchanged from before.

The last known drawing of Eber was made the following day, December 14, 1944, and shows that the canopy of the two later

versions was intended to facilitate the inclusion of an ejection seat. This design has no drawing number.

Two weeks later, on December 28, a full project description was issued. This states: "Required was a disposable device that allows two attacks after being towed by a Me 262 or Fw 190 to the appropriate distance (about 2000m) from the enemy unit. The first attack should normally be made from about 300m above. The attack position for

the second approach must be ensured by rocket-units. The thrust of the rocket-drive should be such that it is possible to attack from an under-elevation of about 700-1000m.

"The original demands went on a ramming flight and a shooting approach. A closer examination of the ramming flight resulted in the following: provided that the aircraft's armour possesses sufficient strength a successful ramming at an approach speed of 150-200m/sec is always carried out. The speed decrease when piercing a fuselage is 6 to 10m/sec. If the ram-fighter performs the impact longitudinally, the accelerations that occur here have the order of magnitude 100 g. It was assumed that the pilot could withstand a maximum acceleration of no more than 16g. The resilient or damped seat assembly is able to reduce the pilot's acceleration load from

ABOVE: The revised Eber with primitive ejection system rather than fuselage split. This rendering in experimental red gives a good idea why the drag ejection system and the vertical fin probably did not go well together.
ARTWORK BY ZOLTÁN CSOMBÓ

100g to 16g, but with a construction that is difficult to accommodate.

"The construction cost is not insignificant, especially when the shock stress is not guaranteed safe except in the longitudinal direction. It must always be expected that even in the direction of high and transverse axes significant accelerations must be recorded, against which effect on the pilot is yet to be estimated. (The values of the shock delay and the acceleration ability of the pilot have not been determined correctly yet.)

"Apart from the fact that the mechanical process after the shock is completely unpredictable, the effort associated with the impact process has led to the view that it would be better to forego the ramming altogether and to make two shooting passes instead.

"For the armament was the choice of the device R4M, the MK 108 and the battery MK 108. Due to its low production costs the R4M device is evidently the most suitable for a disposable aircraft. It also has the advantage that its installation can be recoil-free. The pulse of the MK 108 battery would result in a decrease in speed of 6-8m/sec at launch with a weight of 800-1000kg. High shock sensitivity counts against the R4M however.

"For this reason, the R4M battery was positioned far below the aircraft's armour, so

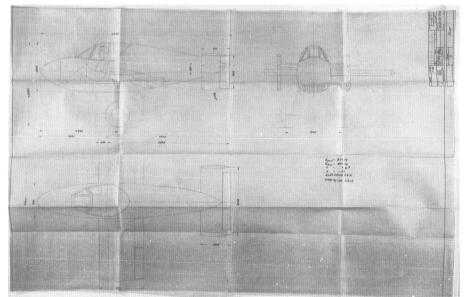

ABOVE: The last known version of the Eber, in a drawing dated December 13, 1944, has a twin fin tail and two rocket motors.

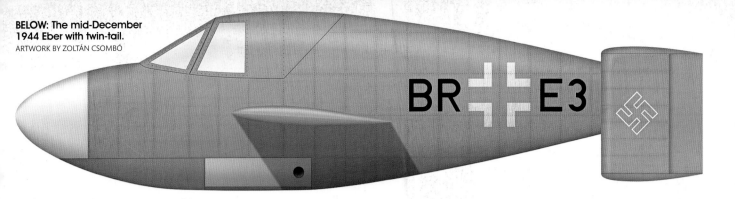

BELOW: The mid-December 1944 Eber with twin-tail.
ARTWORK BY ZOLTÁN CSOMBÓ

BR ✠ E3

that the chances of them meeting from the front are low. For centre of gravity reasons, this situation has proven to be expedient. It was assumed that 20 rounds would suffice for a successful shooting approach. The armour is intended to cover the pilot essentially against fire from the front.

"The fuselage itself was kept as simple as possible for disposability. For this reason, both the wing and the tail unit use the unbroken rectangular shape. Sweepback was deliberately omitted. The critical Mach number must be postponed by high-quality profiling. The choice of the double fin seemed to be expedient, because it was possible to avoid rolling moments at rudder deflection. A certain caution in this regard seemed necessary, since the moment of inertia around the longitudinal axis must be extraordinarily small. The fuselage is designed to be made from wood.

"The Eber should be linked to its towing aircraft with a drawbar. In our experience, between the drawbar and the aircraft only two degrees of freedom should be allowed, namely the rotation to release the transverse and vertical axis, while the towed vehicle in the longitudinal axis is rigidly connected to the towing vehicle. It has been shown that the trailer can be towed unmanned, so during the launch and during the climb no requirements are made to the pilot of the trailer.

"When firing its engines on approach the Eber is expediently set to the correct curve. This includes a well-functioning ram sight, which must be given to the tow plane. To

comply with the straight ramming curve requires the Eber only to have a simple mirror visor. However, there is still the question as to how big the chosen angle can be. That depends on the initial speed of the R4M weapon on launch.

"After a shooting attack the pilot gets out of Eber. The landing was waived, 1) because the aviation requirements of the pilot must be very high, 2) because with unprepared terrain the percentage chance of a safe landing is low and 3) because the transport difficulties of retrieving the aircraft are too great.

"In order to make it easy for the pilot to get out, the following path was taken: a small parachute rips the seat with the pilot out of the plane and gives it a descent speed of about 40m/sec. As the aircraft continues to fly at its own speed, a separation of both should be ensured. The pilot then loosens himself from the seat, which is now braked to about 25-30m/sec. After getting away from this, the pilot opens his own parachute."

Shortly after the end of the war, Professor Ruden described his work for the Allies in CIOS XXXII-66: "The project 'Eber' was worked out from the institute of the undersigned [Ruden] under commission of the research management. The 'Eber' is a short range fighter similar to the Natter with the difference of the Natter where the self start from the ground is abandoned.

"More consideration was given to start and raising the apparatus in pole-tow with help of the Me 262 or the Fw 190. At the altitude of the bomber squadron the 'Eber'

was to be released at a distance of 5-10km behind the squadron and speeded up with rocket apparatus. At a greater height than the bomber squadron of approximately 300-400m. The run was calculated as being sufficient in order to reach and attack the bomber squadron which was assumed with a closing speed of at least 100m/sec. A second attack was possible through the resumed power of the installed rocket apparatus. The equipment of the 'Eber' consisted of a salvo-gun and heavy armament of the pilot.

"At first it was considered to carry out one attack as a ram attack. Closer examination persuaded us to drop the ram attack and perform two attacks. The project was not completed owing to the lack of production capacity and also to the limited capacity for use. The consideration originated from the fact that the towing fighter and 'Eber' at comparably small performance loads experience a loss of speed of approximately 100km/h.

"With strong air superiority it must be reckoned with that the towing and towed pair will be easy prey for the enemy if the latter attacks from greater height."

In short, Eber was originally intended as a rammer but ended up as a two-attacks-only disposable rocket fighter. The project was abandoned because no production capacity was available for it and because it was worked out that the fighter towing Eber would suffer a huge performance penalty, making it extremely vulnerable to Allied fighters roaming unchallenged through German airspace. ●

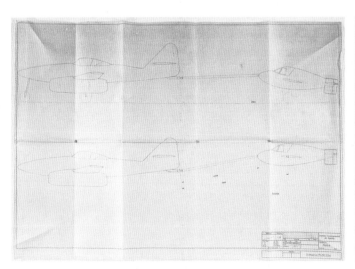

ABOVE: There appears to be no change in the towing procedure for the final version of the Eber in this drawing dated December 13, 1944.

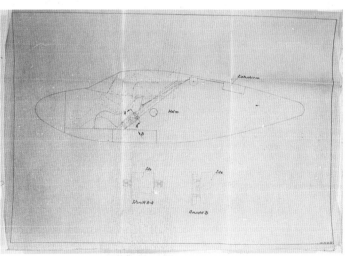

ABOVE: A very basic ejection seat was proposed for the final Eber – a parachute would 'rip' the pilot's seat from the fuselage before slowing its descent enough for the pilot to unstrap himself and open his own chute.

DFS Eber

December 1944

Artwork by Luca Landino

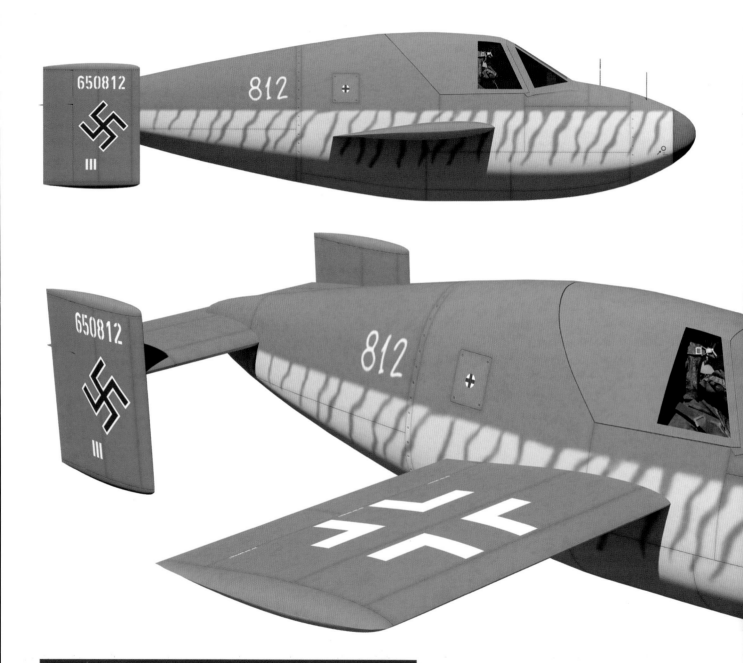

COMMENTS

The tiny DFS Eber measured just 5.15m from end to end, with a wingspan of 4.16m. While it was originally intended that Eber would ram its targets, in the end it was decided that it would make two attacks on enemy bombers using R4M rockets before the pilot bailed out. The main reason was the unpredictable nature of the impact forces involved in the collision. Eber was not a 'suicide' machine and its designers could only provide protection for the pilot from a 100 g impact – at great expense in impact-absorbing materials and mechanisms – if the enemy aircraft was hit dead on. A glancing blow would probably have been fatal.

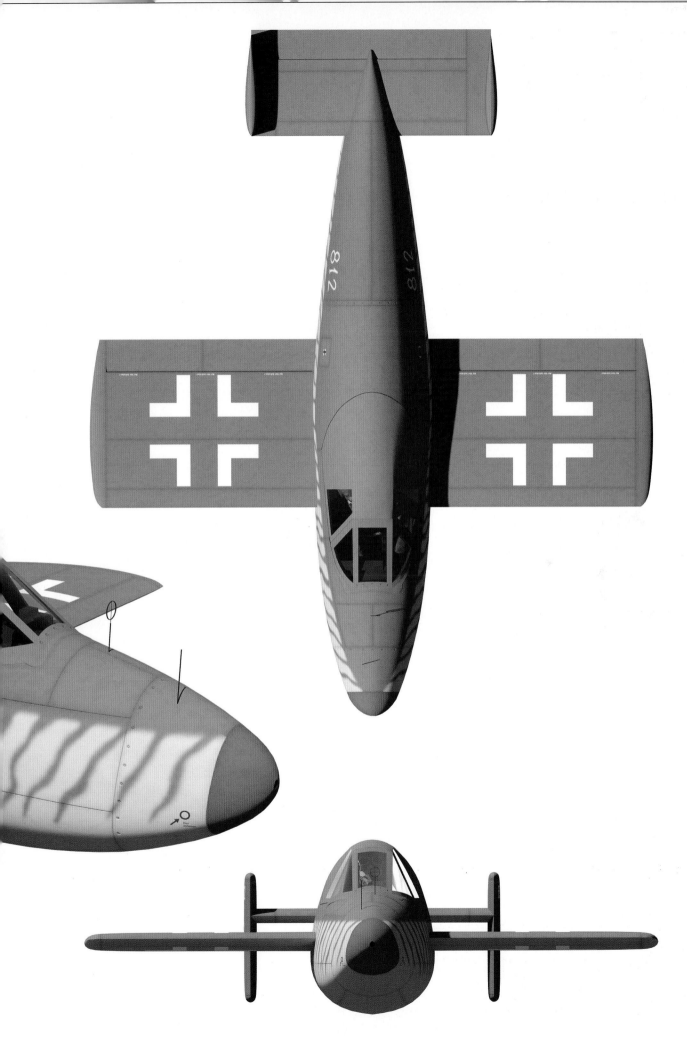

The gliding sub hunter

DFS Lotos

Having originally specialised in gliders, the DFS eventually became involved in a wide range of research projects. It sometimes discovered, however, that a glider could still provide a solution to the most unlikely of problems.

During 1943 the DFS was involved in a remarkably low-tech and evidently rather dangerous series of experiments involving the use of aircraft and electronic equipment to search for submerged submarines.

The organisation had been set the task of finding the best way of using a sonobuoy which consisted of an underwater acoustic search device, 'the diving body', and a float, 'the swimming body', which had to remain attached to the host aircraft via a long cable.

The idea was that the device would be dropped from the aircraft and the cable played out. The aircraft, still attached to the device, would then circle it while the search was conducted before winching it back on board and flying off to the next destination when the search was complete.

The project is outlined in a DFS document entitled Vorschlag zum Verfahren 'Lotos' or Proposal for the procedure 'Lotus' dated January 11, 1944. It states: "The task of the DFS was to find a procedure that allows the detection of submerged submarines, in certain areas, by aircraft. In this case, a known search device should be used, which must lie on the water surface during the search process as far as possible without movement.

"The device is in contact with a diving body, which in turn is about 2-5m below

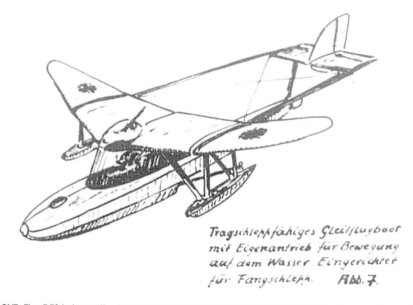

ABOVE: The DFS Lotos anti-submarine glider. The single seat aircraft, fitted with acoustic equipment for detecting submerged vessels, would have been towed to the search location by another aircraft. It would then have been able to manoeuvre on the surface using a powerboat engine. When the search was over, the tow aircraft would then return to pick it up.

the water surface (the aircraft should be in wire connection with the swimming body). Depending on whether the power source is carried in the aircraft or in the swimming body, weights of 50-120kg are used for the swimming body including diving bodies. The flight tests were carried out with dummy bodies of the same weight.

"The DFS's experiments were based on the experience gained from previous attempts to fly an aircraft in full circle around a body on a rope so that the body is at the centre of the circle, virtually without movement."

For these early experiments, carried out in 1938, it was found that a Heinkel He 72 biplane trainer could be flown in circles around a small boat, while attached to it by 800m of rope, without the boat moving.

The first attempt to repeat this feat using a dummy sonobuoy weighing 70kg

and a Focke-Wulf Fw 58 was carried out over the Chiemsee lake in Bavaria on April 14, 1943. The rope linking the dummy and the aircraft was 5mm thick and 1200m long. According to the report: "The rope

ABOVE: The dome-shaped dummy float, to the left of the picture, and the cylindrical rope drum attached to the underside of a DFS-operated Fw 58.

ABOVE: The dummy float used in the early Lotos experiments.

ABOVE: A DFS Habicht glider being towed beneath a Junkers Ju 87. The DFS carried out a huge amount of work on different combinations of gliders and aircraft that could tow them.

ABOVE: A forward view of the rope drum and dummy float.

was wound onto a drum attached to the aircraft so that it was played out when the buoy was dropped ... it was intended to lower the buoy at low tide to the water and then pull up the aircraft and fly in a circle around the buoy.

"An observation point was set up on the lake near the launch site using a motorboat. The dropping of the buoy was carried out without difficulty from a height of 5-10m. The rope was released well from the drum but the aircraft rose relatively slowly (low power of the Fw 58) to the full circle. The angle of the rope between the buoy-airplane and the water's surface was such that the rope with slack got into the water.

"The resistance of the rope being pulled across the water was so great that the Fw 58 lost speed and the ability to climb and could no longer be turned. For the same reasons, the reserve rope was quickly played out of the drum until, with the rope fully played out, there was a violent motion and the buoy was accelerated so that it leaped out of the water. Subsequently, cable break occurred near the aircraft."

No date is given for the "second attempt" but this time the cable drum was mounted on the buoy rather than the

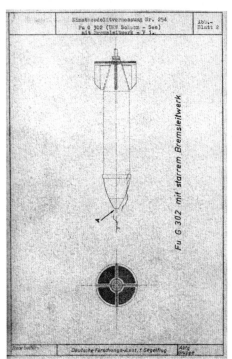

ABOVE: For the fifth attempt, the DFS used a device known as the UKW Schwan-See, also known as FuG 302 and referred to in the Lotos report as the 'Seeschwan'.

aircraft so that the rope wouldn't unwind itself due to its own weight. "The landing of the buoy was again in low altitude flight. Again, the rate of climb of the Fw 58 was too low to avoid water contact with the rope as the rope sag occurred. The course of the second attempt was quite similar to the first attempt."

Two further attempts fared little better. A built in winch and different rope lengths were tried and the 70kg dummy buoy was eventually replaced with a 50kg dummy bomb made of cement.

For the fifth attempt, a DFS aerodynamic device known as the Seeschwan was towed. This also weighed 70kg but "again, the result did not change".

The DFS then determined that "a remedy is only possible to achieve then by a substantial extension of the towing rope and by the aircraft flying with a smaller radius of curvature. However, since there is also the risk of rope dragging in the water here, a solution to the problem on the chosen path must be abandoned as hopeless".

In short, it was realised that flying round and round in circles while attached to a buoy and trying not to move it was probably never going to work. There was always too much risk that the cable would end up in the water and, in the worst case scenario, end up dragging the aircraft down.

However, the DFS had another solution: "After a thorough examination of the available possibilities and evaluation of other tests carried out at DFS, we have come to the following proposal: a single-seat, light and buoyant glider with high surface load (smaller wing) is towed to the search location by a suitable aircraft. Here, the glider is released and glides down to the water.

"The actual search action is carried out by the resting (possibly anchored) glider. After searching a spot, the glider plane must be able to change its position with its own power by means of a built-in engine (possibly a Sturmboot engine). Here, the achievable speed is estimated at about 40km/h.

"After completion of the search operation, the glider is towed back into the air and returned to the port of departure. The initial acceleration for the capture is given to the glider by the engine mentioned."

It was an elegant solution which completely negated the need for a cable attachment between the sonobuoy and the aircraft. The sonobuoy would be installed in a small glider, flown to the search location, and then collected when the search was over.

Presumably the Lotos project was abandoned at this point since there is no known evidence of the anti-submarine glider having been built. ●

ABOVE: A Ju 87 with its propeller removed being towed as a glider beneath a He 111 – viewed from the floor hatch of the He 111.

ABOVE: A DFS 230 glider reconfigured for seaplane operations. Experiments had shown that it was possible for a powered seaplane to tow a glider into the air from the surface of a large body of water – although it was easier if the glider was already moving before takeoff.

ABOVE: Ju 87 towing a DFS Habicht glider (barely visible to the bottom right of the image) into the air on land. This illustration was used in the DFS report to illustrate how the Lotos glider would be collected.

The Tube

DFS Lotos

Among the many strands of research being carried out by the DFS was an ongoing study into the potential of ramjet or 'Lorin' engines. This eventually found expression in the smallest possible ramjet-powered aircraft – the DFS Jabo.

The first work carried out on the ramjet as a potential propulsion system for a fighter aircraft appears to have been carried out by Eugen Sänger at the DFS. In a report produced in October 1943 entitled Über einem Lorinantrieb für Strahljäger or 'On a Lorin drive for jet fighters' he outlined the possibility of constructing a lightweight ramjet fighter by effectively wrapping the basic components of a fighter around a ramjet tube.

The ramjet, commonly known in Germany as the 'Lorin' after its French inventor René Lorin, had a number of disadvantages – it could not begin to work until it was already travelling at high speed, with air literally being rammed into its intake; it could not be throttled (it was either on or off), and it was difficult to design it in such a way that it did not suffer from severe aerodynamic drag.

However, if these issues could be overcome the ramjet had several major advantages – it was very simple and cheap to make, produced a generous amount of thrust and did not require high-grade fuel to work.

Five months after Sänger's initial report, in March 1944, the DFS produced a second report on ramjet propulsion for military purposes, this time offering the propulsion system for either a fighter or fighter-bomber in a report entitled Kurzbaubeschreibung des vorgeschlagenen Jabo bzw. Jägers mit Lorinantrieb or 'Brief description of the proposed Jabo or fighter with Lorin drive'.

In its surviving form, there is no author's name on the document and it is undated. However, it is accompanied by a drawing dated March 16, 1944, which is referred to in the text, thereby offering a good idea of when the report itself was produced. All other drawings and diagrams mentioned in the report text are missing.

The one drawing that is included shows an extension of Sänger's earlier concept and one of the more bizarre-looking German 'secret projects'. It is a 1m diameter tubular ramjet with the pilot lying prone in an armoured capsule over the intake at the front. A narrow vestigial tail emerges from the top of the ramjet tube and two different wing/tail plane arrangements are depicted – one set straight and the other swept. Both side and forward views show a 1000kg bomb suspended from the tube. There is little else to the design except for a skid landing gear.

The report itself begins by discussing how this highly unusual creation was intended

to be operated as a fighter: "The launch takes place by means of rocket propulsion by horizontal acceleration to 800km/h, after which the climb is made using the fuel carried along. The low production costs and the low demands on starting area (runway of 800m length in the main wind direction) allow an increase of the total number of places where it can be used.

"Fig. 1 shows the climb and flight times for different heights. For arming and ammunition 500kg are used. You can see that the fighter reaches an altitude of 7000m after 157 seconds; during this time the target can not have covered 20km at 400km/h. Assuming that the estimated 500kg weapon load consist of launcher ammunition, so could even a single fighter, stationed as local protection of a target at a distance of 30km, break up the enemy formation before it reaches the goal. The actual strength of the device is however in mass use."

This makes it clear that the DFS ramjet fighter was intended to tackle incoming bomber formations in force. It would be cheaply mass-produced then launched in huge swarms to defend vulnerable targets.

The mission profile was somewhat different when the aircraft was used as a fighter-bomber, however: "From the point of view of favourable range, the following use is considered: Mistel start up to 12,000m; launch from the carrier and transition to the dive until the operating speed of 800km/h is reached, then straight flight at 10,000m altitude to the goal. Target approach and attack at speeds around 900km/h; climb with full performance up to 11,000m and return at this altitude.

"With careful consideration of the experimental results available in certain speed and altitude ranges, it seems penetration depths of more than 200km will be achievable. The diagram Fig. 2 illustrates the process. During the combat (approach, dive, climb and return), the speed is so high that attack by enemy fighters or heavy flak seems impossible.

"During the final part of the attack near the ground, frontal attack by machine guns is likely. Against this, extremely strong armour is provided, which covers a large part of the fuselage cross-section in addition to the aircraft pilot. Here, too, the high speed in conjunction

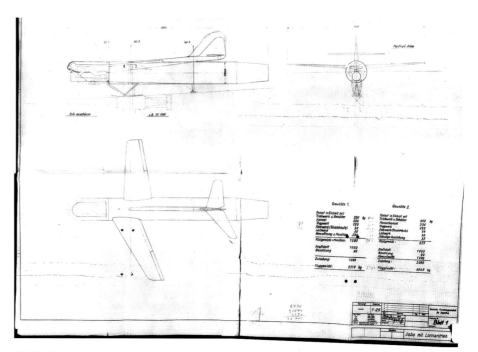

ABOVE: The only known drawing of the DFS Jabo mit Lorinantrieb or 'fighter-bomber with ramjet'. It depicts a tiny aircraft that is little more than a ramjet tube with wings and a small tail attached. It measures 9.3m long with a wingspan of 6.4m.

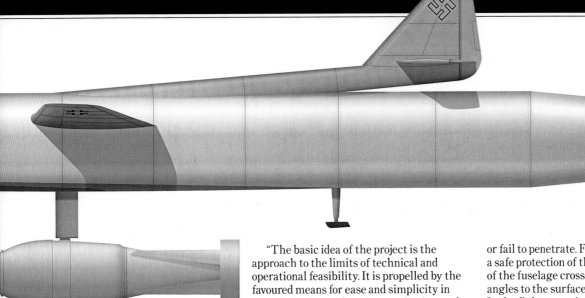

ABOVE: The straight-winged version of the DFS Jabo complete with heavily armoured cockpit. In this form the aircraft would have been carried aloft by a host aircraft – perhaps a Dornier Do 217 or even a Heinkel He 177. Artwork by Zoltán Csombó

with the smallness of the entire vehicle results in an additional measure of security. The landing speed is around 180km/h."

As a 'Jabo', the DFS ramjet aircraft would have been launched at altitude from a carrier aircraft – perhaps a Dornier Do 217 or Ju 88, though no particular type is specified in the report. It would then fly to its target, dive to attack, then climb back to altitude. Close to the ground, the pilot would be protected from defensive machine gun fire by a heavily armoured shroud over the cockpit.

A third use was also envisioned for the ramjet aircraft: "When used as a course-controlled, remote-controlled or television-controlled bomb, there are ranges of over 500km, since no altitude change takes place and there is no return flight. The extremely low production costs make the device particularly suitable for this purpose. By eliminating crew and fuel tank armour, the payload can be increased to about 1400kg = 46% of the flight weight."

"The basic idea of the project is the approach to the limits of technical and operational feasibility. It is propelled by the favoured means for ease and simplicity in manufacturing and engine monitoring, and by focusing on attacking armament, which is made possible by the high speed, so you can do without weapons of defence."

The extreme simplicity of the DFS aircraft would have made it attractive from a production perspective – but getting it to work correctly and in the manner envisioned would most likely have been rather difficult and made it significantly less attractive.

The report next describes the aircraft's structure: "The hull, together with the engine and fuel tank are of sheet metal construction, forming a closed unit. Here are three main frames, which serve to complete the cockpit, wings, load, and tail.

"Frame 1 is the cockpit connection point (also with wing connection), frame 2 as wing and load connection and for the front of the tail boom, frame 3 as burner chamber, spur and tail support. The intermediate space can readily serve as a fuel container, which is restricted only by a smooth tube required as a control channel and plus a recess for the load and skid connection point.

"The cockpit is heavily armoured frontally for attacking bombers so that projectiles striking in the direction of flight or at a slight angle to this encounter a wall thickness of 6cm, measured in the longitudinal direction, so they either bounce

or fail to penetrate. From this one can derive a safe protection of the pilot and a large part of the fuselage cross-section. Hits at right angles to the surface are hard to expect. In the fighter version, the armour can be changed depending on the expected calibre. (Today aircraft guns are at 2cm.)

"In order to avoid viewing slits in the case of the bomber attack, a two-mirror arrangement is provided, whereby only the outer mirror is exposed to the bombardment and can be replaced automatically or by hand from a mirror magazine. An example of such an arrangement is shown in the drawing Bl.2. As entry and exit for the pilot is a large, hinged ejectable hatch, which is incorporated into the armour.

"The prone control offers no difficulties. The pilot's couch is designed in such a way that the pilot has the necessary freedom of movement in a comfortable posture and is well-protected from forces during acceleration. The skid can be arranged in different ways. Bl.1 shows only an example. In the front view the centre of gravity seems to be very high due to the tall skid. However, this applies only to the moment of touchdown, whereupon the struts spring back into the aircraft to a third of their height, absorbing the impact, and do not then change from this point.

"The pilot's instruments are limited to altimeter, airspeed indicator, fuel gauge (rough) and compass. The choice and accommodation of the latter must still be clarified because of the steel masses present at the cockpit. Because of the space restrictions, mirror reading of the instruments is thought necessary, so they would be positioned to the side of the pilot with the mirror showing them in front of him.

"The equipment should also be limited to the minimum of what is operationally required. Radio receivers and signal cartridges can meet the requirements. In addition, there is oxygen equipment and heating, for their simple design good opportunities exist."

The DFS Jabo mit Lorinantrieb is a singularly focused design, produced when Germany still had the resources to put it into production if desired. However, it came at the wrong time. The Jägerstab was being formed, or had already been formed, by March 1944 in order to streamline Germany's aviation industry in favour of existing types that were deemed critical to the war effort. Experimental designs such as this were unlikely to find favour. Whether this was the fate that befell the DFS design is unknown. ●

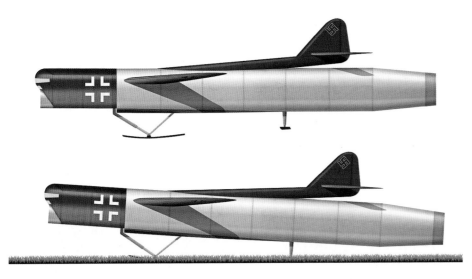

ABOVE: The swept-wing version of the aircraft. The lower drawing depicts it at the moment of landing, with the landing skid uncompressed. As the skid took the force of the impact, it was designed to compress to a third of its fully-extended height. Artwork by Zoltán Csombó

Sabre rattling

Focke-Wulf Ta 152 mit Napier Sabre II

The greatest difficulty Focke-Wulf faced in designing the Ta 152 was its engine. The Jumo 213 suffered ongoing teething problems which had not been fully cured by the beginning of February 1944. At the same time, the RLM was eager to assess the properties and potential of the 'new' British Napier Sabre II engine for comparative purposes. Bringing these two strands of enquiry together resulted was a highly unusual project...

Just as the British and Americans maintained and flew captured German fighters to assess their qualities, so too did the Germans spend a great deal of time examining the newest British and American fighter designs they could lay their hands on.

A number of Spitfires and other Allied aircraft were captured intact or in a condition where only light repair work was necessary to get them airworthy again and during the summer of 1943 a unit known as 2./Versuchsverband Ob.d.L. was established to fly them – its initial complement including a Spitfire Mk.IX coded T9+BB, a P-38F/G coded T9+XB and a Mosquito which was never actually flown.

By the beginning of 1944, however, it did not possess a Hawker Typhoon. Although the RAF had brought the Typhoon into

BELOW: Focke-Wulf drawing number 0310 025-T3 shows the three options examined for installation of the Napier Sabre II engine in the Ta 152. The top drawing shows the Ta 152 with a Typhoon-style chin radiator, the middle drawing shows something more akin to the Hawker Tempest I's wing radiator arrangement (the wing part appears on a separate drawing) and the bottom drawing shows the Ta 152 with a classic German 'ring cooler' positioned in front of the Sabre. This was Focke-Wulf's preferred option.

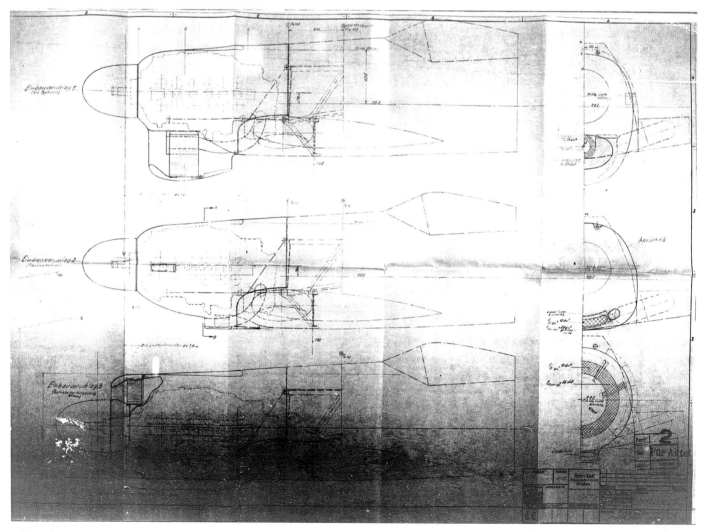

service in 1941, the Germans do not seem to have become aware of its existence before 1943. So when it was identified during that year it was regarded as a 'new' type and there was some concern about what sort of performance capabilities it might possess.

At least one example had evidently been captured but it would appear that this machine was beyond repair so its Napier Sabre II engine, found largely intact, was removed for closer scrutiny.

Between 1942 and 1943, engine manufacturer Daimler-Benz had fitted captured Supermarine Spitfire Mk.Vb EN830 with a DB 605 A-1 engine for experimental purposes but now the German air ministry took the unprecedented step of asking Focke-Wulf to work out how the Napier Sabre II could be installed in the airframe of the latest German single engine fighter at that point – the Ta 152.

The first evidence of this comes from a brief report prepared by Oberingenieur Herbert Wolff of Focke-Wulf's Flugmechanik L department, entitled Betr. Leistungsvergleich Ta 152 A bzw. Fw 190 gegenüber Ta 152 mit Napier-Sabre II or 'Subject: Performance comparison Ta 152 A and Fw 190 compared to Ta 152 with Napier-Sabre II'.

Dated February 1, 1944, this document outlines in brief the task that Focke-Wulf has been set and discusses three different installation possibilities for the Napier Sabre II within the Ta 152.

It says: "Due to the current request to perform the installation examination on the Fw 190 or Ta 152 A with the Napier Saber II engine, performance comparisons have to be made. The documents used are the drawings 0310 025 - T2 and T3, which contain the respective installations. For reasons of gravity and constructional concerns, the fuselage of the Ta 152 is used.

"Installation suggestion 1 – has the arrangement similar to the Hawker Typhoon. Installation suggestion 2 – has the water radiator in the wings. The oil cooler is designed as a ventral radiator.

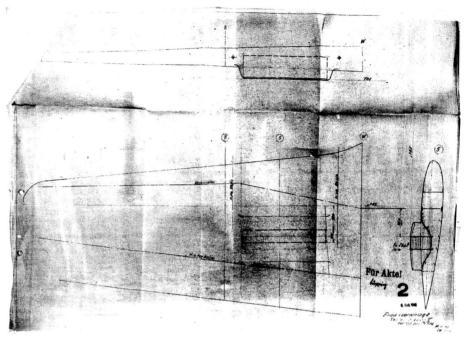

ABOVE: The wing radiator arrangement from installation suggestion 2 – the middle arrangement shown in the other drawing.

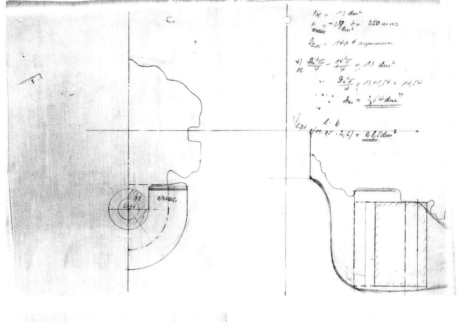

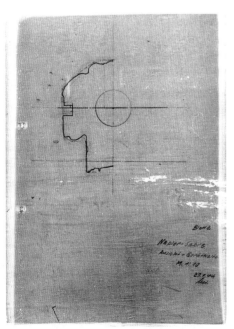

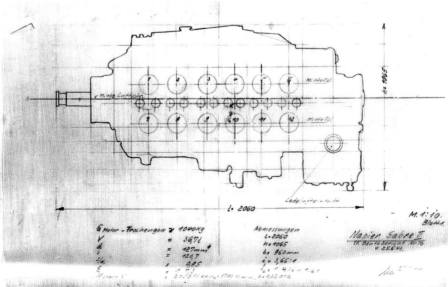

ABOVE & LEFT: Drawings of the Napier Sabre II used by Focke-Wulf to help with working out how it could be installed in the Ta 152.

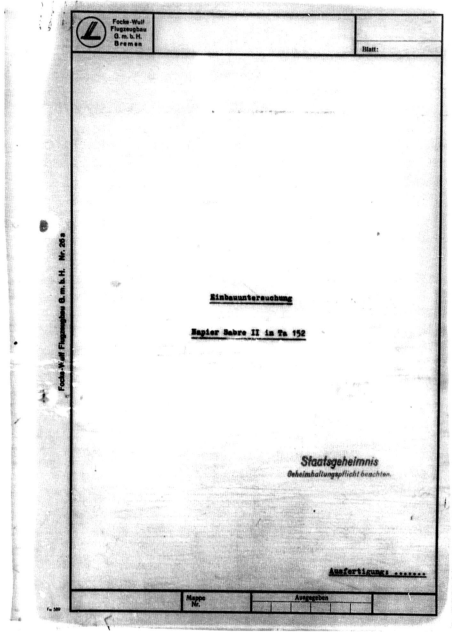

ABOVE: The front page of Herbert Wolff's report on fitting the Napier Sabre II to the Ta 152.

Installation suggestion 3 – shows the axial flow through radiator, if the nacelle housing would be extended by 320mm, radiator head diameter 1210mm. The rest of the fuselage with structure and tail except for the armament is like the Ta 152 A."

The three drawings to which Wolff refers, dated January 28, 1944, are all included. One sheet shows the trio of designs in parallel to one another. At the top is Einbauvorschlag 1 (wie Typhoon) or 'Installation suggestion 1 (like Typhoon). The Sabre engine is bolted onto the Ta 152 A's attachment points and beneath it is a large 'chin' radiator as seen on the Hawker Typhoon. This strange union of a very familiar icon of British Second World War aviation and the distinctive cockpit form of the Fw 190 series certainly makes for an unsettling sight.

In the centre of the sheet is Einbauvorschlag 2 (Flächenkühler) or 'Installation suggestion 2 (wing radiator)'. This aerodynamically cleaner arrangement, with the wing-mounted radiators shown in a separate drawing on a different sheet, is similar to the layout used for the Napier Sabre IV-powered Hawker Tempest I prototype HM599. This aircraft first flew on February 24, 1943, 11 months before Focke-Wulf's study, but it is unlikely that Wolff and his team were aware of it.

Finally, at the bottom of the sheet, is the more familiar Ta 152 annular radiator positioned ahead of the Sabre. The annotation is Einbauvorschlag 3 (Getriebe verlängerung 320mm) or 'Installation suggestion 3 (transmission extension 320mm)'.

A more fulsome report on the project was issued on April 12, 1944. Wolff wrote: "In order to get an overview of the performance of fighter aircraft on the enemy side that can be reached with the Napier Sabre II, and to assess the usefulness of the Napier-built aircraft engine, at the request of the RLM, Focke-Wulf made an investigation of the imaginary installation of the Napier Sabre II in the Ta 152.

"The Napier Sabre II is a liquid-cooled gasoline engine with spool control of 36.7 litres capacity and with 24 cylinders. It is designed as H-engine in horizontal design, its power to weight ratio is 0.46kg per hp at 56hp per litre capacity.

"In view of the purpose of the investigation, it has been assumed that for the sake of a better incorporation changes of a minor nature, e.g. a transmission extension, can be performed. According to the existing engine specifications the installation of the Sabre II in the Ta 152 presents no special difficulties. The basic installation options are shown in three suggestions from the annex (drawing no. 0310 025-T3).

"Installation suggestion 1 shows a similar structure as the Typhoon. The radiator is designed as a belly cooler, whereby the aerodynamic quality of the aircraft is impaired. For suggestion 2, the water cooler is housed in the wing; The oil cooler is located as a belly cooler under the engine. As a result, an aerodynamic improvement is expected.

"Practically, the installation suggestion 3 would be desirable, in which the cooler is designed as a ring cooler. However, this installation requires a motor-gearbox extension of 320mm. Since the best aerodynamic conditions are achieved in the latter arrangement, this is the installation that the weight and performance calculations were based on."

Perhaps the key word to focus on from Wolff's report is 'imaginary'. The original German word he uses is 'gedachten', which does most commonly translate as 'imaginary' or 'imagined' but which can also be translated as 'intended' or 'assumed'. Despite Wolff's explanation, the question of 'why?' hangs over this project like few others. There is no known instance during the entire course of the war of a project being run to determine the properties of a Rolls-Royce Merlin or Griffon, or any other Allied engine, when fitted to any German aircraft.

And if the Germans wanted to determine the likely characteristics of a Hawker Typhoon or other potential Sabre-equipped Allied types in flight, what would be the point of working out how a Ta 152 would perform when fitted with it? It is highly unlikely that the Allied type in question would be a carbon copy of the Ta 152 and its aerodynamics and performance would therefore be different. Surely a better approach – the approach always used in every other instance – would be to capture an intact or nearly intact example, repair it and flight test it. Or even simply capture a pilot from a shot-down example and interrogate him as to how his machine performed.

Spending months working out how a Napier Sabre II could be installed in a Ta 152 airframe and then determining the likely performance of this rather unlikely combination could only result in data relating to that specific design.

There are several documented instances where high-ranking German officials opined that their engineers should simply copy Allied designs – Göring stated at different times that the de Havilland Mosquito and Short Stirling should simply be copied to give the Luftwaffe a fast wooden multirole aircraft and a heavy bomber respectively.

Perhaps the RLM was considering having copies of the undeniably powerful 2200hp Sabre II made. Even with MW50 boost, the Ta 152's intended Jumo 213 E powerplant only made 2071hp.

Such an idea would no doubt have been fiercely opposed by the German engine manufacturers and it is unlikely that even relatively compliant Focke-Wulf would have been particularly happy about fitting a Sabre II copy to its aircraft. Nevertheless, Wolff carried the project through. He set out a table showing the Ta 152 mit Juno 213 E versus the Ta 152 mit Sabre II. Armament would be the same at four MG 151s and two MK 108s and the former would weigh 4770kg compared to the latter's 4800kg.

A second table showed top speed at maximum pressure for five different designs: Typhoon IB with Sabre II – 645km/h (400mph – in fact, the Typhoon's top speed was 412mph or 663km/h at 5.8km altitude) at 6.2km altitude; Ta 152 with Sabre II – 670km/h (416mph) at 6.2km; Ta 152 A with Jumo 213 A-1 – 672km/h (417mph – the closest real life design would be the Fw 190 D-9 with Jumo 213 A, which could manage 428mph with MW50 boost) at 7km; Ta 152 B with Jumo 213 E – 698km/h (462mph – the real life Ta 152 H with Jumo 213 E could in fact do 462mph) at 10.7km and Fw 190 A-6 with BMW 801 D – 651km/h (404mph – presumably verifiably accurate) at 6.5km.

A final version of the report was issued on May 22, 1944. This time the word 'imaginary' has been removed. Wolff begins: "As requested, we submit to the RLM a file on our installation investigation of the Napier Sabre II in Ta 152. To make this investigation with the Fw 190 has no practical value. Because of centre of gravity reasons, this engine for the Fw 190 is out of the question.

"In the course of this war, in the field of enemy aircraft engine design, new patterns have been developed or existing ones improved. So appeared in 1943 in England the Napier Sabre as a fighter engine new at the front. The installation of the Sabre II with 2080hp starting power (speed 3700rpm) was realised in the English fighter Typhoon. The liquid-cooled, supercharged 24-cylinder H-engine (36.7 litre capacity) in horizontal design has an output of 56hp per litre and the favourable power to weight ratio of 0.46kg per hp.

"Thus, at the request of the authorities, it is reasonable to consider the installation of the engine in order to draw conclusions about expected future flight performance with this engine on the enemy side. The task was

conceived and carried out in this form and improvements were even made on the engine design. On the fuselage side a good aerodynamic installation can be made.

"Since exact records of fuselage dimensions and the like of the fighter Typhoon are not available, the model Ta 152 was chosen and the installation investigation was carried out. On the fuselage side, according to the existing engine information on the Sabre II in the Ta 152 no special difficulties were encountered. The basic installation option is shown as suggestion 3 in the appendix.

"In the above list, the same assumptions were made for the performance statement, so the result is a basis for comparison.

No doubt further improvements could be achieved by refinements of the intake shaft on the Ta 152 with Sabre II and thus performance and speed increase."

It would appear that no practical attempt was ever made to actually install a captured Napier Sabre II in a Ta 152 fuselage, particularly as Wolff's calculations correctly suggested that there would be no real benefit in doing so. However, the fact that the RLM commissioned Focke-Wulf to carry out the project at all is intriguing and just the drawing of the Ta 152 fitted with the iconically British Sabre, included with Wolff's reports, is enough to prompt some real 'what if' speculation. ●

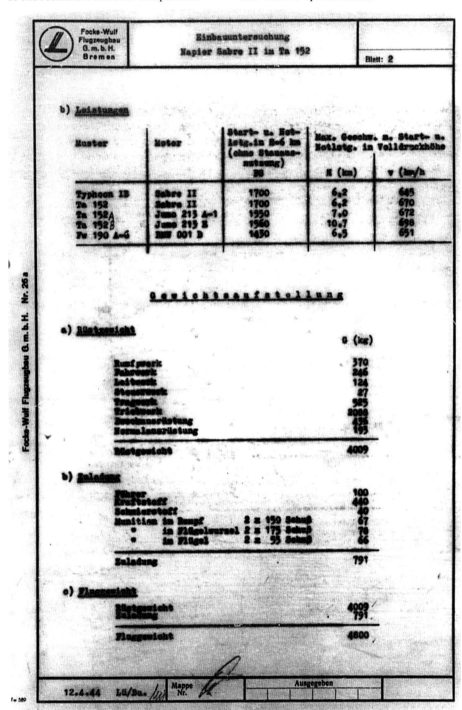

ABOVE: Table from April 12, 1944, showing the anticipated performance of the Napier Sabre when fitted to a Ta 152 fuselage, compared against the Hawker Typhoon, Ta 152 A, Ta 152 B and Fw 190 A-6. Naturally, the Typhoon came out worst – even though in reality its performance was superior to that of the Fw 190 A-6.

Focke-Wulf Ta 152 mit Napier Sabre II

May 1944

Artwork by Luca Landino

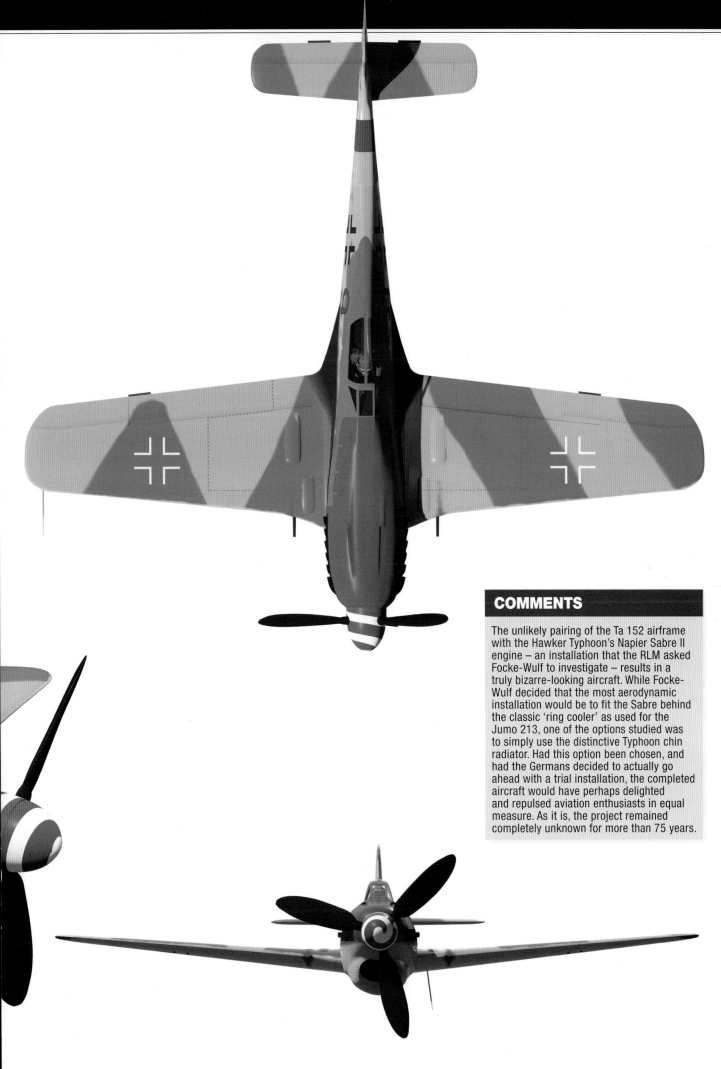

COMMENTS

The unlikely pairing of the Ta 152 airframe with the Hawker Typhoon's Napier Sabre II engine – an installation that the RLM asked Focke-Wulf to investigate – results in a truly bizarre-looking aircraft. While Focke-Wulf decided that the most aerodynamic installation would be to fit the Sabre behind the classic 'ring cooler' as used for the Jumo 213, one of the options studied was to simply use the distinctive Typhoon chin radiator. Had this option been chosen, and had the Germans decided to actually go ahead with a trial installation, the completed aircraft would have perhaps delighted and repulsed aviation enthusiasts in equal measure. As it is, the project remained completely unknown for more than 75 years.

Sensible at first glance

Focke-Wulf Nurflügelflugzeug

There never was a Focke-Wulf flying wing – but the company went back to the all-wing layout again and again. It was previously known that the company studied flying wings in 1942 and 1944 but new evidence shows research stretching back to the third month of the war – November 1939.

Having been head-hunted from the AVA by Kurt Tank himself, aerodynamics whiz-kid Hans Multhopp joined one of Focke-Wulf's two experimental departments – Flugmechanik E – in 1937. Two years later he was tasked with investigating the properties and potential of flying wing aircraft. Exactly what the reason for this was is unclear but Messerschmitt had hired famous tailless aircraft exponent Alexander Lippisch at

the beginning of the year and Focke-Wulf believed itself to be the Augsburg firm's chief rival. In addition, Junkers, Heinkel and Arado had all carried out work on flying wings during the 1930s, which Focke-Wulf would have been aware of.

Finally, Focke-Wulf's proudest achievement at this point was the Fw 200 Condor. It would make sense for a company so heavily invested in large transport aircraft to investigate the potential of the flying wing,

which was anecdotally supposed to be well suited to this purpose.

Multhopp's report, Die Raumausnutzung beim Nurflügel-Flugzeug or 'The use of space in the flying wing aircraft' was published on November 6, 1939. In the introduction he wrote: "One of the most popular arguments in favour of the flying wing construction is the assertion

BELOW: The three flying wing aircraft designs studied by Focke-Wulf engineer Hans Multhopp in 1939.

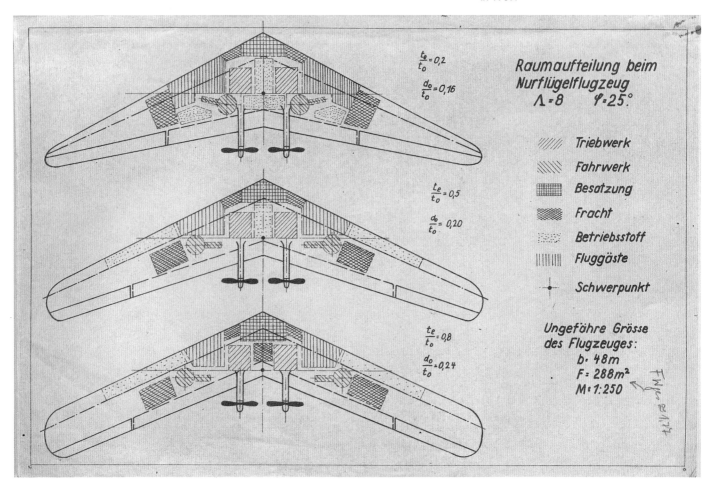

that you can accommodate from a certain size in flying wing everything that such a plane in general carries around, and that you can distribute all weights over the wing so that a minimum on bending moments and transverse forces in the wing comes about.

"From this one concludes again on a very low fuselage weight and the associated performance advantages. All this looks sensible at first glance, but unfortunately such simple considerations usually have a snag at some point; it seemed necessary, therefore, to take a closer look at the space conditions of the flying wing."

The report then examines the theoretical attributes of flying wings in great detail, focusing on three potential twin-engine, tricycle undercarriage layouts. Each design has a wingspan of 48m – 18m wider than that proposed for the Horten XVIII bomber five years later and only slightly narrower than that of the enormous Junkers Ju 390 – with a wing area of 288m² and a sweepback of 25°. In each case the engines, prop shafts and pusher-propellers are positioned tightly around the centre of gravity.

The first design has a near-triangular form with the crew compartment at the forward centre tip of the wing with a small freight compartment to either side. Between the engines at the centre of gravity are two large rectangular fuel tanks. Outboard of the engines at the wing leading edge are two large passenger cabins and beyond them two more freight compartments.

The inwards-retracting undercarriage wheels are positioned just behind the passenger cabins and towards the rear of the aircraft are two more fuel tanks.

The second wing is narrower, with only one fuel tank between the engines and no trailing edge tanks. Instead, two large tanks are fitted into the leading edge of the wing and the undercarriage has been repositioned to retract outwards. The crew, freight and passenger compartments all remain in roughly the same positions.

For the third design, the wing has become a thick constant chord – with more fuel in the wing leading edges and a fifth freight compartment replacing the central fuel tank. Otherwise it is similar in layout to the second design. In each design, the outer sections of the wings are empty.

Multhopp found that none of the three designs was particularly favourable.

He summarised his findings by saying: "A somewhat more accurate comparison of the space and weight ratios of flying wing aircraft and those of a normal design shows that the often-claimed superiority of the flying wing in these questions does not correspond to the real conditions. Rather, one comes, by a somewhat detailed investigation to the following picture:

"1. If one assumes a certain usable volume for any purpose as a given, then it is more efficient to make the wing only so large that it meets the requirements of take-off and landing, and to accommodate the rest in the fuselage, thereby making the wing so big that everything is contained in it. This statement is also true for the largest aircraft conceivable in the near future.

"2. Large parts of the wing space are not usable in the flying wing, since the centre of

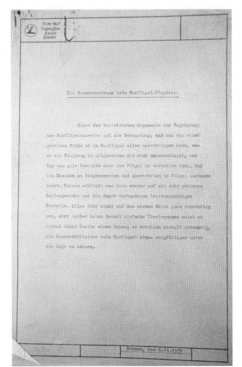

ABOVE: The first page of Multhopp's earliest known report on flying wings.

gravity of the aircraft must be kept within very narrow limits. In particular, a loading of the outer wing is hardly possible.

"3. The necessary concentration of the engines on the middle of the wing and the inability to properly load the outer wing result in an unusually unfavourable mass distribution over the span of the aircraft, which in combination with the larger dimensions and the many required cut-outs in the wing surface, the weight of the flying aircraft increases compared to the normal construction method."

Despite this curt dismissal of the flying wing concept, Focke-Wulf went back to it in 1942 when the company was considering superheavy transport aircraft under the project heading Grosstransporter. Kurt Tank sent a memo to Multhopp, production manager Willi Kaether, project office head Ludwig Mittelhuber and the head of Flugmechanik L, Herbert Wolff on May 13, 1942, telling them: "Since the ongoing development work on large aircraft already has a weight of 120 tons per our discussion, it is appropriate to consider the issue of the flying wing aircraft again.

"The following investigation should therefore be made: at moderate surface loads (200kg per square metre), which still allow a sufficiently high speed, especially in the case of the all-wing type, it is necessary to investigate the weight of the wings as much as the dimensions of the wing, with loads including fuel for very great range in the wing.

"Due to the wide distribution of the loads along the wing span, care must be taken that the bending moments during the flight are reduced to a minimum. In order to keep the impact on the ground as small as possible, it is advisable to distribute the landing gear in the same way as the two Grosstransporter projects along the span in individual bogies, so that the weight is evenly distributed among the wheels on the ground."

He said that there should be no protrusions from the wing either for cockpit visibility or defensive armament during flight "in order to avoid additional drag. The ideal shape of a wing is to be aimed for as far as possible".

He went on: "Since realising such an aircraft type will require a longer development time, engines such as the BMW 803 can be expected. For installation in the wing, the development of the flat counter-piston motors, which starts at Cologne – Deutz, must also be well suited. When installing six such units of 5000hp, the total power of 30,000hp would allow a flying weight of approximately 200 ton.

"The wing required at the given surface load with a relative wing thickness of 20% at the root would have to be sufficient for the required space. In carrying out these investigations, I ask for ongoing information, if necessary to improve the project, to change the task in this or that direction. The basic task of this type is the transport of large loads over very large distances at moderate speed."

Multhopp elaborated on his research into flying wings at a meeting of the Deutsche Akademie für Luftfahrtforschung or 'German Academy of Aeronautical Research' meeting on November 6, 1942. At the event, attended by Heinkel chief designer Siegfried Günter, Professor Walter Georgii, head of the DFS and Franz Nikolas Scheubel, chairman of aircraft and flight technology at the Technischen Hochschule Darmstadt, among others, a presentation was made by Alexander Lippisch entitled The Evolution of the Tailless Aircraft and there was a discussion afterwards, all of which was recorded for posterity.

Multhopp said: "We also have been thoroughly occupied with this problem, because the industry has been continuously approached with the project of tailless aircraft.

"With regard to the flying performance we, as well as Herr Günter, obtained different results from those of Herr Lippisch. We were less interested in the tailless fighter aircraft than in the tailless super-aircraft and particularly in the all-wing aircraft. The all-wing construction is extraordinarily difficult for large aircraft which are built either for the transport of very heavy and bulky goods, or for long-range flying."

He went on to list problems with engine positioning, fuel tank positioning and other centre of gravity issues. Designing the structure to ensure that stresses were not unacceptably high led to weight increases and low speed performance was expected to be poor.

Focke-Wulf looked at flying wings again from March to August 1944, based on the knowledge that Reichsmarschall Hermann Göring had paid 500,000 RM each to Lippisch and the Horten brothers to develop flying wing designs. The conclusion was that the tailless aircraft offered no real advantages over the conventional aircraft.

Finally, in January to March 1945, while working on a series of night fighters, Focke-Wulf came up with another flying wing layout – but little is known of this design. Perhaps it shouldn't come as a great surprise that a major aircraft manufacturer would spend time examining cutting edge technological concepts that might ultimately lead to the next stage of aircraft development – but it is difficult to see why Focke-Wulf kept going back to it despite concluding again and again that it had no merit. ●

X-planes

Focke-Wulf Strahlrohrbomber

Ramjet aircraft designs were worked on at Focke-Wulf from February 1944 to at least October of that year, resulting first in the slender Strahlrohrjäger with two podded ramjets to the rear and then the Triebflügeljäger with its three spinning wingtip ramjets. But a sketchy third design also makes a brief appearance amid the company's 'X' series ramjet designs – the Strahlrohrbomber.

The earliest known mention of a '2 Strahlrohr Jäger' or 'two ramjet fighter' in surviving Focke-Wulf company documents is on a number of handwritten papers dated February 11, 1944. At least a week prior to this, the company was studying the shape of ramjet tubes.

The earlier history of Focke-Wulf's involvement in ramjets is revealed in a US report on the interrogation of company aerodynamicist Dr Otto Ernst Pabst on May 21, 1945: "Pabst stated that his last job was on the ramjet motor. This project originated from a visit of [ramjet pioneer Eugen] Sänger to [Focke-Wulf chief designer Kurt] Tank. Sänger had built and flown a ramjet motor, but it was no good because it was too long and had high drag and high skin friction.

"In fact the skin friction alone was so high that there was no net thrust. Pabst suggested to Tank that he could do a better job, i.e. get lower drag."

According to a British report, Pabst stated that he had begun work on ramjets in 1941, Focke-Wulf having already been made aware of the technology, and simply kept a close eye on reports of Sänger's work as it progressed. This latter seems more likely since Focke-Wulf was renowned for keeping close tabs on all developments in propulsion.

Whatever the truth, a research station under Pabst was set up at Kirchhorsten in 1943, just to the north of Focke-Wulf's design and research headquarters at Bad Eilsen, and work was begun on combustion problems with the goal of making the ramjet a viable means of propulsion.

The earliest Focke-Wulf ramjet aircraft design, for which no drawing seems to have survived, was designated X1 and had a wingspan of just 7m with a wing area of 10m². It was to be a single-seater powered by a pair of ramjets and had a takeoff weight

of 5000kg. This was compares to a takeoff weight of 4900kg for the Fw 190 A-8.

The X2 had followed by April 24, 1944. This had 45° swept wings which, despite retaining a wingspan of 7m now had a much

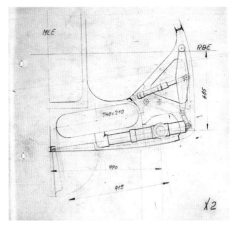

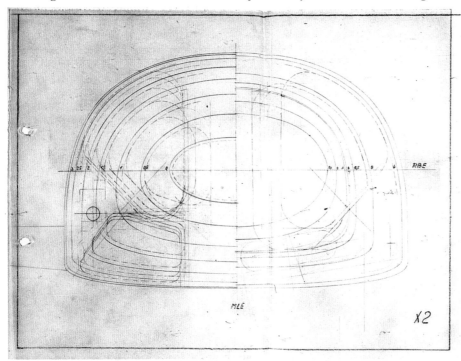

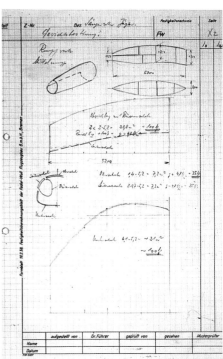

ABOVE & RIGHT: Fuselage and landing gear sketches for Focke-Wulf's X2 Strahlrohrjäger.

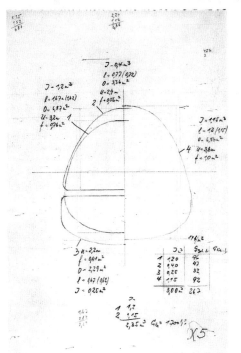

ABOVE: Sketch showing a cross section of the X5's fuselage.

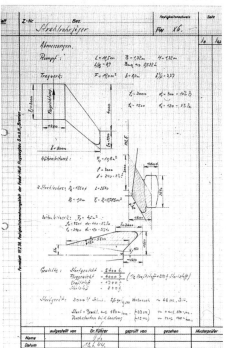

ABOVE: Designs for the wings, ramjet booms and tailfin for the X6.

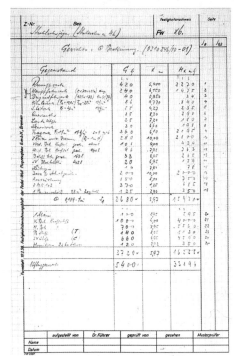

ABOVE: Weights of the X6's different component parts.

larger wing area of 17.5m². The fuselage appears to have been quite broad and flat with very short undercarriage legs, judging by an existing fuselage cross-section drawing. It was to have been armed with three MK 103 cannon – which appear in a table of weights for the aircraft's components.

By May 16, the sequence had reached the X5 with nothing of the X3 or X4 appearing to have survived. The X5 had a more oval-shaped fuselage, only two MK 103s and a single rocket motor with 3000kg thrust for starting from the runway, since ramjets cannot work at a standstill when no air is being 'rammed' into them. Its nosewheel was to measure 380 x 150 and its two main wheels 740 x 210. Its maximum takeoff weight was 5072kg.

The X6 had taken over by June 6, 1944. This had a wingspan of 8m and a wing area of 16.8m², later amended to 19m². Again, it had two MK 103s and a tricycle undercarriage arrangement but now the nosewheel was 475mm by 173mm although the main wheels remained 740mm by 210mm. A table of weights cites drawing number 0310 246/10-01 but this may no longer exist. The maximum takeoff weight is 5400kg.

By June 13, 1944, the X6 was becoming a much more fleshed out aircraft design, with details being given for how long the 3000kg thrust rocket motor would fire for on takeoff – 48 seconds – and the shape of both the aircraft's ramjet motor nacelles and its tail fin. It was calculated that it would take 2.4 minutes for the X6 to reach an altitude of 11km (36,000ft), while overall flight time was 50 minutes and range was 800km. It would measure 11.85m long and 2.9m high with a wing sweep of 45°.

On July 5, 1944, the X6 was the subject of a full Focke-Wulf baubeschreibung or 'construction description' – Nr. 283 Strahlrohrjäger. Later the company would produce Baubeschreibung Nr. 290 Ta 152 C and Baubeschreibung Nr. 292 Ta 152 H, indicating

that the construction description number was not the project's 'Fw' or 'Ta' number. So the X6 Strahlrohrjäger was never the 'Ta 283' – this postwar designation was the result of a simple misunderstanding about the nature of Focke-Wulf's project numbering system. The

company knew the design formally as the Strahlrohrjäger or Baubeschreibung Nr. 283 aircraft' and internally as the Strahlrohrjäger or X6 but not the 'Ta 283'.

The introduction of the document states: "The ramjet fighter is a particularly

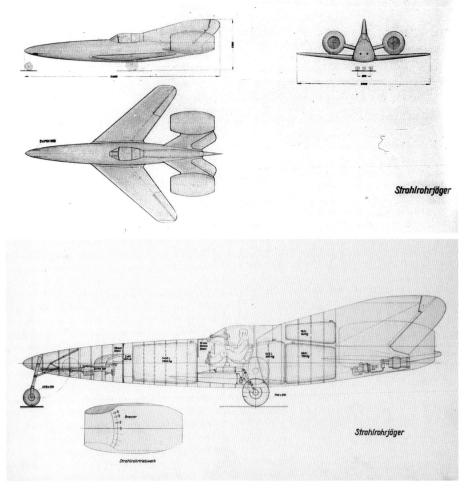

ABOVE & RIGHT: X6 – the finished design, now known simply as the Strahlrohrjäger and described in Baubeschreibung Nr. 283.

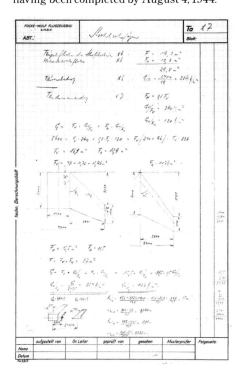

ABOVE: Weights of the X6's different component parts.

fast aircraft, with a high ceiling and good climbing power. The use of such fighters calls without doubt for new tactics, which must be developed accordingly. Their high rate of climb and horizontal speed allow their use against bombers with 700km/h average speed, which fighters with Otto engines cannot fight successfully. Their speed superiority of about 500km/h, compared with the normal bomber formations makes pursuit possible to a greater distance than with Otto engine fighters.

"In combat itself, an approach directly from behind is often the most favourable, for it offers the longest time of fire. There is possibility for the installation of two MK 103, four MK 108 or four MG 213. Considering the short duration of attack, density of fire must be preferred to an extended flight path

with possible greater range, so that the installation of four MG 213 appears to answer the purpose best.

"Nor must it be forgotten that a synchronising of the speed of the ramjet-propelled fighters with the bomber speed can hardly be possible, because of the limited controllability of their engines."

Shortly before work on drafting a presentable version of this document commenced however, on June 23, 1944, the ramjet designers examined what a Pabst type ramjet would look like attached to the wing of a Focke-Wulf Fw 190 A-10. The following day, they sketched an astonishing theoretical design for a ramjet powered bomber based on the X-series work. Labelled simply 'Strahlrohrbomber', this design had a wing area of 134m² and a wingspan of 32m. By comparison, the Heinkel He 177 had a wingspan of 31.44m and a wing area of 100m² but its wings were straight rather than swept. The Junkers Ju 90 had a wingspan of 35.02m and a wing area of 184m².

No figure is given for the length of the fuselage, but using the wingspan for scale it should be about 35.5m. The He 177 was just 22m long and the Ju 90 was 26.3m. Even the enormous Ju 390 was only 34.2m long, though it had a wingspan of 50.32m and a wing area of 253.6m².

The Strahlrohrbomber had a maximum takeoff weight of 25,000kg and its bomb load was 3000kg. Range is given as 2000km at an altitude of 16km (52,500ft). The He 177's range for comparison was 5600km and its bomb load was 2500kg internally or up to 7000kg with underwing attachment points.

There does not appear to be any indication of how many crew the Strahlrohrbomber was going to have – although it would seem logical that it had more than two, given its size.

The story of the X-series doesn't end with Baubeschreibung Nr. 283 though, this having been completed by August 4, 1944.

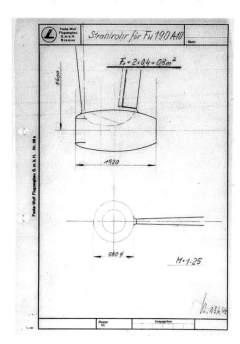

ABOVE: This drawing showing ramjets attached to the wingtips of a Fw 190 A-10 comes from the same file of notes and sketches as the X-series and the Strahlrohrbomber.

An X7 Strahlrohrjäger was then designed which seems to have gone back to the smaller earlier designs of the series, with a wingspan of 7m and a wing area of 15m². It had a maximum takeoff weight of 3600kg and was armed with two MK 103s. Nothing is known of the X8, if there was one, but finally there was the X9 Strahlrohrjäger with a wing area of 31m² and a wingspan of at least 10m. Incredibly, its wings had an 80° sweepback and while a drawing of the wing survives, there is no further visual representation of either.

After this point, Focke-Wulf seems to have given up on the Strahlrohrjäger design with its podded ramjets and switched to the even more radical Triebflügeljäger. ●

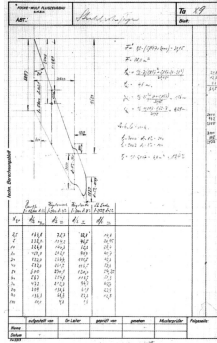

ABOVE: A page from the official report based on the characteristics of the X6.

ABOVE: A progression of the Strahlrohrjäger beyond the X6 to the X7.

ABOVE: Sharply swept back wings would have been a feature of the X9 – the last known design in the series.

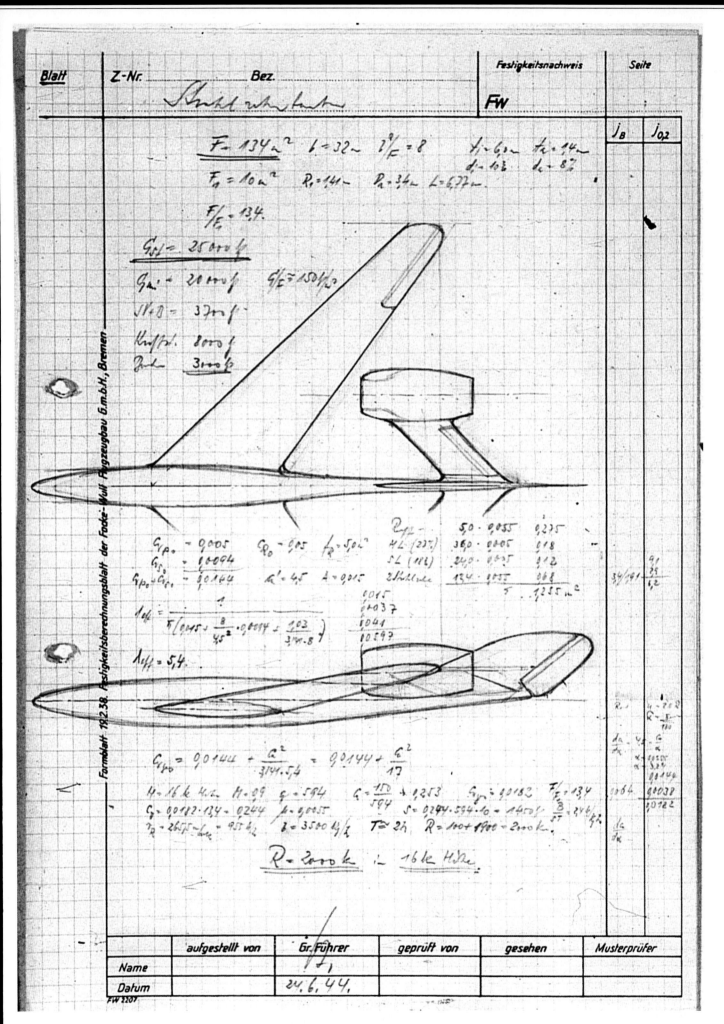

ABOVE: The Strahlrohrbomber was an impressive – almost alien-looking – design.

The sting

Gotha Rammstachel and Bombenflugzeug

During the Second World War a remarkable number of outlandish aviation-related patents were filed by the Gothaer Waggonfabrik company. From rammers to armoured ground-attack rocket aircraft, Gotha had them all.

Even among Gotha's more novel patents the 'Rammstachel für Flugzeuge' or 'ram sting for aircraft' stands out. The undated design is the work of prolific 'wonder weapon' inventor Oberingenieur Walter Wundes – 'Herr Wundes' appears at the top left of the drawing and the legend 'Rammflugzeug' or 'ram aircraft' appears to the bottom left.

The aircraft itself is very similar to several of Wundes' other creations, with a teardrop-shaped fuselage, thickly armoured cockpit, high wing position and rocket motor propulsion. The major difference is the spiky device attached to its back.

According to the patent: "A ramming aircraft should approach as close as possible to the aircraft it is attacking and destroy it by damaging flight-important airframe parts. Due to the collision, the ramming aircraft itself is usually so heavily damaged that another attack is no longer possible.

"In order to allow the destruction of the enemy aircraft without direct collision, it is proposed to attach to the ramming aircraft a protruding arm (spike) in which one or more explosive projectiles are installed, and which breaks off when touched with the enemy aircraft and with the help of barbs, a tack or ropes that loop around parts of the enemy aircraft, it remains hanging.

"The sting with the explosive bullets is now stuck to the enemy aircraft and it cannot shake it off or remove it. The subsequent explosion will bring the enemy plane to crash. The protruding arm is usually folded into the aircraft, so as not to cause drag, and deployed just before the attack. In addition, several arms can be provided, which are extended one after another, so that various attacks can be performed."

Where Wundes had previously advocated simply smashing an armoured rocketplane into enemy bombers, wrecking the rammer but ensuring the pilot's survival, his thoughts were clearly now turning to a more reusable design. The rammer would approach the enemy bomber stream, flip its spiky explosive 'sting' up into a vertical position, then fly close enough to an individual bomber so that the 'sting' snagged on it and then became embedded – detaching as the rammer flew away. The explosives would then detonate, destroying the target.

Assuming that the patent's final provision

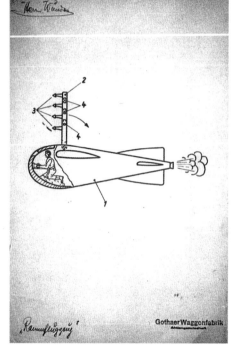

RIGHT: The drawing which accompanied the 'Rammstachel für Flugzeuge' patent. The title in the bottom left corner reads 'Rammflugzeug' while the note in the top left appears to read 'Herr Wundes'. The drawing itself shows a heavily armoured rocket-propelled rammer aircraft with a pop-up explosive 'sting' fitted to its spine. The idea was to dig the spikes into the target aircraft then fly away, leaving the sting behind – which would then explode.

was followed, the armoured rocketplane would then simply flip up another 'sting' and perform another attack.

The concept would undoubtedly have been difficult to implement in practice. Just getting the heavily armoured rocketplane airborne without wasting its fuel on the climb would have been tricky. Actually ramming a target aircraft when approaching at high speed would have been difficult but attempting to just slightly miss a target to get the sting embedded would have required a pilot of exceptional skill. If the explosives failed to go off, the attack might easily fail to bring down the target – and if they did go off, despite its armour the rammer could easily suffer damage sufficient to make it unflyable.

Luckily no one ever attempted to put the idea into practice.

BOMBENFLUGZEUG

While researching Luftwaffe: Secret Designs of the Third Reich, the author discovered a Gotha patent entitled Flugzeugführersitz für Notausstieg bei grossen Geschwindigkeiten in Bodennähe or 'Pilot's seat for emergency exit at high speeds near the ground'. This consisted of two written sheets and three sheets of drawings showing different but very similar designs on each sheet for a monoplane aircraft with an oval-shaped fuselage, twin boom tails and the titular 'pilot's seat for emergency exit', which was essentially a rocket-propelled escape capsule which fired out between the booms.

A third written sheet bundled with

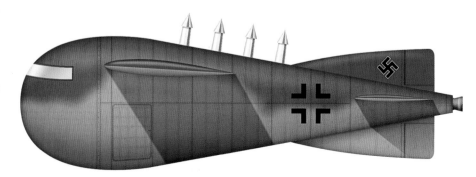

ABOVE: Gotha's rammer aircraft with its 'sting' retracted for aerodynamic efficiency during flight.
ARTWORK BY ZOLTÁN CSOMBÓ

the patent described a proposal for suicide attacks using piloted flying bombs. The latter appeared to make little sense until the author read BIOS Interrogation Report No. 187 of October 7, 1946 – one of several interrogations of German test pilot Hanna Reitsch. This one is titled: 'Main Interest: German Version of the Suicide Weapon'.

It describes Reitsch's attempts to secure a suitable aircraft for her fanatical volunteers to crash into Allied targets. Initially, it was decided that the Messerschmitt Me 328 would be used. Work on the Me 328 as a pulsejet-powered light bomber was stopped on September 3, 1943, when it was concluded that the vibration and noise problems of the Argus As 014 pulsejet were incurable. Efforts to 'save' the project as a single-jet fighter are detailed elsewhere in this publication but what really gave it a stay of execution was Reitsch's intervention.

The British interrogation report states: "The aeronautical characteristics most important for the intended use of the plane were: 1) Excellent visibility. 2) Ample cockpit space to afford the pilot sufficient room and comfort in controlling the aim. 3) Excellent manoeuvrability. 4) Good flight stability.

"In the degrees required the Me

328 fulfilled all of these requirements. These tests at Hörsching airfield were completed in April 1944. Thereupon the Flugzeugbau Gothaer-Waggon Fabrik in Gotha, Thuringen, was ordered to undertake the assembly-line production of the plane. Unexplained difficulties and delays prolonged the construction until it began to appear to Reitsch and her volunteers that there was some sort of official sabotage afoot to delay or prevent the suicide project.

"When it began to appear that long months would still be required before the Me 328 was available in any sufficient quantities, the suicide group began to look about for some sort of makeshift plane that would still fulfil the purpose and, most important, be immediately available. The decision was reached to use the manned V-1."

This would appear to explain Gotha's sudden interest in rammers, bombers and other designs which involved some sort of 'sacrifice' in the name of destroying the enemy during the early months of 1944. It also explains the suicide attack 'proposal' which could conceivably have come to Gotha from Reitsch's group and been bundled with the 'Pilot's seat' patent.

Furthermore, it now appears that the 'Pilot's seat' patent was actually an extract from an earlier document. Another patent has come to light which features basically the same 'Pilot's seat' at the beginning but then goes on to offer further inventions that Gotha hoped to patent.

This is entitled simply 'Bombenflugzeug' or 'Bomb aircraft'. It states: "In the normal bomber, bombs are dropped from considerable height, but this significantly impairs their accuracy. In particular, ship targets are hard to hit, as the ships are constantly changing direction. On the other hand, it is desirable to destroy the target with a single bomb of large weight.

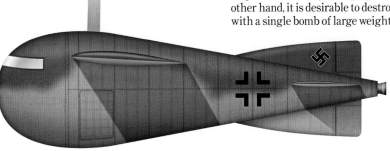

ABOVE: The rammer with its 'sting' extended in readiness for an attack. ARTWORK BY ZOLTÁN CSOMBÓ

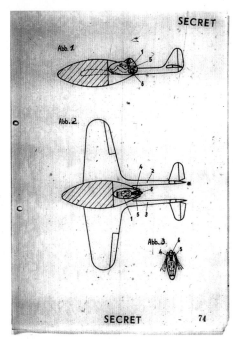

RIGHT: The first page of illustrations accompanying Gotha's 'Bombenflugzeug' patent. This shows side and top views of an unpowered twin-boom glider laden with explosives. At the rear, and shown separately, is the pilot's seat – designed to detach and fly clear using retro-rockets before the glider hit its target.

"It is therefore necessary to steer the large-calibre bombs until the last moment before they hit their target and so that all unforeseen influences that affect the accuracy are avoided. Also, in a normal bomber the amount of explosive material transported amounts to only a part of the aircraft's own weight, including the amount of fuel to be carried, which must also be sufficient for the return journey.

"This invention provides a bomb carrier aircraft for total deployment in that the aircraft itself is designed as a gliding bomb. In this case, a precaution is to be taken so that the aircraft pilot can part with the gliding bomb when it is reaching the destination. The pilot's seat is therefore carried by the gliding bomb in a conventional manner. Here, the pilot's seat is equipped with retro-rockets that are triggered when separating the seat from the aircraft.

"As a further braking measure, the pilot's seat can be equipped with a parachute, which is extended after switching on the rockets or at a certain time determined by the aircraft pilot."

It goes on to explain that a light aircraft could be employed rather than a rocket-propelled seat. This would be attached to the flying bomb and the pilot could simply detach before the point of impact. At the last moment, the bomb's flight controls could be locked in position, "thus, the direction of flight of the gliding bomb when separating the pilot's seat or light aircraft remains unchanged from the glide bomb".

Three pages of additional drawings show how the light aircraft could be attached to the flying bomb in various different ways. This was effectively an attempt to patent the Mistel concept – which would have presumably failed because the Mistel already existed by early 1944 as a combination of a Ju 88-based flying bomb and a Bf 109 F 'light aircraft'. Perhaps this explains why the patent was trimmed back to just the pilot's rocket seat invention. ●

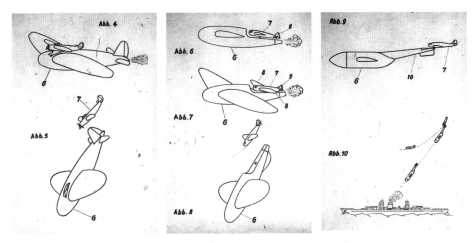

RIGHT: Gotha's 'Bombenflugzeug' patent attempted to protect three different ways of attaching a light aircraft to a glider filled with explosives. Unfortunately, similar combinations had already been built and flown by the DFS and Junkers – which seems to have resulted in Gotha ditching the Mistel aspect of the patent and concentrating instead on the rocket-powered escape seat.

British wings

Horten airliners

Immediately after the war the British spent months gathering together as much useful German technological research as they could at Göttingen in Lower Saxony. As part of this effort they drafted in tailless aircraft pioneer brothers Walter and Reimar Horten to design a new flying wing airliner.

The saga of the Horten brothers and their incredible story of subterfuge and persistence in attempting to get their flying wing aircraft built in wartime Nazi Germany despite official apathy or even opposition is well documented.

In short, the Hortens began the war as Luftwaffe officers designing sports gliders on the side for their superiors – but by the end they were regularly invited to meetings attended by the most important figures in Germany's aviation industry and were working on a large flying wing bomber propelled by four turbojets.

During the war years they had managed to scrape together sufficient resources to build, or at least start building, more than 20 flying wing aircraft, two of them powered by a pair of piston engines, one by two jet engines and the rest being gliders.

Having been captured by advancing American troops on April 7, 1945, the Hortens were initially held in Germany before being transported to London on May 9. They were interviewed by Kenneth Wilkinson of the Royal Aircraft Establishment from May 19 to May 21 before being transferred back to Germany by the Americans towards the end of the month to help track down some of their surviving aircraft.

The components of the part-built H VIII

were found at the Horten brothers' makeshift factory – a former highways maintenance depot in the British zone at Göttingen.

The British had intermittent contact with the Hortens during August and on the 27th Reimar, staying at Göttingen, was informed that the Ministry of Aircraft Production wanted construction of the Horten VIII to be completed. According to notes made by Operation Surgeon coordinator Group Captain Geoffrey Mungo Buxton, "Reimar thinks that two months will be needed to remake the drawings and three months to complete the aircraft".

It was hoped that the H VIII could be completed at another Horten brothers workshop – Peschke Flugzeugbau in Minden – but "Peschke is now building agricultural machinery in a small hangar at Mindenheide but would be prepared to build two H VIIs. To do this, he would need one to one and a half years at least. The shop is too cold for gluing and too small for the job. It is now clear that he was a furniture builder dragged into light aircraft construction and has little knowledge of building prototypes".

A team from the RAE's Tailless Advisory Committee visited Buxton and his team on September 14 and conducted further interviews with the Hortens. There was a breakthrough

on September 26 when it became clear that a cache of H VIII drawings, hidden by the Hortens' sister Gunhilde near Munich, had been discovered by the Americans. However, when the British tracked these down they found that "only 30 prints concern the H VIII".

It then transpired that "near Eilenburg, 26km north east of Leipzig, in the Soviet zone, a quantity of original tracings of Horten VIII drawings are buried in the ground and suitably protected. A man named Pützer at Bonn knows where they are hidden and it will be necessary for him to go with any expedition to recover them. If we can not recover calculations and drawings, it will take six months to produce new ones. This is providing that we can assemble a suitable design staff.

"If we do recover suitable calculations and drawings, it will take three months to complete them for the whole machine. Highest authority should be invoked to recover the above. Furthermore, I am still waiting for the admin officer to deal with German and military authorities regarding setting up the Horten factory. As yet, the factory at the Strassenmeisterei [road maintenance depot] is occupied by the military, but there is no reason why we should not start temporarily at the AVA (Göttingen)."

Detail of precisely what happened next is lacking but within two and a half months both Horten brothers were indeed working for the RAE at Göttingen. Initially, however, they were not working on the H VIII but rather a passenger transport based on their earlier bomber work. Dated December 12, 1945, the only known drawing of this design, labelled 'Project Horten', shows a flying wing aircraft with seats for 102 passengers and five crew plus large quantities of baggage. The only measurement given, in feet and inches, is the wingspan: 262ft 6in (80m) – the same as a modern day Airbus A380.

Like the Hortens' wartime H 18 bomber design, the crew were housed beneath a large blister canopy at the centre of the wing's leading edge. The passengers sat in six blocks beneath six large glazed strips – three on either side of the centreline. Most passengers wouldn't be able to see anything outside the aircraft except the sky. The baggage compartments were positioned around the aircraft's centre of gravity and six engines drove six pusher props arrayed along the aircraft's trailing edge.

Twin nosewheels retracted into a bay beneath

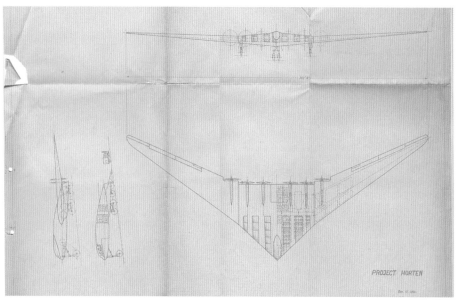

ABOVE: The first Horten aircraft designed for the British – 'Project Horten'. This design, dated December 12, 1945, had an 80m wingspan and could carry 102 passengers, albeit without giving them a particularly good view outside while they were in transit.

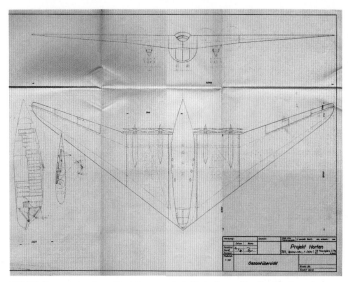

ABOVE: The second and last known aircraft designed by the Hortens for the British, known as 'Projekt Horten'. This 70 ton design could carry 48 passengers when set up for daytime rather than overnight flight.

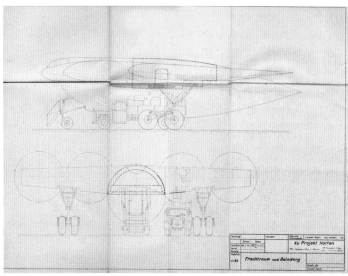

ABOVE: Loading baggage into the Projekt Horten was more difficult than getting passengers on board – it had to be winched into the wing from a lorry. This drawing is dated April 26, 1946.

the cockpit and there were four mainwheels on either side retracting into faired housings.

Evidently this design was not what the British were looking for, however. So the next job for the Hortens was to produce fresh drawings for the H VIII and an accompanying brochure for the design. The drawings are dated January 22 to February 19, 1946, and the brochure was dated simply 'February 1946'.

Years later, Reimar Horten told historian David Myhra: "When I was working for the RAE in Göttingen designing an all-wing passenger aircraft with a propeller for passenger transport, one of the RAE officials there said that the British Air Ministry was really interested in all-wing passenger transport planes. I thought that if I did a really good job then for the RAE, they would want me to go to England and help them build the passenger transport I was then designing. This would not be.

"However, in designing the all-wing passenger transport, great concern was given that every passenger have a window for a view of the outside. Also, they wanted a design with a high wing so that the passengers could have an excellent view all around and not have anything hidden by the wing. I think that my

plans called for about a 40-passenger aircraft. I think that the plans called for Rolls-Royce Merlin engines in this proposed all-wing passenger plane for production of these engines was being continued after the war."

The last known aircraft designed by the Hortens for the British – presumably the one referred to by Reimar – was labelled 'Projekt Horten' (as opposed to the December 1945 design, which was 'Project Horten'). Rather than being a pure flying wing, the 70t 'Projekt' featured a deep central fuselage housing luxurious accommodation for 48 passengers in day fight configuration or 24 when arranged for overnight travel.

In the former, passengers sat in private booths with sliding doors on the lower level – portholes offering them a good view from the side of the aircraft. If they needed to use the lavatory, they left their booth to enter a corridor, walked to the end, climbed a flight of stairs and found the toilets waiting for them at the top. Beyond that was a lounge area with tables and comfy chairs. And towards the rear was a kitchen area where the cabin crew could prepare meals.

Passengers would climb aboard via a simple flight of stairs which unfolded from a hatch beneath the nose. The aircraft itself had a

wingspan of 48m and a wing area of 363m². Like the December 1945 design, and the H VIII, it had a twin nosewheel but unlike the earlier designs it had eight mainwheels, four on each side, which were all fully retractable into the wing.

Four unspecified engines were to drive contra-rotating props in the usual pusher configuration and 16 of the 24 separate fuel tanks were positioned along the leading edge of the wings – the remaining eight positioned centrally, four in each wing. The drawing dates of this project show that it was worked on between March 25, 1946, and April 26, 1946. There appears to have been no report to accompany the project though – just a series of drawings.

This last project appears to have been the zenith of the Hortens' flying wing transport designs – an aircraft tailored to the requirements of a mainstream postwar airline. But as with the December 1945 transport and the H VIII, it does not appear to have been sufficiently interesting for the British to pursue it further. Reimar Horten would try, unsuccessfully, to get a job at the Fairey Aviation Company in 1947 before leaving Europe to work with Focke-Wulf's Kurt Tank in Argentina where he would eventually remain. ●

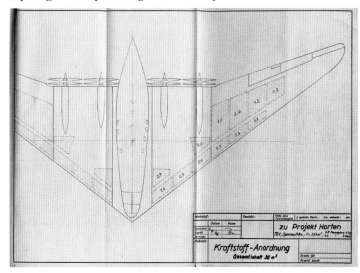

ABOVE: Drawing of April 4, 1946, shows the fuel tank positions of Projekt Horten.

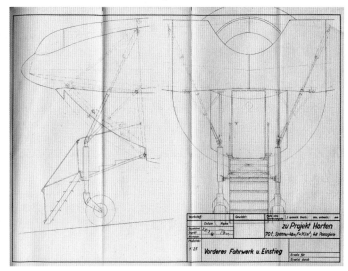

ABOVE: Climbing into the Projekt Horten airliner was simple – this drawing of March 25, 1946, shows the aircraft's extendable nose ramp which led to a door behind the curved hatch.

Horten 'Projekt Horten'

April 1946

Artwork by Luca Landino

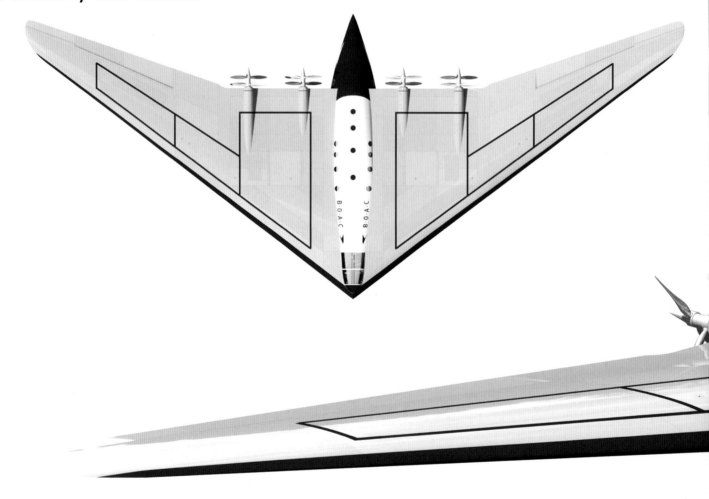

German wings

Junkers Nurflügel-Flugzeug Entwurf

Ordinarily an airliner project from 1930 – before the formation of the Luftwaffe – would fall beyond the scope of this publication but the design details included here were presented at conference on flying wing aircraft held in Berlin on April 14, 1943, which gives it a little more relevance.

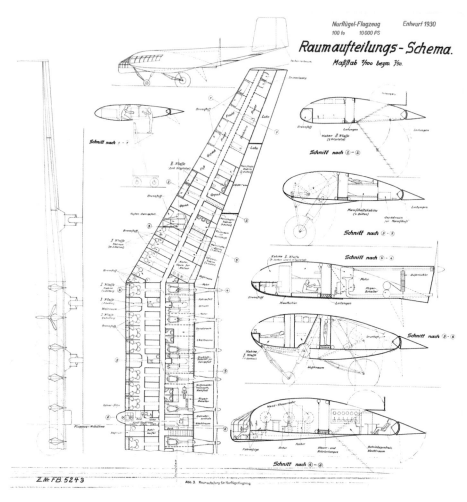

LEFT: Detailed plans for the 100 ton Junkers flying wing passenger airliner of 1930.

actual application of the flying wing aircraft – the fast mass transportation of people and goods over very large distances with the least possible effort – it is far superior to the normal aircraft. For the transport of very large single loads, in terms of weight and space, for the stratospheric flight and for extreme fast flight, the flying wing aircraft is less suitable.

"The idea of the flying wing aircraft originates from Professor Hugo Junkers (patent 253788 from February 1, 1910). It is plausible that a simple reduction in drag and weight must occur through the simple omission of gondolas, fuselage and tail, but the feasibility of this measure raises doubts. So it was only natural that in the Junkers-Forschungsanstalt works were carried out to examine the possibility of realising this thought.

"Admittedly, the department responsible for 'flow technology' at the Junkers research institute was so heavily burdened by cooperation with the Junkers aircraft company in the development of new aircraft designs that there was little time left to work on fundamental questions of non-immediate urgency.

"Only in the years 1929 to 1932 (the economic crisis – through which the Junkers factories were particularly hard hit – and in the subsequent transitional period until the dissolution of the Junkers research institute and transition of the flow technology department to the aircraft factory) could – albeit with more and more merging staff – handle work on flying wing aircraft."

He said that in order to clarify whether a flying wing could be built as a practical aircraft and whether, once built, it would be better than a conventional aircraft, "a flying-wing aircraft was designed with the flying weight of 100 tons, which at that time seemed very high, but which was far from being fantastically high. It seemed to be the minimum in order to make flying wing construction worthwhile. The aircraft was intended to serve long-distance passenger transport, a purpose for which this type of construction is particularly well suited and where the profitability of air transport (for example, Europe-America) is virtually certain.

There were six speakers at the event – which was titled Flugzeugkonstruktion: Bericht über die Sitzung Nurflügelflugzeuge or 'Aircraft construction: Report of the session on flying wing aircraft' – and organised by the Lilienthal-Gesellschaft für Luftfahrtforschung.

They were August Quick of the DVL on 'Flight mechanical properties of the swept wing at normal speeds', Adolf Busemann from the LFA on 'Swept wings at high speed', 'The tailless aircraft in comparison to the aircraft of conventional design' by Franz Nikolaus Scheubel from Darmstadt, Walter and Reimar Horten on 'Stability considerations of swept wings' and then again on 'Ten years designing fast flying wing aircraft' and finally Philipp von Doepp

from Junkers on 'Flying wing aircraft. Report on the work of Professor Junkers, Dessau, Department of aerodynamics'.

Just a few months after his presentation, the last speaker, von Doepp, would begin designing the forward-swept Junkers Ju 287. But here he was looking back to the past. He began by saying: "In the years 1925 to 1931 at the Research Institute Prof. Junkers conducted work which should clarify the feasibility and the advantages and disadvantages of the flying wing aircraft. In addition to experiments on swept wings, they included the design of a 100 ton flying-wing transoceanic plane. It turned out that although some difficulties arise, their overcoming is likely to be quite possible."

He said that "if you confine yourself to the

"The basics that were assumed in this design corresponded to the state of the art about 13 years ago and are now long since out of date. This applies in particular to the aerodynamic drag, the weight and space requirements of the engine and the permissible level of landing speed.

"The aircraft has the following main characteristics: flight weight at departure: 100t, wing area: 1070m , span: 100m, power: 10 x 1000hp diesel engines. Altitude control is done by a centre flap, the side control by vertical vanes, which act both by their lateral forces, as well as unilateral resistance increase."

He said some people had dismissed flying wings because simply removing the fuselage on a conventional aircraft would leave a very thin wing – but this was misunderstanding the benefits of designing an aircraft as a wing from the outset.

"For the purpose of our proposal – long-distance passenger transport – a spatial distribution was carried out to clarify the question of space, from which it can be seen that for 100 passengers and 20 crew plus the fuel and all accessories ample space is available. In any case, the passengers are better accommodated than in a passenger train, which is sufficient for the short travel time compared to the ship."

He said that in order to understand the design it was necessary to look carefully at the accompanying picture – which is the one featured on these pages.

"As you can see, there are some deviations from the pure flying wing form for the reasons of a safe landing particularly to accommodate the large chassis wheels in a simple manner. In addition, extensions had to be provided to take out the propeller shafts and a cockpit protrusion for better pilot visibility. Incidentally, you can see that the space delineated by the profile outline can be used quite well in practice and that only the interior of the flap remains unused."

Von Doepp points out that the aircraft's fuel supply has been distributed around the aircraft's interior rather than kept in a small number of large tanks: "This made it possible to avoid shifting the centre of gravity as the consumption progressed, nor to degrade the spanwise load distribution too much. That the accommodation space for the fuel (diesel oil) is partly adjacent to the passenger rooms – although hermetically sealed against them by solid walls – is, however, a beauty defect.

"The passengers can also move in the spanwise direction as well as in the longitudinal direction (during the transition from sleep to daytime living rooms). The former is harmless, since even for space reasons, a strong one-sided shift in passenger weight – which makes up only about 6% of the weight – is not possible."

The Junkers 100 ton flying wing consisted of three main parts – the section in front of the walkway, the stiff central walkway which served as a spar and the rear section. The undercarriage consisted of six main wheels and a two nosewheels although it was anticipated that the short distance between the main wheels and nosewheels could cause difficulties.

The aircraft's range was 7000km at an

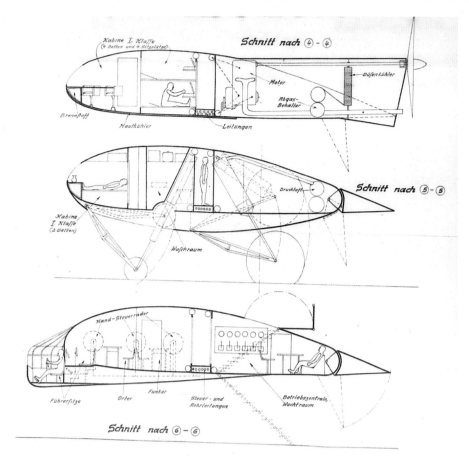

ABOVE: These sectional views, in close-up, show the luxurious interior of the aircraft – where passengers could gaze out of the huge wings in the wing leading edge, take a nap or freshen up in the washroom.

altitude of 3km but von Doepp points out that a modern version of the design would be able to comfortably manage 10,000km without payload.

A single major flaw had been identified with the flying wing airliner however: "With regard to safety we must point out that based on our draft the emergency landing on the water without floating is a major source of danger." This would be mitigated through the use of 10 separate engines, which could be accessed and worked on mid-flight by the crew. Running out of fuel was also dismissed as a possibility since with modern navigation systems and radio it would be nearly impossible to get lost, he said.

The potential for 'flutter' vibration was an unknown quantity: "With regard to the risk of fluttering the wing and the risk of vibration when rolling on the ground, a clarification would have to be made.

"The low landing speed, the multiple subdivision of the chassis with two nosewheels and the very large suspension travel (2m) allow a particularly safe landing even on the worst terrain. Based on the above considerations and calculations, the feasibility of the aircraft and its usefulness for long-distance passenger transport are well demonstrated. However, the usability for some other purposes by this, of course, is not proved yet."

Flying very heavy and bulky single loads, such as tanks, would not be possible because the centre section of the wing would have to be made extremely large. High altitude flight would also be difficult

because it would not be possible to sufficiently stiffen the outer wings without making them too heavy.

However, the flying wing was well-suited to work as a military transport and "for droppable loads (bombs, parachute loads) the accommodation in the rear centre section is even particularly favourable, as it could then take place in the gravity line and the discharge would cause no change in load."

There was a more outlandish Luftwaffe possibility too: "A perhaps promising military use would be the aircraft carrier and flying fuel station. Jet and bomber jet aircraft – whose range is comparatively low – could be hung under the flying wing aircraft and so can be transported over long distances.

"They would carry out their attack operations from the mother plane and be provided with fuel and ammunition. The aircraft carrier could carry its own fighter protection. By the way, a flying-wing airplane is less endangered than a conventional plane, since it has no tail fin or tail planes, without which one is no longer able to fly."

While the sheer ambition of Hugo Junkers' 1930 design for a monstrous airliner is breath-taking, it is clear that the reason for revisiting a 13-year-old Junkers project in 1943 was to see what lessons might be learned for future military flying wing aircraft. It is perhaps fitting, therefore, that Junkers' last project of the war was the design of a large flying wing bomber – the EF 130. ●

Junkers Nurflügel-Flugzeug Entwurf

1930

Artwork by Luca Landino

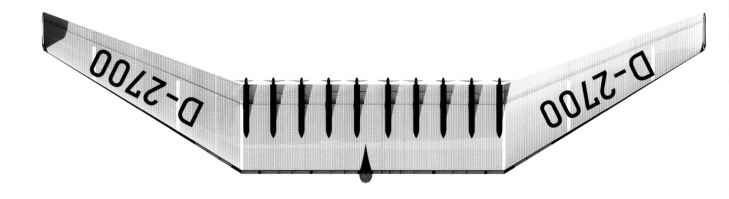

COMMENTS

Junkers' enormous flying wing passenger airliner design of 1930 weighed 100 tons, had a wingspan of 100m and 10 diesel engines developing 1000hp each. Designed to carry passengers from Germany to the United States, it would have been a relatively slow but undoubtedly comfortable way to travel. In 1943, Junkers suggested that a flying wing based on the same design principles but using modern materials, engines and construction methods would have made an effective military transport or bomber.

By way of a size comparison, even today's Airbus A380 – the world's largest passenger airliner – only has a wingspan of 79.75m. Howard Hughes' infamous H-4 'Spruce Goose' Hercules has a wingspan of 98m. The twin-fuselage Scaled Composites Model 351 Stratolaunch, however, finally surpassed them all with a wingspan of 117m.

Tunnel visions

Junkers early jet designs

The very earliest days of jet engine development at Heinkel in 1937 are reasonably well known but the development of jet aircraft designs at Junkers a year later remains shrouded in mystery. Recent discoveries have shed a little more light on this work and uncovered some interesting new 'projects'...

Jet engine pioneer Hans von Ohain's first successful jet engine, the HeS 1, was completed at Heinkel's Marienehe facility in March 1937 and the world's first jet-propelled aircraft, the He 178, first flew on August 27, 1939.

It would seem that some time around the beginning of 1938 – perhaps nine or 10 months after von Ohain's first successful engine test – Junkers began designing aircraft that could be powered by jet engines. The only available information about these designs appears to come from wind tunnel test reports which give very little information about anything other than the aircraft's physical layout.

Until recently the only known images of these designs were very basic, almost childlike, sketches, three wind tunnel model photos and some similarly basic information about armament and a handful of other details. The 'known' designs were sketches of the EFo 08 bomber, EFo 09 fighter, EFo 11 record attempt aircraft, EFo 15 bomber, EFo 17 fighter, EFo 18 fighter and EFo 19 fighter, and photos of the EFo 12 bomber, EFo 15 and EFo 17.

Some gaps can now be filled in with photos and some drawings showing wind tunnel models of the EFo 11-02, EFo 11-22, EFo 11-03, EFo 11-04, EFo 11-05, EFo 12, EFo 13 and EFo 14/1.

The drawings present in the newly discovered set are very similar if not identical in style to the previously known drawings – suggesting that these are also drawings of aerodynamic wind tunnel models, rather than detailed designs for aircraft. This would seem to call into question some of the suggested uses of the designs as bombers, fighters and record-setting aircraft, not to mention the dimensions and performance statistics that have been attributed to them. The data sheets accompanying the recent discoveries offer none of that detail.

They are dated, however, which offers a clear timeline for the development work. This goes from July 20, 1938, for the EFo 11-02 and -22 through to December 16, 1938, for the EFo 14/1 – still eight months before the He 178's first flight.

As to the designs themselves, the EFo 11-02 and -22 are similar to, if not the same as what was already known as the 'Rekordflugzeug-Projekt' with twin engines positioned ahead of the wings on forward-projecting booms. The EFo-03 is described as an 'experimental

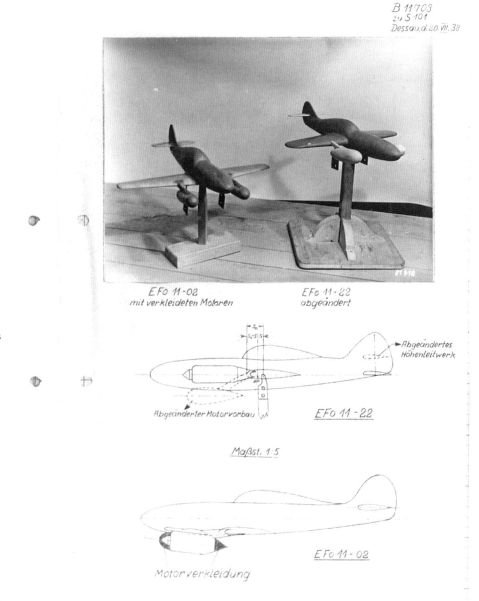

ABOVE: The EFo 11-02 and EFo 11-22, from a document dated July 20, 1938. The -22 appears to have been the same as the -02 but with repositioned tail surfaces and modified engine attachments. As with the other wind tunnel models, the actual aircraft's intended purpose can only be guessed at.

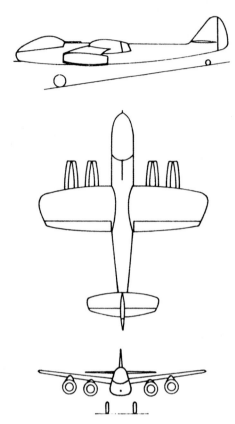

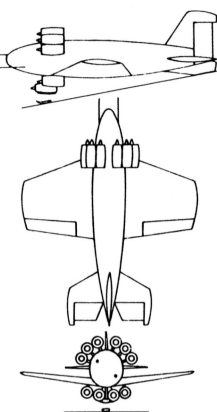

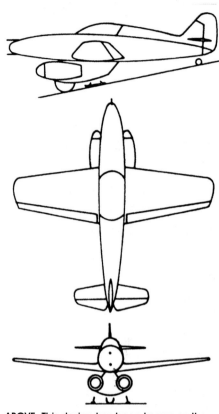

ABOVE: The Junkers EFo 08 is said to have been a bomber with four jet engines, a pressure cabin, two crew seated back to back and a single MG 151/20 20mm cannon in the nose. Assuming that the drawing shows a wind tunnel model, and it would be impossible to extrapolate the other details from that, those details must be regarded as suspect.

ABOVE: The bizarre EFo 09 was supposedly a tiny interceptor with the pilot lying prone in its nose, ringed by small turbojets. Armament was said to be two MK 108s – which is odd because this design would have been drawn up at least two years before the MK 108 existed even as a concept. Again, it is probably a drawing of a wind tunnel model and the other details have been guessed at by those writing about it later.

ABOVE: This design has been known as the EFo 11 until now – a fighter with two jets and two MG 151s. It seems more likely that, in fact, this design is a late addition to a whole sequence of EFo 11s and that its purpose is unknown.

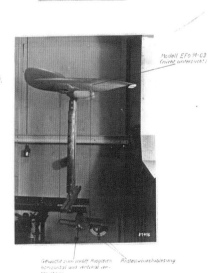

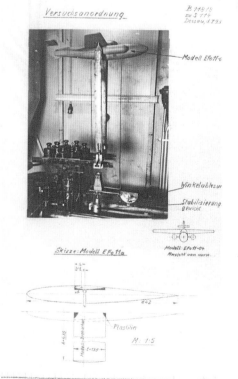

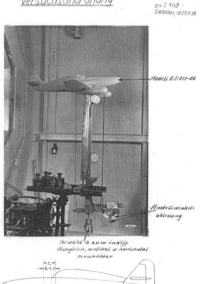

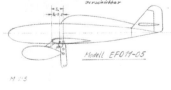

ABOVE: The radical EFo 11-03 of July 20, 1938, was not developed further than this wind tunnel model. Even so, with its streamlined fuselage and presumably integrated cockpit/fin it looks impressive.

ABOVE: A later development from the EFo 11 series – the 11-04 – had a high wing, a reshaped fuselage and fin, and its engines attached to the fuselage at the front. It is dated September 9, 1938 – later than the EFo 11-05.

ABOVE: The EFo 11-05 of July 29, 1938. This design features a taller tail fin than earlier 11-series models and a raised spine extending back from the cockpit.

E.Fo-12
Versuchsanordnung

B. 1.1995
zu S. 128
Dessau, d. 25.11.38

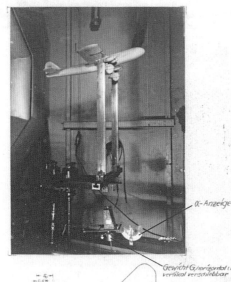

α-Anzeige

Gewicht G, horizontal u.
vertikal verschiebbar

α-Anzeige   G, horizontal u. vertikal verschiebbar

M. 1:5

E.Fo.12 - Doppelmotor - Fahrgestell
Mod.-Maßst. 1:5

B. 12074
zu S. 133
Dessau, d. 28.11.

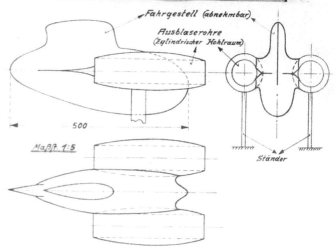

Fahrgestell (abnehmbar)

Ausblaserohre
(Zylindrischer Hohlraum)

500

Maßst. 1:5

Ständer

E.Fo-13, Mod.-M. 1:20
Versuchs-Anordnung

B. 12033
P. 2659
Aufg. 598
zu S. 133
Dessau, d. 6.1.

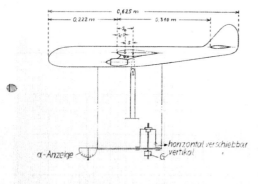

0,625 m

0,222 m   0,310 m

α-Anzeige

horizontal verschiebbar
vertikal

G

Maßstab 1:5

D 0,44 m

Triebwerk

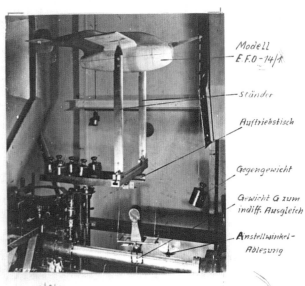

Modell
E.F.O-14/1

Ständer

Auftriebstisch

Gegengewicht

Gewicht G zum
indiff. Ausgleich

Anstellwinkel-
Ablesung

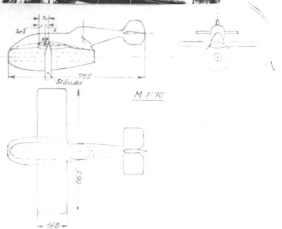

Ständer

755

M. 1:10

665

160

OPPOSITE LEFT: When it has been written about previously, the EFo 12 – oddly and inconsistently written as 'E.FO-12' on the original document – has been described as a four engine jet bomber with two crew and fixed undercarriage. This, while likely inferred, probably isn't too far from the truth. The document is dated November 25, 1938.

OPPOSITE TOP: The engine nacelle for the EFo 12 – this time written as 'E.Fo. 12'.

OPPOSITE BOTTOM LEFT: The EFo 13, from a document dated December 6, 1938. The length of the model is given as 0.625m and scale as 1:20, so the aircraft would have been 12.5m long – slightly shorter than the Ar 234, which was 12.64m long. The wingspan would have been 8.8m –

incredibly short compared to the Ar 234's 14.41m. Even the diminutive Me 163 B had a wingspan of 9.3m.

OPPOSITE BOTTOM RIGHT: Dated December 15, 1938, the EFo 14/1 appears to be a single jet aircraft. The scale is 1:10 so the fuselage length appears to be 7.55m and the wingspan 6.65m. By way of comparison, the single jet He 178 was 7.48m long with a wingspan of 7.2m. Presumably the undercarriage would have folded up into the engine housing. The EFo 14/1 would appear to have been a contemporary of the He 178 – making it one of the two earliest known single-jet aircraft designs in history.

arrangement', perhaps with the cockpit moved into the tailfin for aerodynamic reasons and a more pointed nose. An annotation on the photo suggests that this radical departure from the rest of the EFo 11 series was not pursued.

The EFo 11-04 is another variation on the same theme, this time with a high wing arrangement and the two engines attached to the sides of the aircraft's nose rather than its wings. The tail too is somewhat different with a small under-fin in evidence or perhaps an integrated tail skid.

A somewhat less radical halfway house between the EFo 11-02 and EFo 11-03 is the EFo-05. This features a cockpit canopy integrated into a smooth sloping spine which runs back to a reshaped tail, similar to the spine and tail arrangement seen on what was previously known simply as the 'EFo 11' – presumably this design is actually part of the EFo 11 sequence later than -05.

The EFo 12 appears the same as

the design already known but can now be dated: November 29, 1938. The not-dissimilar EFo 13 can also be dated: December 7, 1938.

The most interesting and arguably the most radical design among the new discoveries is the EFo 14/1. This is described in the notes as a "high-speed aircraft with a new drive (propulsion nozzle)" and appears to be a single jet aircraft built around a large turbojet – certainly larger than the units planned for the other designs. The turbojet's housing makes up most of the fuselage, with the wings attached on either side and the cockpit positioned above the exhaust. The small rear fuselage and tail fin extends backwards from the cockpit.

Assuming this is what it appears to be, it would be perhaps the earliest or second earliest known German single jet aircraft design – the other being the He 178 itself. Alexander Lippisch's Messerschmitt P 01-116, the next earliest, would not be committed to paper until April 1939. ●

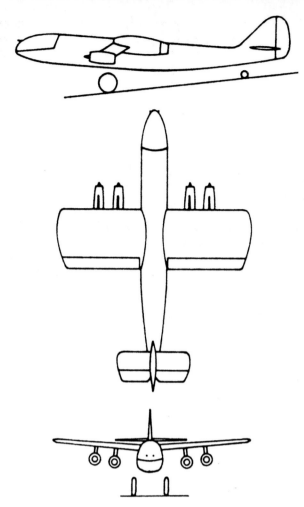

ABOVE: The EFo 15 appears to have been very similar to the EFo 13 but with a slightly more tapering fuselage and a higher wing position. It has been said to have had two MG 151/20s in the nose but there appears to have been no evidence for this and it is not entirely impossible that the simple drawing was doctored to fit this theory.

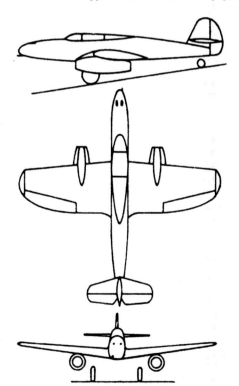

ABOVE: It is easy to see why the EFo 17 has been regarded as Junkers' competitor for the Me 262 and He 280. But whether it was or not is unknown.

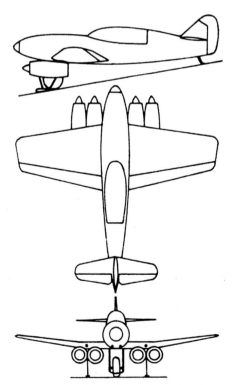

ABOVE: The EFo 18 is said to have been a four-jet fighter version of the EFo 11w with two MG 151/20s and two MK 103s but again this design might well pre-date the design of the MK 103.

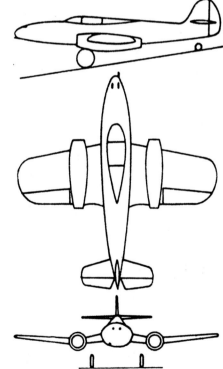

ABOVE: Another design speculated to have been a competitor for the twin jet designs of Messerschmitt and Heinkel, the EFo 19 features engines integrated into its wings.

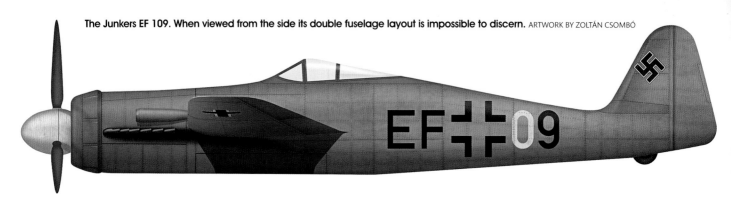

The Junkers EF 109. When viewed from the side its double fuselage layout is impossible to discern. ARTWORK BY ZOLTÁN CSOMBÓ

The fantastic four

Junkers EF 109, 110, 111 and 112

Dornier's P 231 design was declared the winner of the Schnellstbomber competition at a meeting on January 19, 1943 – defeating Messerschmitt's Me 109 Zw. The Arado entry fell by the wayside and Heinkel's work was redirected along a path that would lead to the P 1068 and He 343 – but what about Junkers?

The Schnellflugzeug concept was first set out during in May 1942 – an unarmed and unarmoured light bomber so fast it would be impossible for enemy interceptors to catch. The initial specifications were: 2000km range, 500kg payload and a maximum speed of 800km/h – or no less than 750km/h without GM1 or water-methanol injection.

Early designs resulting from these stipulations varied widely – from the tailless Messerschmitt P 10 with a single pusher prop, designed by Alexander Lippisch, to Blohm & Voss's large triple-engined two-seater P 170. Focke-Wulf produced a number of more conventional twin-engine designs.

It was clear that some guidance was needed as to the aircraft's engines and layout so towards the end of September or in early October, Generalfeldmarschall Erhard Milch commissioned Heinkel to assess a wide range of different configurations and see whether an optimal design approach for this fast bomber could be identified.

The results were then reviewed at a meeting of the RLM's development committee on November 13, 1942. According to a summary of the minutes published on November 21, 1942, the six configurations assessed were: "two motor normal, double engine the fuselage, three motor, two motor/double fuselage, single engine tailless, single engine normal. For the comparison was also used: Ar 234 (reconnaissance aircraft with two TL engines, also single-seated and 2000km range), Blohm & Voss project P 170 (two-seater, three engines with the outside engines in wing nacelles, 2400km range), Ju 288 with special cabin and heavily reduced armament, Fw 190 Jabo.

"Furthermore, the influence of the multi-engine layout on build cost and performance

level should be clarified in principle."

A list showing the six configurations and the four comparison designs "with statistics was handed over before the meeting". And "the investigation showed: More than two motors leads to very high production cost with hardly increased performances. The required speed is achieved with 2 x BMW 801 E or DB 603 G or Jumo 213. Jumo 211 and DB 605 are eliminated. The aircraft must be redeveloped with a special design. Using the basis of an existing design is not appropriate.

"Proposal: double fuselage construction is preferred. The project already presented by Heinkel seems favourable and takes into

account the demands of mixed construction. For a solution later the development of the jet engines is to be promoted by all means. The development of a Jumo 222 single-engine fast bomber is also to be considered."

The meeting next heard a statement from Junkers technical director Heinrich Hertel. He said: "A 'fast bomber', which is supposed to be superior to the (single-engine) fighter, has to have lower weight and drag values with greater power (i.e. twin-engine, since a significant superiority of its own engines can not be expected). In other words, it must be less than two fighters.

"The immediate solution requires design and

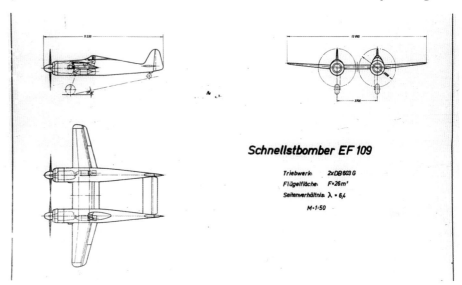

Schnellstbomber EF 109

Triebwerk: 2xDB 603 G
Flügelfläche: F=26 m²
Seitenverhältnis: λ = 6,4

M·1:50

ABOVE: The Junkers EF 109 twin fuselage Schnellstbomber. At a meeting on November 13, 1942, it was decided that this was the optimal layout for an unarmed bomber capable of outpacing the best fighters the Allies had to offer. The drawing is dated December 10, 1942.

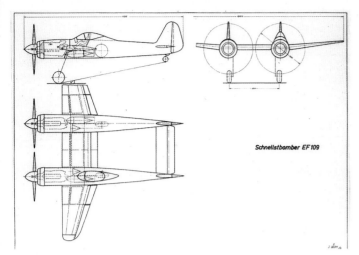

ABOVE: Although it looks similar to the other EF 109 drawing, this version actually has a slightly shorter wingspan and a longer fuselage. This undated three-view appears to have been the more recent of the two EF 109 drawings.

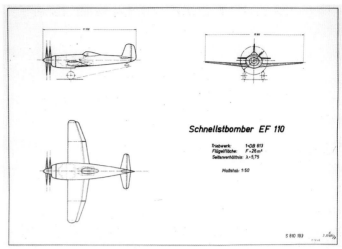

ABOVE: Putting two linked DB 603s, a DB 613, in the EF 110's nose gave it an extremely wide forward fuselage but expected performance was still calculated to be slightly better than that of the EF 109.

components that are already adequately available today. This rules out tailless design, pressure and counter-rotating propellers. In order to keep the development time as short as possible, despite the high-quality construction and the high-speed problems, research on the broadest basis is needed and pre-testing of all new parts on a quick-to-build flying mock-up. In accordance with C-E 2, double-fuselage design is specified.

"However, such an aircraft may not weigh 9.2 tons (Heinkel project), but only 7.5 tons (compared to a fighter weight of 4 to 4.5 tons). Specifically, the following conditions must be met without compromise: no armour, no armament, no fuel tank protection, fuel unprotected in the wing (densely riveted surfaces), restriction in the equipment, limitation in the load assumptions (H 3), internal bomb carriage, opposite propellers, no weight reserves for GM 1, the best material (duralumin-wing, at least mixed construction fuselage), landing aids (brake parachute).

"With these specifications, it will be possible to create an aircraft that is actually superior in speed to the fighter by about 40km/h and which will be effectively combated only by an unarmoured, lightly armed, special, 'Überjäger' which the enemy could decide to develop. For future development, promotion of high-speed research and development of the land brake and contra-rotating prop is to be demanded."

There then followed a series of six 'individual points'. First up was 'single seat': "C-E, K.d.E. and L In 2, it is not necessary to carry a special radio, as the second man required to

operate it would result in a loss of speed, the weather at the home station can be determined with sufficient accuracy for the short duration of the mission, and special procedures for targeting and pitching will be provided."

Secondly was 'strength' which addressed structural issues, then there was 'bomb load': "Initial demand was taking a 500kg bomb. At the suggestion of Junkers it should be possible to carry 2 x 500kg or 4 x 250kg bombs on short routes. A normal 1000kg bomb will not fit. The possibility of an SD 1000 or PC 1000 without RS-part has to be investigated, but is not decisive for the project."

The Schnellkampfflugzeug's 'attack method' was next: "In addition to dropping bombs from high altitude in horizontal flight via Lotfe [bombsight], with additional sight (Zeiss) as the main attack method sling throwing and flat sliding attack are intended. This targeting system development is to receive special attention. Actual dive-bombing attack is not provided."

The fifth point was 'other uses': "An aircraft superior in speed to the enemy fighter should be much in demand by the Luftwaffe fighter force. For this purpose, as a military load, rather than bombing equipment heavy weapons can be provided. For reconnaissance use, photographic gear can be housed in the bomb room. Installation of ship search equipment at the current stage of development contradicts the task. If the enemy later launches a special anti-fast aircraft fighter, fixed backward weaponry with periscope sight can be installed."

The sixth point was 'development':

"The development of jet engines, tailless construction and Mach number research are urgently to follow for a later development of the Schnellkampfflugzeugs."

Finally the summary concludes: "The Generalfeldmarschall underlines the accuracy and necessity of the planned Schnellkampfflugzeugs and orders the launch. In view of the importance and the multiple use possibility of the aircraft, production must be reckoned in larger numbers. At the suggestion GL/C chief, Heinkel and Junkers will be commissioned to prepare a project and a schedule. In four weeks the Generalfeldmarschall is to review it here."

The next meeting to discuss what had initially been the 'Schnellflugzeug', then the 'Schnellkampfflugzeug' and was now being called the 'Schnellstbomber', was duly held on December 12, 1942.

The summary of the minutes of this meeting, released on January 4, 1943, begins with a brief recap of the competition to date, stating that a double-fuselage layout was the preferred design choice and "On this basis, Junkers and Heinkel have made new investigations. Irrespective of this, Messerschmitt study on Bf 109- or Me 309-Zwilling, in its interpretation, has yet to be voted on with the other projects already in full compliance."

Specifically for this meeting, Junkers had come up with four new Schnellstbomber designs – designated EF 109, EF 110, EF 111 and EF 112. Each was intended to meet the same specification with the same engines but within a different airframe layout. Although the drawings show

The Junkers EF 110 was a handsome-looking aircraft in profile. ARTWORK BY ZOLTÁN CSOMBÓ

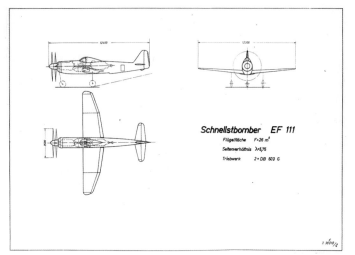

Schnellstbomber EF 111
Flügelfläche   F=26 m²
Seitenverhältnis λ=5,75
Triebwerk   2×DB 603 G

ABOVE: Junkers technical director Heinrich Hertel believed that the EF 111's single fuselage, twin engine, double prop layout was superior to the double fuselage layout of the EF 109. The design was dropped before it could be pitted against Dornier's push-pull P 231, which went on to become the Do 335.

ABOVE: The second drawing of the EF 111 with a slightly reduced wingspan. Neither EF 111 drawing is dated but it seems likely that both were drafted between December 10 and December 11, 1942.

the designs with DB 603 G engines, the preferred choice, accompanying documents also gave their anticipated performance with the BMW 801 E and Jumo 213 B.

The starting point was the EF 109 – a double-fuselage design that was precisely what had been prescribed at the previous meeting. It was an uncomplicated tail-sitter and each fuselage had a DB 603 G up front with a small bomb bay behind it and a conventional tail fin. The left hand fuselage also contained the cockpit. In the first drawing, dated December 10, 1942, length was 11.22m, wingspan 12.89m and wing area 26m². A second drawing was also presented, which appears to have been more recent, showing length at 11.35m and wingspan at 12.8m.

Hertel briefly described this design, saying it would "reach a maximum speed of 760km/h at a gross vehicle weight of 7.3 ton and a surface area of 25m² [presumably he is referring to the second drawing with the smaller wingspan]. It can also accommodate 2 x 500kg bombs inside (7.8 ton flight weight). Restricting to load factor n=3.5 is considered to be fully adequate. Engines are normal.

"Air-cooled engines would be an advantage. The stats are more favourable than with a central fuselage and the overall structure is easily manufactured."

Heinkel chief designer Siegfried Günter then "submits documents to the Generalfeldmarschall about the newly worked Heinkel project. Special features: half of the fuel is protected in the fuselage; the right-hand, unmanned fuselage has been shortened for

visual and centre-of-gravity reasons".

Hertel then moved on to the EF 110, EF 111 and EF 112. The EF 110 was a single fuselage design with a massive DB 613 – effectively two DB 603s but linked together – in its nose driving contra-rotating props. This resulted in the aircraft having a very wide fuselage, conveniently providing room for two 500kg bombs to be positioned side by side in its internal bomb bay. The only drawing of the design, dated the day before the meeting, December 11, 1942, gives a wing area of 26m², length of 11.55m and a wingspan of 12.3m.

The EF 111 appears to have been Hertel's favourite. It features two single DB 603 Gs mounted within the fuselage – one in the nose and one behind the pilot driving a double propeller. A tricycle undercarriage is used and two 500kg bombs are squeezed into the very narrow fuselage directly beneath the pilot. Length is given as 12.4m in the first, undated, drawing. Wingspan is 12.3m and wing area again is 26m². A second drawing, also undated, gives the same length but wingspan is again reduced, this time to 12.2m.

The EF 112, shown in a drawing dated December 11, 1942, features a short cramped fuselage with engines to the front and rear driving props in a push-pull arrangement. The same fuselage also contains both the cockpit and bomb bay. The tail consists of two booms housing the undercarriage and, presumably, much of the fuel. The overall length of the aircraft is just 10.7m with a wingspan of 12.8m. As with the other three designs in their first iterations, wing area is 26m².

The meeting minutes summary says: "Following a presentation by Mr Gropler, Junkers is investigating a mono-fuselage project with 2 x DB 603. The first engine sits in the front, the second behind the pilot and works via a shaft that passes through the cannon hole of the front engine. There are two normal propellers used, which are applied to a special base construction. The efficiency is increased by the contrast of 72% to 76%.

"The gyroscopic moments are completely balanced, and the flight characteristics become favourable due to the concentration of the masses. The interference resistances of a double-fuselage construction drop away, and the speed increases from 760 to 805km/h. Nose wheel is possible. The bomb room is sufficient for 1 x 1000kg bomb or 2 x 500 or 3 x 250 or 10 x 50kg. This design gives the highest speed under otherwise identical assumptions."

The EF 110 and EF 112 are dismissed with: "Other solutions (with DB 613 double engine, etc.) would not come over 780km/h. Daimler-Benz informed us, on request, that the chosen engine arrangement is quite possible in itself. However, it may be necessary to change the gearbox housing on the front engine. Negotiations between Junkers and DB are continuing. Accelerated creation of an engine test vehicle (Ju 52) is a prerequisite for the timely execution of the task."

RLM staff engineer Walter Friebel, referred to by the name of the RLM department he represented – 'C-E 2', was not convinced by the EF 111 at all however, preferring to stick with the double fuselage

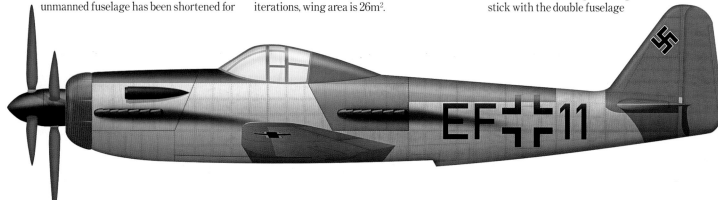

The Junkers EF 111, though designed as a bomber rather than a fighter, looks almost Thunderbolt-ish in profile. ARTWORK BY ZOLTÁN CSOMBÓ

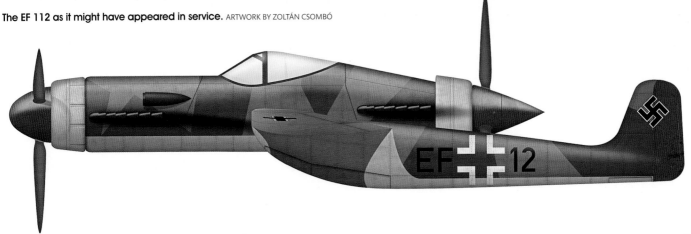

The EF 112 as it might have appeared in service. ARTWORK BY ZOLTÁN CSOMBÓ

layout. The record states: "C-E 2 expresses vivid concerns, as experience in the provision of the test carrier, which in turn is still dependent on the delivery of the engines, shows that delays are to be expected. The twin-fuselage aircraft would be at least one year earlier than the proposed single-fuselage aircraft and will also present a smaller developmental risk for the future as more powerful engines will be the easiest to deploy there later."

Milch ordered that this assertion be investigated.

In the 'general questions' section of the meeting which followed, Luftwaffe representative Colonel Theodor Rowehl spoke up, saying that he "considers a second crew member to be indispensable for reasons of weather. [The RLM's] Lieutenant-Colonel von Lossberg explains that the second man matters very much, not only for navigation, which can be helped by special equipment and procedures, but especially for the operation of the Lotfe on approach, which otherwise would require a three-axis control of 95kg weight and for the aircraft pilot to be robbed of any view for one and a half minutes on approach.

"On the other hand, the TSA would force it to give up the advantage of height. But if a second man is taken in, you have to give him the best possible view, so that he can effectively support the pilot in the ground orientation even in bad weather days. Colonel Vorwald stressed after further discussion of the question (accommodation of the second man staggered behind the pilot or in the second hull) that the two-man crew must be regarded as an indispensable requirement."

On the subject of armament, Milch said he "would be very grateful for a strong attacking armament (two cannon facing forward) to hold down the defence at the finish". It was pointed out to him by Vorwald that these would suffer

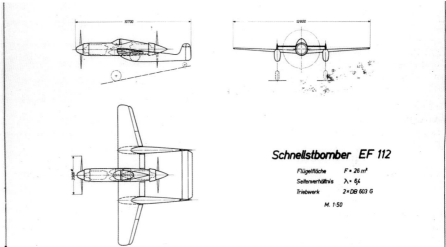

Schnellstbomber EF 112

Flügelfläche   F = 26 m²
Seitenverhältnis   λ = 6,4
Triebwerk   2 × DB 603 G

M. 1:50

ABOVE: Junkers placed little faith in the double-boom push-pull EF 112 – the fourth and last of its Schnellstbomber designs. The concept was similar to that of the Do 335 but the need for tail booms made the EF 112 significantly inferior. The drawing is dated December 11, 1942.

from low accuracy at long distance and that the speed of the aircraft would be impaired by providing space and weight allocation for the armament and ammunition. It was further mentioned that providing self-sealing fuel tanks was even more important than attacking armament and Hertel said that this was "the right thing to do".

Milch summed up the meeting and at the end it was found that "several points need further clarification: The question of the second crew member is decisive for the attack method and the possibility of deployment. Since the protection cannot exist alone in the speed, fuel tank protection, armour and armament must be carefully examined. If compromises have to be made, this is more likely in terms of payload and range than speed."

The next Schnellstbomber meeting

date was set for January 8, 1943 and "in addition to Heinkel and Junkers, Professor Messerschmitt is to be called in to report to the Generalfeldmarschall on his proposal for Me 309 Zwilling. Furthermore, the question of jet engines for the projects has to be investigated".

This meeting would eventually be pushed back to January 19, 1943, and would feature full project submissions from new entrant Dornier alongside the Messerschmitt, Heinkel and Arado designs – all four of the Junkers proposals having been dismissed. A description of this meeting and its outcome is included in *Luftwaffe: Secret Designs of the Third Reich*. In short: Dornier won and the innovative push-pull single fuselage twin-engine P 231 was ordered into production as the Do 335. ●

This Junkers EF 112 wears the colours of the Royal Hungarian Air Force. ARTWORK BY ZOLTÁN CSOMBÓ

The flying soufflé

Messerschmitt Me 109 S

One of the more obscure and heavily modified proposed variants of the Me 109, the Me 109 S, was designed to suck in air through a ventral intake and blast it out over the trailing edge its wing onto the flaps – increasing lift at low speeds and giving the aircraft a shorter takeoff run. But why was this necessary?

The Me 109 S dates back to before April 16, 1942, the point at which the Aerodynamische Versuchsanstalt (AVA) at Göttingen commenced work on a pair of 'blower' systems. According to a Messerschmitt report entitled Lagebericht Me 109 Ausblaseversuchsträger (Stand vom 14.2.44) or 'Management report Me 109 blower test vehicle (as of 14.2.44)', the blower systems were completed and sent to specialist gear wheel manufacturer Zahnräderfabrik Augsburg on February 13, 1943.

At this point the project appears to have been put on hold for three months before recommencing. The Messerschmitt report states: "In the middle of May 1943, the dormant work on the two blower testers was resumed (S-instruction no. 2128, supplement 2) and, in part due to new findings, the project was completely reworked.

"Delivery of the new project (III) took place on July 31, 1943. In the meantime, work had already begun at a number of different companies on the basis of provisional documents. The problems occurring in the pre-realisation of blower test vehicles were of various kinds. The selection of the Me 109 G-6 as the fuselage resulted in a number of changes or conversions. Due to the installation of the air channel in the new wings (the old outline form was larger), to ensure the least possible influence on the flow at the wing, the radiator could no longer be fitted the same way."

It had been decided that rather than a conventional radiator, the test vehicle would feature an evaporative cooling system for its engine. This would reduce flight time to approximately 20 minutes at maximum power. The original design was to have included a wide-track landing gear "which was desirable in terms of the experiments" but "in order not to complicate the conversion even further and in view of the task, a chassis using the old struts and wheels rigidly fixed in position was used".

With this aspect of the design decided, it was realised that the normal Me 109 G-6 tail unit was no longer suitable without modification so a fuselage extension was required. Furthermore, "in order to avoid an unfavourable influence on the blower intake, the oil cooler previously mounted under the engine was moved into the left wing (in front of the main spar) so that hardly any influence on the test results is to be expected".

Five organisations were involved in making the Me 109 S – Caudron in Paris was contracted to build the airframe, Daimler-Benz in Stuttgart was to modify the engine with Zahnräderfabrik Augsburg working as a subcontractor, Zahnräderfabrik Augsburg itself was to produce the engine/blower gearbox, the AVA was building the actual blower and the electrical part of the system was being designed by VDM of Frankfurt.

The AVA's W. Schwier produced report Nr. 43/W/66, dated December 29, 1943, which outlined work done on the blower system and said: "In the various wind tunnel tests carried out to increase lift, the entire inside of the wing, which was only interrupted by a few stud bolts, was used as the air duct in the wing itself. As a result, there was always a sufficiently uniform distribution of the blown air, without any special measures, along the

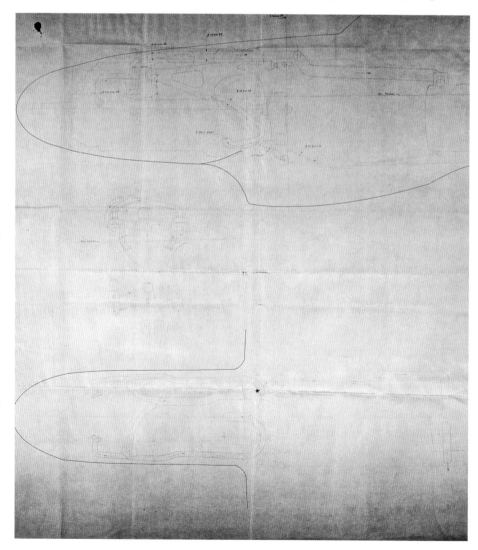

ABOVE: Profile and top view of the Me 109 S showing the shape of the ventral intake as well as the pipework for the type's evaporative cooling system. Barely visible to the bottom right in white is the text 'Me 109 S Janvier 44'.

span. The interior of the wing was almost completely smooth, so that the flow losses there were comparatively low.

"In a practical use of the blow-out for the purpose of boosting lift the air duct is not the entire interior of the wing, but in general only the space behind the rear spar available. On such an original wing, the distribution of the blown-out air was examined.

"The experiments were carried out at the suggestion and with the support of Messerschmitt AG, Augsburg."

So the idea originated with Messerschmitt some time prior to the AVA's involvement. Meanwhile, the Messerschmitt project management report concludes that as of February 1944, Daimler-Benz was still working on the engines but that these were expected to become available "in the worst case" by the end of April. In the meantime, "the authorised agencies will clarify some pending questions by the end of February and will prepare an experiment at the beginning of March on an aircraft yet to be determined. The trials are expected to be completed by the end of March".

Given that no Me 109 S was anywhere near completion at this time, it seems likely that the 'experiment' and the 'trials' mentioned would have taken place using a lightly modified 109 or other aircraft to test some specific part of the blower design.

The last part of the report shed some light on what was to follow: "It should also be mentioned that at Caudron for reasons of secrecy only dummies of the gears, blowers and evaporator systems are installed."

The first British intelligence knew of the project appears in A.I. Report No. 65965 of February 20, 1944, six days after the Messerschmitt project management report had been produced. It says: "Alterations to the Me 109 for use on aircraft carriers. Work being carried out at the Caudron-Renault works, 4 rue Diderot, Paris. This factory is engaged in alterations to the Me 109 namely in its length which is increased by one metre.

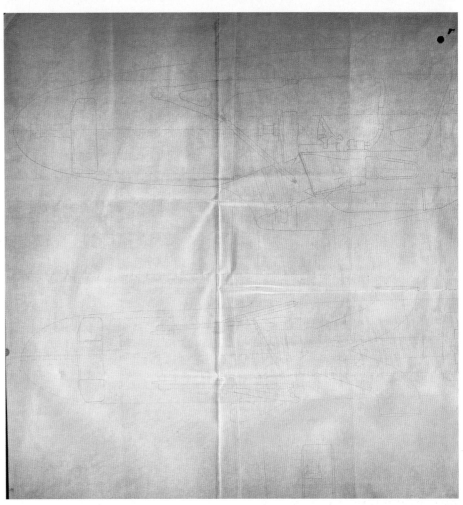

ABOVE: Another profile and top view of the Me 109 S but this time giving detail of the intake system itself. Air entering it could either be fed down ducting into the wings or vented through an exhaust at the rear of the intake.

"A large air intake is added underneath the fuselage, and fitted with a ventilator driven by an electric motor. An air stream is directed from this intake by means of a duct on to the aileron and elevator in order to facilitate taking-off and landing. This aircraft is foreseen

for use on aircraft carriers."

On June 16, 1944, Messerschmitt engineer Pieckert produced a report entitled 'Messungen an der Tragflügel-Attrappe des Ausblaseversuchsträgers Me 109' or 'Measurements in the wing mockup of the

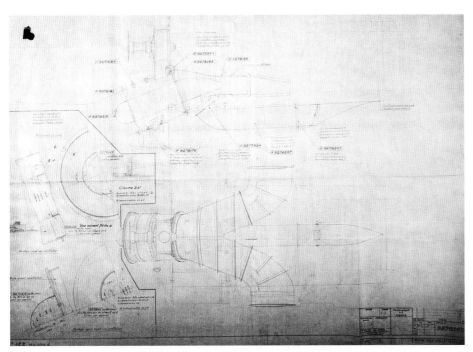

ABOVE: French drawing on Messerschmitt paper, dated January 30, 1944, showing the fan at the mouth of the Me 109 S's intake which would spin at 9000rpm to drive air into the wing blower vents – generating lift at low speeds.

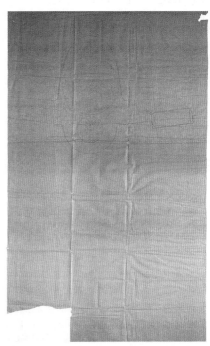

ABOVE: A forward view of the Me 109 S's circular ventral intake. The object in the left wing is the oil cooler.

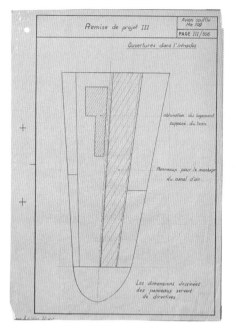

ABOVE: The experimental Me 109 S would have had a fixed undercarriage – which meant that the wheel wells in the surface of the aircraft's wings would be unnecessary and could be faired over. This French design drawing is dated August 11, 1943.

blower test vehicle Me 109'. This suggested changes to the shape of the duct based on alterations and measurements made to a test rig at Messerschmitt itself in Augsburg. Pieckert concluded: "The flow losses in the performance and in the air duct are about 25% lower than the values measured by Schwier in Göttingen on a Me 109 wing mockup."

A further Allied report was prepared by the Combined Intelligence Priorities Committee (CIPC) following a visit to the Paris-based Caudron-Renault factory in September 1944, not long after its liberation. The report is entitled 'Me 109 with air discharge from wings' and states: "Information and drawings on this scheme (Me 109 S) were obtained in discussions with M. Schmitt, technical director of Caudron-Renault (SAAC) 19 rue Lord Byron, on September 5 and 7. Partially completed prototypes were seen at Caudron factory at 12 rue Diderot, on September 5.

"In this scheme a large air scoop is mounted below the fuselage just aft of the engine. Air entering the scoop is speeded up by a fan driven from the rear of the engine by a gear train through a hydraulically controlled clutch, ducted through the wings and discharged through a narrow slot along the whole span just ahead of the ailerons and flaps.

"The maximum speed of the fan was said to be 9000rpm, but no details of it nor of its drive were available, the Germans having supplied wood mock-ups only. Guide vanes were fitted in the bends in the duct, and the flow can be controlled by butterfly valves in the branch pipes and main entry, as well as by varying the engine rpm.

"The discharge is directed above the noses of the ailerons and flaps are inclined slightly upwards, and three alternative widths of slot are available, the best width being chosen by trial and error. These widths are 0.3, 0.5 and 0.7% chord. Drawings of the layout and slots were obtained.

"No data as to the volume or rate of air flow are available, the Germans having supplied details of duct and inlet sizes to the firm. Three sets of wings had been ordered, and two fuselages. Two alternative shapes of flap leading edges were to be made, one symmetrical and the other approximating to a Frise nose. The aileron noses are symmetrical. Drawings were obtained. Auto slots are fitted over the whole span.

"M. Schmitt said he understood that the object of the scheme (which was a purely experimental installation) was to increase the lift when landing on a deck. This installation prevents retraction of the undercarriage, and the wing ducting also prevents the normal engine coolant radiators being fitted. Instead of placing the radiators elsewhere, an evaporative cooling system is proposed, with two condensers mounted forward on either side of the engine and a 200 litre tank in the fuselage aft of the pilot. A sketch of the system was obtained, but no details, wood mock-ups only being supplied by the Germans.

"The weight and siting of the installation and of the water tank moves the centre of gravity too far aft, so that the length of the rear fuselage has been increased by adding a section one metre long, aft of the pilot. A fixed inverted slot covering the whole span of the tailplane has also been designed. Caudrons had spent nearly two years on the design and construction, and considered their work to be within three months of completion."

Another report, prepared by Wing Commander G.E.F. Proctor of the Air Ministry's Deputy Directorate of Intelligence (2) in December 1944 and entitled simply 'The Me 109 S (with air discharge over the wing)', offers the most complete account of exactly what the Me 109 S was and how its unique blower system was intended to function.

It says: "Experiments have been carried out (by Caudron-Renault in Paris) with an Me 109 modified to enable air to be discharged over the wing in front of the ailerons and flaps in order to obtain a smooth air flow at slow speeds. This sub-type has apparently been designated the Me 109 S. Two versions were projected, the main difference being the provision of a conventional or tricycle type of undercarriage could be fitted without extensive modification to the airframe.

"The experiments were carried out with the object of increasing lift and control to facilitate take-off and landing in a confined space, probably on the deck of an aircraft carrier.

"General description: A large air scoop (illustrated in the attached drawing) is mounted beneath the fuselage and below the rear of the engine. Air entering the scoop is accelerated along a duct by a fan driven from the rear of the engine. A hydraulically controlled clutch is incorporated in this drive.

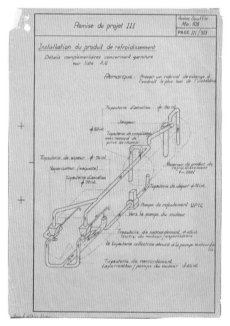

ABOVE:The complicated new cooling system employed by the Me 109 S is shown on this drawing dated August 11, 1943.

BELOW: Largely standard Me 109 G-6 tail components would have been used for the Me 109 S. These French drawings date from August 11 and 12, 1943.

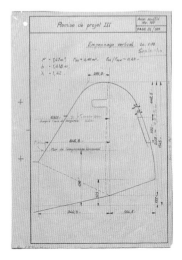

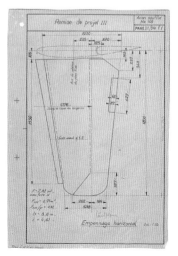

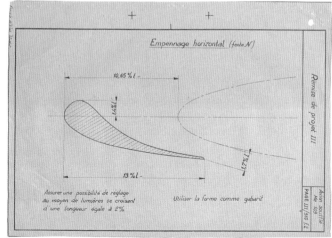

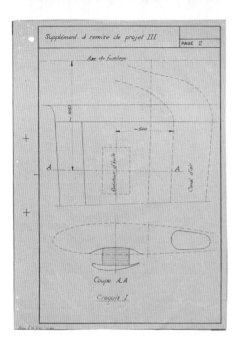

ABOVE: With significant modifications having been made to its fuselage, the Me 109 S's radiator needed a new home – so it was repositioned under the port wing.

"Behind the fan the main duct is divided into three smaller ducts, one leading along each mainplane and one to an exit orifice beneath the fuselage, the area of which is controlled by a butterfly valve. It is believed that a similar valve is fitted in the main air scoop.

"The ducts in the wing are situated behind the main spar and the air is discharged through a narrow slot along the whole span and in front of the ailerons and flaps. Experiments were carried out with two different types of flap, one with a symmetrical leading edge and the other with a Frise type of leading edge. The leading edges of the ailerons are symmetrical.

"Mainplanes. The wing is very similar in construction to that employed on the Me 109 G-6 but has the following modifications: a) The fitting of an air duct between the main spar and the subsidiary spar to which the flaps and ailerons are attached. b) Wing flaps extending to root end of wing. c) Leading edge slat throughout the complete span.

"The air discharge is directed above the leading edges of the ailerons and flaps, the width of the discharge slot being found by trial and error. Four widths of slot are available.

The air ducts in the wing preclude the use of normal coolant radiators and an evaporative cooling system has been evolved.

"Engine and coolant system. The engine mounting is similar to that employed on the Me 109 G-6, but the DB 605 A engine has been raised above the normal position. Vaporisers are fitted on each side of the engine and the vapour is passed into a 44-gallon tank situated in the fuselage behind the pilot. The condensed coolant is pressure fed back to the normal coolant pump on the engine and after circulating around each cylinder block is passed to the two vaporisers. Pipes from the vaporisers also feed coolant to the inlet side of the engine coolant pump. The oil radiator is fitted under the port wing, forward of the air duct.

"Fuselage. The installation of the coolant tank altered the centre of gravity considerably so that an additional fuselage section about a metre long is fitted immediately behind the pilot. The addition of this section also raises the tail unit above the normal position. The air ducts in the wing prevent the undercarriage being retracted, and a fixed undercarriage of wide track has been adopted, the oleo legs being attached to the wing instead of to the fuselage, but the exact position is not known.

"Tail unit. The fin and rudder are identical to those fitted on the Me 109 G-6, with an inset mass-balanced rudder and a servo tab in the trailing edge. The tailplane has a fixed inverted slat along the whole leading edge, but the slat can be adjusted within certain limits. The slat is illustrated in the attached drawing.

"Performance. The maximum speed is given as 250mph and the minimum speed without flaps is 125mph.

"General. Caudrons had spent nearly two years on the design and construction of the Me 109 S and considered that the work was within three months of completion. Some French documents are available at A.I.2(g), which give details of construction, dimensions of the control surfaces, and the layout of the engine coolant system."

ANALYSIS

While Messerschmitt was clearly developing one or more experimental Me 109 S airframes to test the 'blown flaps' concept that it had originated some time prior to April 1942, it is unclear exactly why this work was being carried out – or indeed what the test aircraft was actually going to be called.

The French who worked on the design at Caudron-Renault in Paris certainly referred to it as the 'Me 109 S' and were reasonably clear in

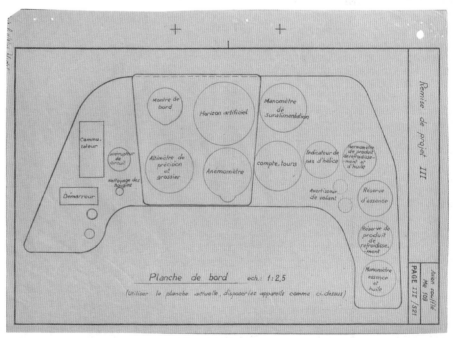

ABOVE: Cockpit dashboard layout for the Me 109 S – with gauges for the cooling system to the right.

BELOW: The Me 109 S's intake, fan and split ducting.

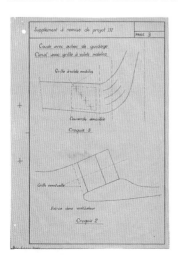

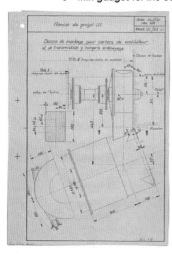

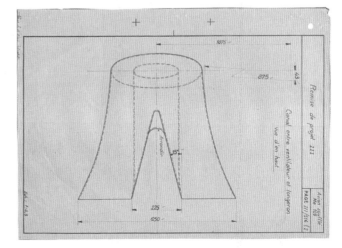

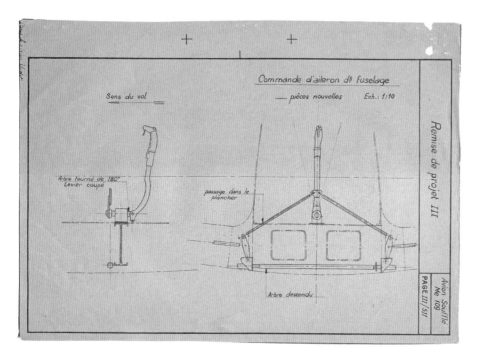

ABOVE: The control system.

of this work had been carried out on in Paris by Caudron, subcontracting for Messerschmitt. This timing roughly matches the development history of the blower system – which was put on hold in February 1943.

While the Me 155 A's high-altitude sibling, the Me 155 B, was handed over to Blohm & Voss for further development in the summer of 1943, it has always been assumed that the Me 155 A was simply dropped. However, a Messerschmitt document from April 1944 entitled Waffenanlage Zeichnungen für eine Anzahl von Messerschmitt Modelle or 'Weapon equipment drawings for a number of Messerschmitt models' shows side and front views of a 'Trägerflugzeug Me 155' or 'Carrier aircraft Me 155'. This appears alongside drawings of other contemporary Messerschmitt types including the Me 163 B, Me 109 K, Me 109 H and Me 410 A-1. While there is little detail

BELOW: The 'baumuster' type shown on this page from a Messerschmitt report of June 16, 1944, demonstrates how Messerschmitt typically referred to the blown flap Me 109 – as the Me 109 Ausblaseversuchsträger.

their understanding that the high-lift system was intended for a carrier-borne fighter. French drawings on Messerschmitt-supplied paper dated January 1944 are clearly marked 'Me 109 S', while drawings from an earlier French report, dated August 11, 1943, call it the 'Avion soufflé Me 109' or 'Blown aircraft Me 109'. It doesn't take too much of a leap to suggest that the 'S' in 'Me 109 S' actually stands for 'Soufflé'.

Neither of the two known Messerschmitt reports on the design – dated February 14, 1944, and June 16, 1944, actually refers to it as the 'Me 109 S'. The designation the company uses in both cases is the rather less snappy 'Me 109 Ausblaseversuchsträger'. The AVA report doesn't refer to the aircraft directly – only the system it was intended to carry.

The Me 109 S itself was definitely a purely experimental design, since it was unable to retract its landing gear, its top speed of 250mph was nothing like that of a fighter in 1944 and its endurance of 20 minutes made it useless for anything other than tests. None of the three original German reports offers any clues as to what the ultimate goal of all this research was. However, there remains the tantalising prospect that the system fitted to the Me 109 S was intended for something else – another design that would be suitable for combat.

Presumably this aircraft would have been powered by a single piston engine, since otherwise the blower system would have needed huge modifications and a complete redesign. Also, the design developed relies on a ventral intake with its clever system allowing air to be either blasted into the wings or vented underneath the fuselage when takeoff assistance was no longer required. This would surely preclude a 'rough strip' takeoff, since any dirt or debris kicked up by the propeller blades would immediately be sucked into the intake – potentially damaging the blower system.

In fact, the system would make the most sense if it were applied to a carrier aircraft. Messerschmitt had worked on the Me 409, later redesignated the Me 155, a DB 605-powered carrier-borne fighter, from early 1942 until it was 'stopped' in early 1943. Much

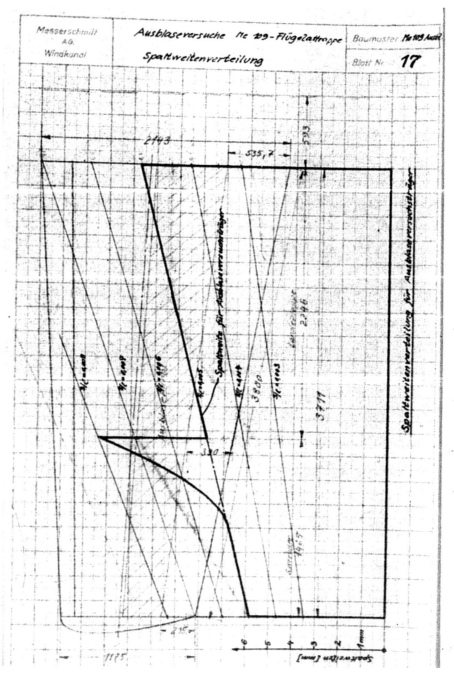

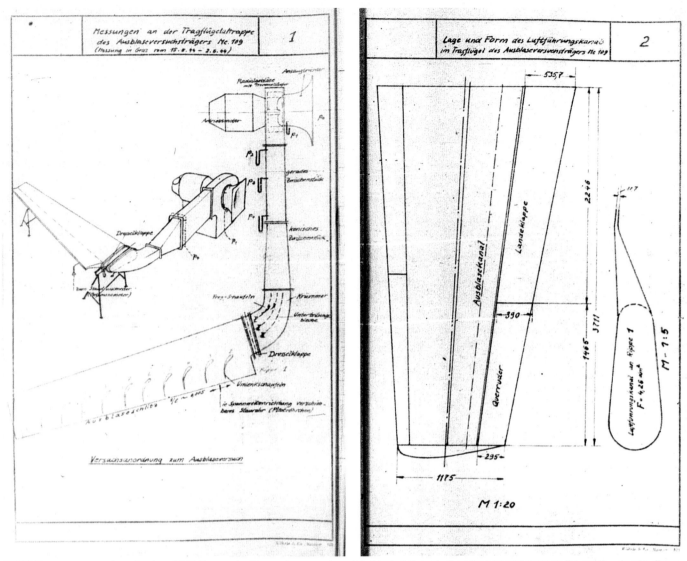

ABOVE: Two more pages from the June 1944 Messerschmitt report on experiments to blast air through aircraft wings and measure the results – showing the experimental setup.

present apart from the aircraft's armament, it is clear that the design is based on the Me 109 but features a significantly extended tail unit. There is certainly no suggestion of an intake below the fuselage centreline, but then there are no radiators or intakes or any sort pictured at all.

By this time, the Me 155 designation had been given a 'B' and applied to a high-altitude fighter before being officially redesignated BV 155 B by the RLM. Could it be that Messerschmitt entertained hopes of reviving its carrier aircraft against all the odds in 1944 by giving it an innovative blown-wing system?

There was one final British report on the system, BIOS Evaluation Report No. 13 of September 22, 1945. This states: "Boundary layer suction. The use of suction or blowing of air over the wings to increase the maximum lift was in an experimental stage and considered to need too much power.

"Regenscheidt had carried out some wind tunnel tests and a Me 109 had been built with jets fitted in the gap in front of the flaps so that air was blown over the upper surface. The only work in the tunnel in connection with this scheme had been to determine the correct width of slot along the span."

It would appear that, perhaps, the blower system was finally abandoned in June 1944 because it simply required too much of the engine's power to make it work effectively. ●

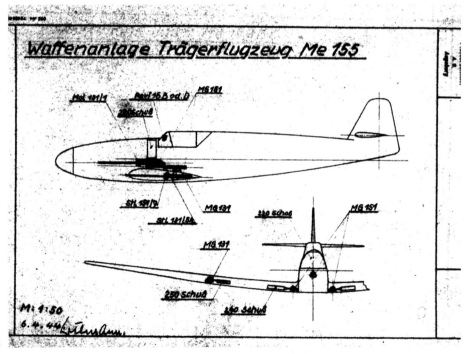

ABOVE: This drawing, from a Messerschmitt report of April 1944 entitled Waffenanlage Zeichnungen für eine Anzahl von Messerschmitt Modelle or 'Weapon equipment drawings for a number of Messerschmitt models', shows the long-tailed Trägerflugzeug Me 155. This is odd because Messerschmitt had handed the high-altitude Me 155 over to Blohm & Voss over seven months earlier. Could this have been the model intended to receive the Me 109 S blown flap system?

Messerschmitt Me 109 S

June 1944

Artwork by Luca Landino

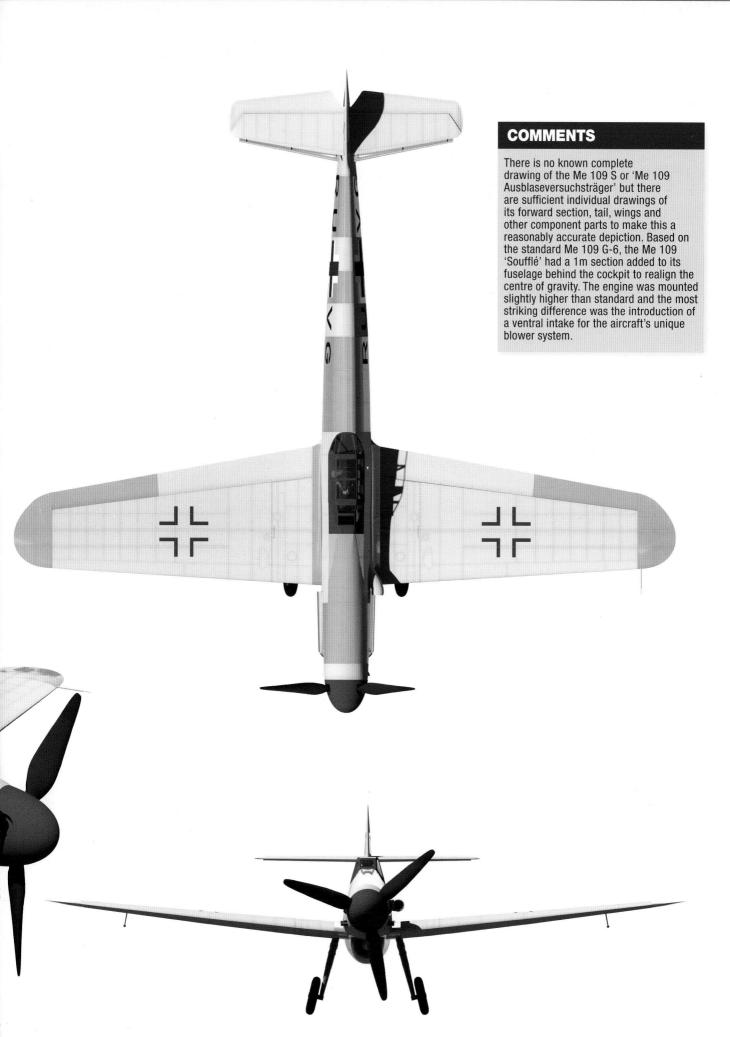

A tail of woe

Me 210 with V-tail

The sorry saga of the Me 210 wrecked careers and directly impacted on the Luftwaffe but even after the dust had settled Messerschmitt continued to investigate exactly what went so badly wrong...

Abb. 1 und 2

ABOVE: Wind tunnel model of the Me 210 with V-tail, tested by the DVL between June 1943 and June 1944. The V-tail in combination with a longer fuselage was expected to have a positive effect on the aircraft design – instead tests showed it made it even worse than the single fin, short fuselage version.

Shortly after the Messerschmitt Bf 110 twin-engined heavy fighter entered service in 1937 plans were drawn up for its replacement: the Me 210. The aircraft was a significant departure from its predecessor in some ways, with new wings, a short nose and a new cockpit design – but it did retain the Bf 110's twin tail.

The Me 210 V1 W.Nr. 210 0001 D-AABF made its first flight, lasting 10 minutes, with Messerschmitt chief test pilot Hermann Wurster at the controls on September 2, 1939. A second flight of eight minutes followed on September 4 and Würster kept the landing gear extended each time.

In a report written on September 5, he commented that the aircraft seemed very tail-heavy in all flight conditions and stability was poor around the vertical axis but he hoped these issues would be resolved when the landing gear could be retracted. He was to be sadly disappointed.

The Me 210 suffered from severe instability, stalled easily, vibrated strongly at speed and could enter an unrecoverable spin – and Messerschmitt's engineers were at a loss to explain why. Following Wurster's comments, attention initially focused on the twin-tail design which had largely been carried over from the tried and tested Bf 110. A single fin was fitted but this had little if any impact on the aircraft's problems.

Work went on throughout 1940 and into 1941 but the Me 210 continued to be plagued by the same problems, as well as numerous other technical issues such as engine fires and undercarriage failures. The Luftwaffe was desperate for its new heavy fighter though, so series production commenced before the problems had been resolved. After a series of crashes and many complaints from pilots production was eventually halted in March 1942.

Development proceeded however, and the aircraft's fuselage was lengthened, which helped, and this combined with alterations to the shape of the wings, the introduction of leading edge slats and a change of engine from the DB 601 to the DB 605 and then the DB 603 eventually cured the problems – but not before Messerschmitt as a company had taken a huge financial hit and a significant loss of prestige. Willy Messerschmitt himself was made to suffer personal consequences such as enforced demotion from company chairman to chief designer and the loss of his Me 108 personal aircraft. Production finally restarted in November 1942 with the aircraft redesignated as the Me 410.

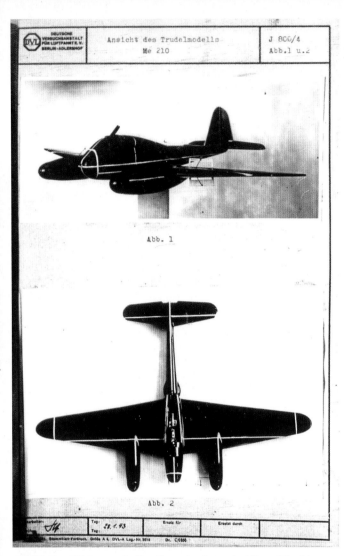

ABOVE: The DVL began testing the spin characteristics of the Me 210 with a model featuring the type's short fuselage, single fin configuration. Tests confirmed that near-total occlusion of the rudder during a spin made the aircraft very difficult to recover.

ABOVE: Drawing of the DVL's single-fin Me 210 model dated January 28, 1943. By this point, deliveries of the Me 410 to Luftwaffe units were already under way.

A British intelligence report of March 30, 1943, AI Report 47680, marked 'secret – do not quote', offers an interesting perspective on the source of the troubled aircraft's failures: "At the outbreak of the war, two Me 163s (Jaguar) [actually the Bf 162, first flown as a prototype in 1937 – and apparently never known as the Jaguar outside the German press of the day] had been constructed by Messerschmitt, Augsburg. This aircraft, which was highly thought of by Mr Messerschmitt, did not meet with the approval of the RLM. For this reason, the construction of the Me 210 was undertaken.

"In order to avoid the usual long delays before a new type could be produced a number of Arado engineers were taken over by Messerschmitt (probably at the instigation of the RLM) for the purpose of designing and constructing the Me 210.

"The Me 210 was intended to serve as an all-purpose aircraft (Mehrzwecke-Flugzeug), one of the main purposes, however, being ground attack. The RLM rejected the original twin-fin version and insisted on a single fin. The RLM also ordered that the drawings of the Me 210 should be completed in the design office without going through the 'Fertigungsburo' [production office].

"The design and construction has been greatly influenced by the Arado engineers: Messrs. Rethel and Fröhlich. These two

engineers, in co-operation with Messrs. Messerschmitt, Krauss and Schmidt, were the five persons principally responsible for this aircraft [Messerschmitt, Krauss and Rethel received their own personal copies of Wurster's initial flight test reports while Messerschmitt chief designer Woldemar Voigt received two]. The incorporation of the Arado engineers was apparently for the purpose of, as far as possible, avoiding individual work and to construct the aircraft by more mass production methods than is usually the case with Messerschmitt. For instance, to avoid pressed, cast and forged pieces, welding was preferred to riveting.

"The result of this was that the general conception came from Messerschmitt, but the details from Arado; in other words, the aircraft has a Messerschmitt fuselage combined with an Arado wing; while split flaps were introduced. The detail construction was improved and simplified. This is not only due to the Arado influence, but also to the experience the Germans had with the Me 109. The number of different parts for 'left' and 'right' was reduced. The undercarriage was considerably improved.

"The following details concerning the construction are known to Source: fuselage – monocoque, Dural Z.B.1/3. Undercarriage – VDM construction based on Messerschmitt

drawings. Control surfaces - fins covered with sheet metal; rudders covered with fabric, metal noses. Flettner rudder statically balanced. Steering – by push and pull rods and by wires. Wing – single spar with auxiliary spar; nose and end ribs in Dural, tip slots, split flaps, airbrakes.

"Engines – 2 x DB 601 (?) with block radiators in wing. Engines hold by cables ('Fangseile') (ordered by RLM?). Tankage – 2 x 2 flexible tanks in the wing roots before and behind the spar. Airbrakes – landing flaps and cooling flaps coupled.

"Considerable trouble was experienced with the control surfaces. The fin had to be enlarged five times with the result that the torsional forces in the fuselage were increased, thus defeating the result which they had hoped to obtain by rejecting the original twin-fin design.

"In diving tests at Rechlin, the elevator broke, whilst the aircraft was diving from a height of 4km and levelling out at $2^1/_2$km (70 degrees against the horizon). As a result of this, diving tests were abandoned. When in level flight, the wing broke repeatedly at about two-thirds of its span.

"The serial production, which had started, had to be stopped for a considerable time, when only 200 aircraft had been manufactured; this took place towards the end of 1941 and the 200 aircraft were grounded as no use could be made

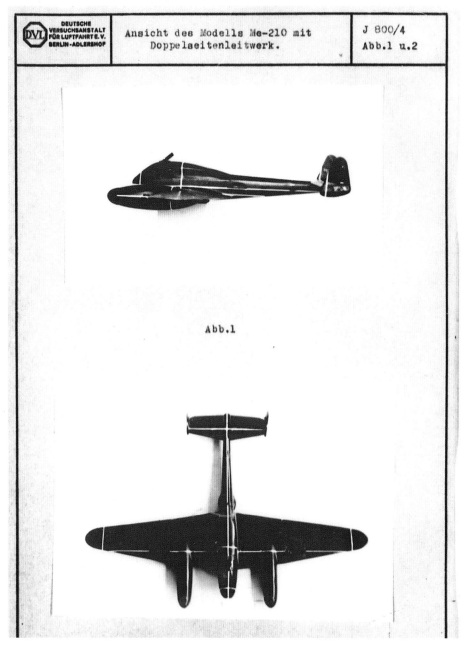

DEUTSCHE
VERSUCHSANSTALT
FÜR LUFTFAHRT E. V.
BERLIN-ADLERSHOF

Ansicht des Modells Me-210 mit
Doppelseitenleitwerk.

J 800/4
Abb.1 u.2

Abb.1

ABOVE: DVL tests of an Me 210 model with a twin-fin tail and short fuselage showed that, in fact, the type's initial configuration had been fine all along – it was the aircraft's wings that were at fault.

of them. However, the speed of the Me 210, when compared to the Me 110 – given equal engines – was approximately 20% higher, while the early troubles which Messerschmitt had concerning the manoeuvrability of the aircraft appeared to have been overcome.

"The fact that the Me 210 was not a success, created great difficulties between the Messerschmitt firm and Hitler. Relations got very strained and at one time Hitler threatened to take over Messerschmitt and put it under State control."

Identifying the Me 210's problems as related to the wings and fuselage appeared to largely exonerate the twin-tail layout which had originally been blamed, but could greater improvements in the aircraft's stall and spin characteristics be made via further alterations to the fuselage and tail? Messerschmitt commissioned the Deutsche Versuchsanstalt für Luftfahrt (DVL) to investigate through an extensive programme of wind tunnel testing.

The first DVL report, on an Me 210 model

with a short fuselage and single fin, was produced on February 15, 1943. This gave unsurprising results – the aircraft was very difficult to recover from a spin because in such a condition the rudder was almost completely ineffective, being extensively blocked by the "unfavourable tail assembly". Dive brakes "provide no significant contribution to the termination of the spin" and "at 10km altitude, none of the possible rudder movements suffice to disturb the flat state of the spin".

For its second report, of June 2, 1943, the DVL presented the results of tests involving a model of the Me 210 with a short fuselage and twin fin – the original configuration of the Me 210 V1. These results were a little more surprising: "By using the double-sided stabiliser instead of the central vertical stabiliser, a considerable improvement in the turbulence properties of the short-fuselage Me 210 was achieved. The reason for this is the much more favourable blocking ratios for a double-sided tail.

"The spin properties of the Me 210 short-fuselage and double-fin tail model can be described as satisfactory on condition that the model test results can be applied to the large-scale test. As part of the systematic spin test on the Me 210, the following variations of the fuselage and tail assembly are provided and in preparation: III. Extended fuselage with larger construction height and central rudder. IV Extended fuselage with larger overall height and V-tail. V. Short fuselage with high position tailplane. VI. Short fuselage with brought-forward tailplane."

Incredibly, the DVL's tests had proven – nearly four years later – that the Me 210's original short fuselage and twin-fin tail were actually fine. The aircraft's 'Arado' wings really had been the problem all along. Switching to a single fin layout had been a terrible mistake, because it introduced the unrecoverable spin characteristic which made the aircraft so dangerous.

Had the wings been identified as the source of the problem from the outset, the type might have entered service by the end of 1940 – too late for the Battle of Britain but in time for the invasion of the Soviet Union in 1941.

Further testing was now to be undertaken with a lengthened fuselage and single fin – the layout the Me 210 had ended up with in service as the Me 410 – followed by testing with a radical V-tail arrangement, then tests with the original short fuselage and two further tailplane arrangements intended to negate the spin problem.

The report on the 'III.' model is missing and the report on the V-tail configuration would not be made until June 15, 1944 – by which point production of even the Me 410 was just two weeks away from cancellation. Willy Messerschmitt himself seems to have been very fond of the V-tail layout and appears to have entertained high hopes for it in production.

The DVL shared this view initially. The report states: "After completion of the spin test of the Me 210 model with extended hull and central rudder (model III), tests were carried out on the same model with a V-tail (model IV). In this version, the entire tail consists only of a surface with a strong V-form. Because of the lack of blocking of the vertical stabiliser by the tail fin, which can occur in a normal tail, favourable tail air properties were to be expected in this tail form, in particular with

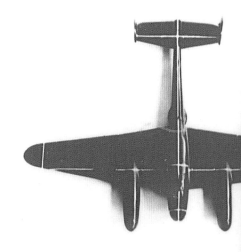

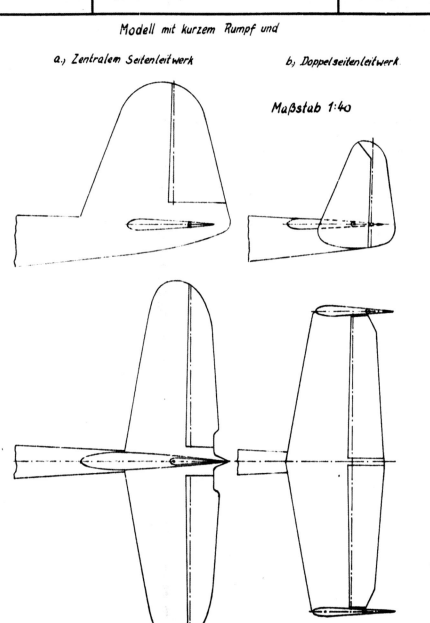

Modell mit kurzem Rumpf und

a.) Zentralem Seitenleitwerk

b.) Doppelseitenleitwerk

Maßstab 1:40

ABOVE: May 26, 1943, drawing showing the single and twin fin layouts of the Me 210's tail tested in the DVL's wind tunnel. Swapping the single fin for a twin fin actually cured the aircraft's dangerous spin characteristic. Had Messerschmitt stuck with a twin fin from the outset, many of the Me 210's problems might have been avoided.

regard to the rudder efficiency to emerge from the spin.

"However, the results did not confirm these expectations. It turned out that the flat spin was very irregular; in terms of rudder efficiency, the V-tail proved to be inferior even to the normal tail and thus represents the most unfavourable of the four fuselage and tail combinations previously studied."

So switching to a V-tail arrangement would have been an even greater blunder than fitting a single tail fin.

Interviewed on September 7, 1945, chief project engineer Woldemar Voigt gave a more succinct summary of the Me 210's history: "The Me 210 was first flown in the early days of the war. Its rearward-firing, remotely controlled armament in the fuselage barbettes enabled it to defend itself from behind, but resulted in a speed loss of approximately 20-30km/h.

"The Me 210 was the only Messerschmitt type to give serious trouble in the flight testing; and in this case the difficulties were very great. Among the chief sources of trouble were: rather big trailing edge angles of wing, ailerons and tail surfaces, resulting in irregularities in the lift and moment curves; breakdown of the airflow at the wing root at take-off, caused by a divergent flow between the rather convergent shape of the fuselage and the big trailing edge angle of the wing; effect of the crew's cabin (specially designed to give a good field of view rearward and backward, therefore rather clumsy and not aerodynamically clean) on the intersection of elevator and rudder with their respective tabs; dangerous spin characteristics which were not discovered until the aircraft were in the hands of the service pilots.

"The last-mentioned item led to a complete cessation of production just after the first production aircraft were delivered. The fault was remedied within some weeks, but the order to resume production was not given until about six months later. The series was then equipped with the DB 603 engine and renamed the Me 410. Production ceased altogether in 1944 when the Me 410 was dropped in favour of the single-seater fighter programme." ●

BELOW: Three of the four models tested by the DVL for comparison – the only one missing is the long fuselage single fin arrangement which was tested at some point between June 1943 and June 1944, presumably towards the end of 1943.

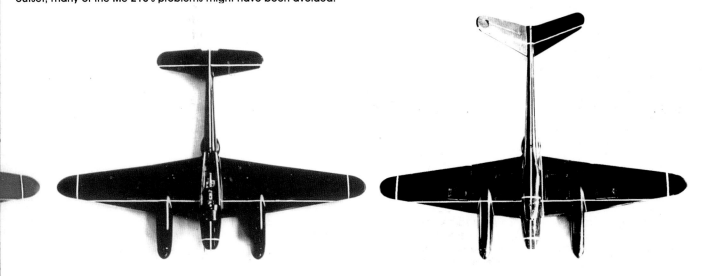

A nose for trouble

Messerschmitt Me 328 C

Development of the pulsejet-powered Me 328 had faltered throughout the spring and summer of 1943 until it was eventually halted on September 3, 1943, but there remained two potential options for continuing with the type – either as a jet fighter or a suicide bomber.

Messerschmitt's Abteilung L had begun working on single-jet fighters before the Second World War but the concept was shelved relatively quickly when it became clear that Germany's early turbojets were not sufficiently powerful for such an aircraft.

When preliminary performance figures for the next generation of turbojets – the HeS 011 and Jumo 004 C – were made available, however, the idea was revived and Abteilung L's last project prior to its dissolution was the design of a single-jet fighter, a '1-TL-Jäger', based on the Me 163. This portly-looking little aircraft was designated 'P 20' and the earliest known drawing of it was produced on April 16, 1943.

The previous month, on March 3, 1943, a brief report was written by Me 328 designer Rudolf Seitz comparing the dimensions of the 'Me 328 C' to those of the Me 262. The Me 328 in question is presented with a wing area of 18m² compared to the Me 262's 21.6m² – not much smaller. And the aircraft's fuselage has a surface area of 30m² compared to the Me 262's 31.6m². However, data on the Me 328 with an extended fuselage is also presented – showing it with a significantly larger surface area than the Me 262. It is not entirely clear whether this Me 328 has turbojet rather than pulsejet propulsion but it would appear that it does not.

That same month, Focke-Wulf had also begun working on a single-jet fighter design loosely based on the Fw 190. The true designation of this design is unknown but it would be retrospectively described in a report of August 1944 as '1. Entwurf'. Although it would most likely have been an entirely new machine if built, the design shows it with what might have been the wings and tail of an Fw 190. The cockpit was moved to the nose and the turbojet was slung underneath it.

Both of the Focke-Wulf '1. Entwurf' and Messerschmitt P 20 designs were discussed at a meeting of the RLM's development committee on May 28, 1943, without representatives of either company present. According to a summary of the meeting issued on June 12, 1943, the designs were presented by Staff Engineer Walter Friebel who had said "it was suggested by Focke-Wulf and Messerschmitt to provide an existing fighter (Fw 190 or Me 163)

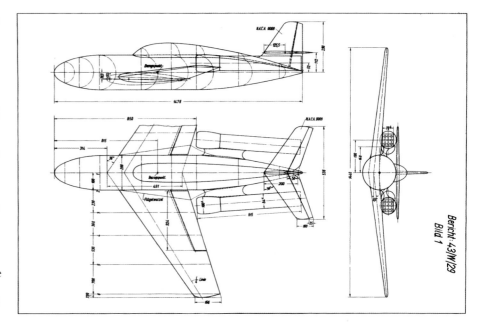

Bericht 43/W/29
Bild 1

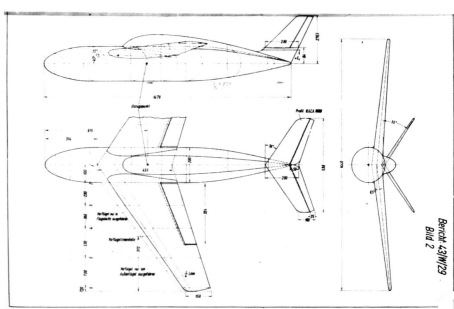

Bericht 43/W/29
Bild 2

ABOVE: A report of July 14, 1943, published by the AVA gave the results of wind tunnel tests carried out on a 1:5.5 scale model of a stretched Me 328 fitted with 36° swept wings and a V-tail. Full scale, this aircraft would have measured 8.118m long, compared to the Me 328 B's 7.05m and its swept wingspan was 7.92m compared to the straight wingspan of the Me 328 B at 6.9m or 8.6m with extensions. Four months earlier Messerschmitt had compared specifications for an enlarged 'Me 328 C' against the Me 262 – could these designs represent the original Me 328 C?

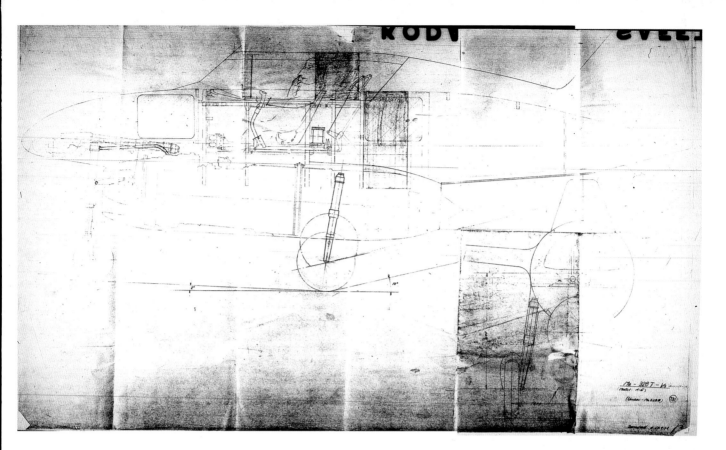

ABOVE: The Me 328 T – V1, dated September 20, 1943, as designed by Jacobs-Schweyer Flugzeugbau. This unarmed turbojet-powered version of the Me 328 has a fixed shock-absorbing undercarriage fitted close to its fuselage, a long nose and small fuel tanks. In brackets after 'Me 328 T – V1' the inscription says 'Umbau Me 328 B' or 'Modification Me 328 B'.

with a TL device with the least amount of design effort. Working through the design showed that a complete reinterpretation was inevitable. The possibilities and prospects of such 1-TL-Jägers have been investigated.

"Advantages: horizontal speeds 150km/h larger than the Otto [piston engine] fighter. Climbing speeds are as great as the maximum possible horizontal speeds of Otto fighters. A pursuit in the climb would therefore be possible.

"Central installation of several heavy weapons in the fuselage means strong concentrated firepower like that of the two-jet fighter Me 262, which is preferably used against bombers. Special advantage over Me 262 is the possibility of fighter to fighter combat (manoeuvrability). Saving of material about 20%, saving in hours spent manufacturing the airframe about 25%, saving on engines 50%. Disadvantages over the Otto fighter: a) fuel consumption at least twice as high. b) significantly shorter flight duration for the same route.

"Capacity availability: Although Focke-Wulf has been able to complete the task, the RLM believes it is certain that it will have a detrimental effect on Ta 154. This view is confirmed by the special representative for Ta 154. Whether Heinkel from the end of 1943 between taking care of the He 177, He 277 development and He 219 development as well as He 274 can still be charged with a jet fighter is being investigated. Heinkel is also heavily involved in the jet bomber project.

"Most likely, Messerschmitt would be suitable for the new task provided that it would be tackled only after completion of the

Me 262 development (about the end of 1943) to avoid division of effort."

Staff Engineer Eick then submitted project sketches by Messerschmitt, Focke-Wulf and Heinkel. Apparently "the designs are not even aligned due to the shortage of time. For performance reasons, the HeS 11 engine is to be considered in addition to the weaker Jumo 004 C".

In the discussion section, General of Fighters Adolf Galland said that "the need for the 1-TL Jägers also alongside the (expected to be one year earlier) Me 262 is beyond doubt, since with that aircraft only locally and temporarily on certain fronts can air superiority be achieved. In the interest of manoeuvrability, this aircraft must be very small. Service ceiling should be at least 13km".

Commander of the test establishments Colonel Edgar Petersen "indicates the danger of damage to the tail by the hot jet. For lift increase and reduction of the surface load for slow flight 'tactical Fowler' would be a big advantage".

Technical Office Chief of Staff Major General Wolfgang Vorwald "expected that there was a danger of the tail surfaces being affected by the exhaust, so that a tailless construction method is not indispensable for this reason, especially as tilting and centre-of-gravity difficulties must be expected".

Friebel then said that "the very high strength requirements of a tactical Fowlers make the steel wing appear desirable. However, housing the Fowlers will be difficult with the thin wing profiles".

Professor Dr Friedrich Seewald of the FoFü,

ABOVE: The cartoonish 'pilot' of the Me 328 T appears to pick his long nose in reference to the aircraft's own unique forward profile.

"emphasizes the importance of the piston engine for speeds up to 900km/h despite high weights for propellers etc. But since a corresponding engine is not yet available, the need for the use of TL devices from the Otto point of view is beyond doubt".

In the 'decision' section of the summary it says: "The Field Marshal [Erhard Milch] orders that the project of the 1-TL Jägers be pursued with the utmost vigour. In the interpretation the two versions a) highest

▶

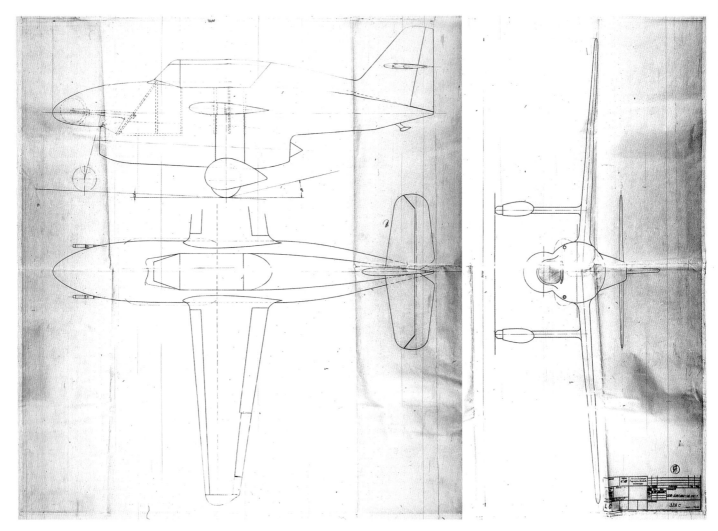

ABOVE: A three-view drawing of the apparently renamed Me 328 C dated October 6, 1943, on Jacobs-Schweyer Flugzeugbau paper. Unlike the Me 328 T, the undercarriage of the 'C' is fixed to the wings, much further away from the fuselage, with large gaiters and spats over the wheels. The top and front views show the bulged fairings necessary to accommodate a pair of MK 103 cannon.

speed, b) a service ceiling of at least 13km are to be considered. Scheduling and performance suggest using the HeS 011 engine. With the execution of the task, which will be decided at a later date, it would be appropriate to entrust a fighter company – such as Messerschmitt or maybe Focke-Wulf. Also Heinkel is to be involved in the project work at first".

A date is set for a further discussion of single-jet fighters – June 25, 1943 – but the summary of that day's meeting includes no mention of them.

From this point on, both Messerschmitt and Focke-Wulf began programmes of single-jet fighter development. Messerschmitt's next move was to create the P 1092 – a new single jet fighter design which had its engine beneath its nose and cockpit like the P 20 but with a more conventional tailed rather than tailless layout.

A Messerschmitt report of July 3, 1943, compared three different versions of the P 1092 – the P 1092/a, P 1092/b and P 1092/bH – with the P 20 and Me 262. It concluded that the twin-engine arrangement of the Me 262 was superior in every respect except for cost and production time. A single jet fighter would only require 55% as much material as an Me 262 to build and the process would take between 10 and 15% fewer man hours.

Precisely when the idea of turning the Me 328 into a single-jet fighter arose is unclear but a drawing of September 20, 1943, shows the 'Me 328 T – V1' – the Me 328 pulsejet fighter reimagined as a single jet aircraft. The drawing is also marked 'Darmstadt', suggesting that it originated with Darmstadt-based Jacobs-Schweyer Flugzeugbau, which had been charged with building the prototypes for the Me 328 B.

The Me 328 T – V1 has an upper profile similar to that of the Me 328 B but slung beneath the fuselage is a single turbojet. The characteristic bullet nose of the Me 328 is replaced with a beaky looking nose housing a nosewheel and the aircraft has a non-retractable mainwheel strut housing – visible in the forward view. There is also a small tail skid. Comically, seated within the cockpit a cartoonish pilot is depicted picking his correspondingly beaky nose.

The date is interesting because Messerschmitt had ordered that all work on the Me 328 pulsejet fighter be stopped on September 3, 1943. However, a letter written by Willy Messerschmitt to Seitz on September 29, 1943, suggests that Seitz himself had pushed for a jet-propelled Me 328 to take the place of the pulsejet version, allowing work on the project to continue.

Messerschmitt's letter is headed "Ihre 'Stellungnahme der Entwicklungsleitung Me 328 zum Stoppbefehl vom 3.9.43'"

or "Your 'Statement of the development management Me 328 to the stop command of 3.9.43". It is his response to Seitz's reaction to the 'stop' command.

He writes: "A final decision on whether to accelerate the 1TL [single jet] aircraft and start it in series depends on the following conditions: 1) The likelihood that the flight characteristics will not cause any difficulty. 2) The time needed for the entire process from the exact planning including series preparation to the time of the production of at least 100 aircraft per month. 3) The performance of the aircraft a) with fixed undercarriage b) with retractable undercarriage. 4) The capacity available for the production of the standard aircraft.

"This is the quickest way to do it, but I would like to point out that it needs to be handled very carefully. If this result shows that in a relatively short time larger numbers of an aircraft are to be created, which will have better flight performance with sufficient defensive armament than the best enemy aircraft with piston engine may have, the flight performance may of course be worse than that of the 262, if the aircraft is cheaper accordingly."

A week later, on October 6, 1943, a number of drawings were produced showing a turbojet-powered Me 328 that was largely the same as the 'Me 328 T' drawing. One of these is marked 'Darmstadt' while another actually appears on official Jacobs-Schweyer Flugzeugbau drawing paper. These are marked 'Me 328 C'. Presumably the designation had been reapplied from the much larger 'Me 328 C' of March 1943.

Although similar to the Me 328 T, the rechristened Me 328 C is armed with a pair of MK 103s which require bulged fairings on either side of the fuselage. A much larger fuel tank now sits above the nosewheel housing, the nosewheel strut itself is now straighter and angled forwards, the fuel tank behind the cockpit is enlarged and the biggest change involves the undercarriage mainwheels, which have been repositioned further away from the fuselage and given full aerodynamic housing, including spats.

It would appear that Seitz was unable to demonstrate the merits of the turbojet Me 328 C and it went no further – although the Me 328 project itself would stagger on into 1944 as a vehicle for Hanna Reitsch's suicide attack project.

It has been suggested that the Me 328 C was derived from the Messerschmitt P 1095 single-jet fighter project or vice-versa. The only known primary source evidence of the P 1095 is an undated memo entitled 'P 1095 Vorbemerkung' or 'P 1095 preliminary note'. This appears to follow the Messerschmitt philosophy outlined elsewhere in the Luftwaffe: Secret series by using as many components from existing or apparently soon-to-exist full production aircraft types as possible. It says: "In the following, the proposal is made to develop a 1-TL-Jäger

whose components are largely taken from the current or just beginning full production series fighters.

"Investigations conducted so far show that with today's tangible jet engines (up to approx. 1000kg thrust) superiority of the single TL aircraft over the two TL aircraft (apart from turning and landing behaviour) cannot be fully achieved, but on the other hand only about half the fuel is needed.

"A completely new development for the 1-TL-Jägers with the TL engines of today is hardly worthwhile, but on the other hand, it is urgently necessary in the current air warfare and fuel situation to develop the 1-TL-Jäger, given its great performance superiority over the enemy aircraft with piston engines. A compromise solution suitable for this purpose may be the following proposal: From the series of the Me 262 and Me 209, as many parts as possible are taken over with or without slight changes for the one TL aircraft project P 1095 to be created from them.

"The development and production costs are then reduced to a minimum. In the enclosed short description the parts that are acceptable for the series are listed for the 1 TL-Jäger and their share in the overall production is estimated. It is irrelevant whether the metal version or the later wooden version of the Me 262 is used.

"The following is a summary of the main possible uses: Taking off under its own power (without or with launch rockets) – 1) Light fighter. Ranges and flight duration approaching today's requirements for single-

engine propeller-driven fighter. Armament 2 x MK 103 with 60 rounds or 3 x MK 108 with 60 rounds each in the fuselage nose. 2) Fighter with stronger armament. Basic armament the same as 1.) but additionally 2 gondola weapons each with 1 x MK 108 or 2 rocket launchers. 3) Ground-attack aircraft with up to 5 MG 81. 4) Destroyer.

"Taking off under its own power but with the aid of rockets – 5) Fighter-bomber. Basic armament as fighter with 2 x SC 250 bombs or up to 4 rocket launchers. 6) Long-range fighter. Possible by enlarging the fuel system. For catapult, towing or carrying towing start only – fast bomber with up to 2000kg bomb load."

The P 1095 was to consist of Me 262 wings and forward fuselage, including pressurised cockpit, tail from the Me 209, controls from the Me 262 and/or Me 209, undercarriage from the Me 262 and Me 209, and a single Jumo 004 B-2 turbojet. Wing area was to be 15.3m^2, wingspan was 9.77m. These figures seem slightly at odds with the rest of the description since the Me 262's wings, with a turbojet each, gave the aircraft a wingspan of 12.6m and a wing area of 21.7m^2.

Re-drawn pictures of the P 1095 purportedly dated October 19, 1943, do appear to show the aircraft with slightly swept wings similar to those of the Me 262 and with a tail which may be derived from that intended for the Me 209. This would suggest that the P 1095 was separate from the Me 328 C and came about after the Me 328 programme had been switched to Reitsch's suicide weapon project. ●

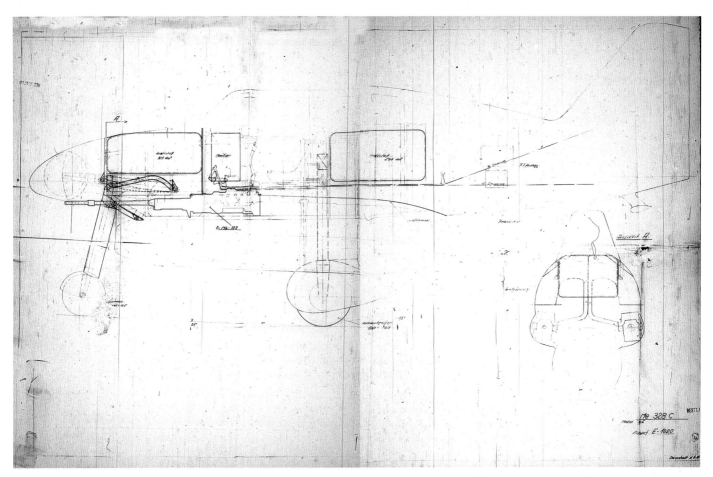

ABOVE: A detailed side view of the Me 328 C, also dated October 6, 1943, showing the MK 103 installation from the side and as a cutaway from the front.

Tailless takeoff tangent

Messerschmitt patents

The designer of the Messerschmitt Me 163, Alexander Lippisch, was undeniably one of the Third Reich's more creative aviation pioneers. A set of patents from the autumn of 1941 illustrates his inventive mind at work...

ALL IMAGES THIS CHAPTER: IOWA STATE UNIVERSITY LIBRARY SPECIAL COLLECTIONS AND UNIVERSITY ARCHIVE

Whenever Lippisch found himself at the end of a major project cycle he seems to have abruptly branched out into new areas of research or begun investigations leading off at a tangent from his previous efforts.

Having just gone through months of disagreements and focused development work to determine the form of the Me 163's successor (the Me 163 B as it turned out - see p116-121) and seen Heini Dittmar become the first man to fly faster than 1000km/h on October 2, 1941, Lippisch turned to more conceptual designs.

Between October 11 and October 13, 1941, he sketched out at least three separate patent applications, each of which seemingly arose from the need to improve the characteristics of tailless aircraft during takeoff and landing. The first of these saw him returning to research he had carried out five years earlier while working at the DFS – forward-swept wings.

In his book, Ein Dreieck Fliegt, Lippisch wrote: "We should not omit mentioning a special project of 1936 which was of unusual design. In England Professor Townsend had shown that by sweeping the wing forward and strongly tapering it toward the tip, stalling at the outer wing section could be effectively postponed.

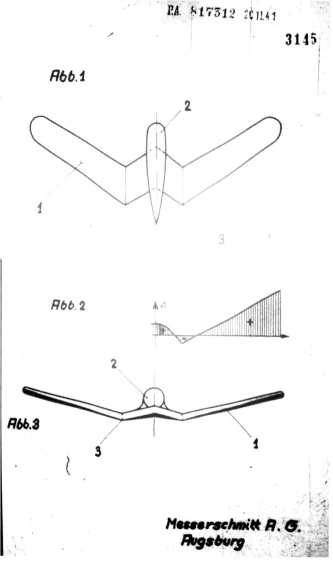

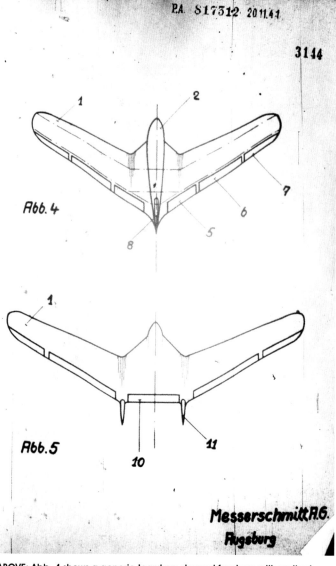

ABOVE: Drawings from Alexander Lippisch's patent for a W-wing arrangement intended to improve the takeoff and landing characteristics of tailless aircraft. Abb. 1 shows a plan view of the unusual wing form, Abb. 2 shows the 'twist' applied to the wing leading edges and Abb. 3 shows a forward view of the design.

ABOVE: Abb. 4 shows a generic teardrop-shaped fuselage with vertical fin and rudder to the rear with another unusual wing planform. This time only the leading edge has the 'W-wing' shape, while the trailing edge is straight. This results in extremely deep wing roots. Abb. 5 shows a similar arrangement but with twin fins and a straight horizontal stabiliser.

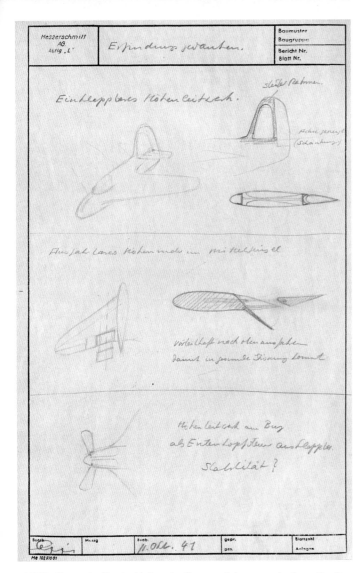

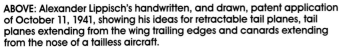

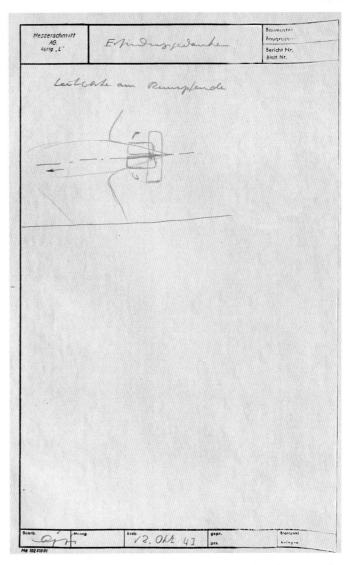

ABOVE: Alexander Lippisch's handwritten, and drawn, patent application of October 11, 1941, showing his ideas for retractable tail planes, tail planes extending from the wing trailing edges and canards extending from the nose of a tailless aircraft.

ABOVE: Drawing showing the fourth of Lippisch's ideas for pop-out tail planes – similar to the first idea but with the planes hinging out horizontally rather than dropping down from a vertical position.

"Even at large angles of attack and low speeds, roll stability could thus be maintained, as opposed to the normal swept-back wing where stalling started at the wing tips. To study this problem we designed an experimental glider Kormoran DFS 42 with forward sweep of the wings, which was built in 1936.

"We observed the flow by means of filaments and clearly observed the Townsend phenomenon. We took a number of photographs of the wing flow on subsequent flights. However, although the flow on the outer wing remained steady, the flow over the midsection of the wing stalled relatively early causing loss of longitudinal stability and lower maximum lift.

"We therefore installed an additional rudder over the midwing section which prevented the incipient loss of lift. On the whole, these experiments were interesting but failed to prove any superiority of the wing with forward sweep, since on normal swept-back wings stalling of the outer wing could be prevented by installing wing slots which produced higher maximum lift. From that time on no further experiments with swept-forward wings were carried out by us."

While there is no evidence to indicate that Lippisch did conduct further practical

experiments, he evidently did return to the problem and his employer, Messerschmitt AG, patented what he considered to be a potential solution on his behalf.

Entitled 'Flugzeug mit nach vorne gepfeilten Flügel' or 'Aircraft with forward swept wings', the patent says: "Swept aircraft wings with both positive and negative arrow position (wing ends swept back or swept forward) are made inherently stable by appropriate twisting (setting angle at the leading parts larger).

"The negative arrow position brings greater security against stalling, because in contrast to the positive arrow position no flow can take place from the boundary layer to the outer wings and the boundary layer instead flows inwards towards the middle of the wing. This means, however, that the flow, which has already been disturbed by the influence of the fuselage, is even easier to break off in the middle part of the wing; the result is great additional resistance and loss of lift even at moderately high angles of attack.

"The present invention is based, then, by appropriate shaping of the wing plan to direct the boundary layer where it can do the least damage. According to the invention, in an aircraft with a negative arrow position,

with predominantly forward-facing wings and at the front of all wing-ends, which are connected to the hull and, where appropriate, to engine nacelles, with positive sweep. The result is that the destructive boundary layer flow is not only kept away from the tips of the wings, but also from near the fuselage, where there are already favourable flow conditions.

"It is sufficient if the positive sweep to be used according to the invention at certain points extends to the leading edge of the wing; this is enough to divert the boundary layer in the desired sense. The twisting of the wing according to the invention depends on what has been said above: the setting angle becomes larger the farther the relevant wing part is from the fuselage.

"A further improvement of the flight characteristics can be achieved in a further embodiment of the invention in that the wing receives a weak W-shape not only in the top view, but also in the forward view."

The patent is illustrated with five diagrams. The first shows Lippisch's W-shape design from above, the second shows the wing 'twist' he proposes and the third a forward view of the same design, indicating a slight gullwing effect. The fourth drawing shows "another embodiment in plan view;

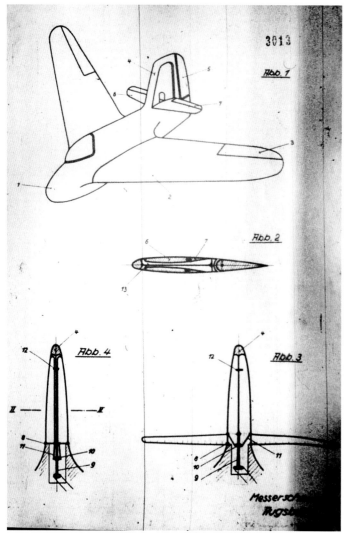

ABOVE: The first page of illustrations from the formal submission of Lippisch's ideas to the Reich patent office by Messerschmitt AG. This shows the flip down tail planes.

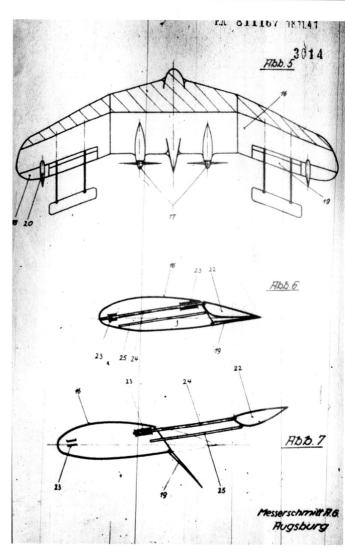

ABOVE: A flying wing with 'tail planes' that can extend from the trailing edge of its wings.

the positive sweep in the area of the fuselage (2) is limited here to the leading edges. This leads to a strong increase in the wing depth against the fuselage and therefore allows a very favourable connection of the wing (1) to the fuselage (2). For the control, three pairs (5), (6) and (7) of wing flaps are attached, as well as a central rudder (8).

"The inner flap pair (5) serves as an aileron and is just as actuated as the elevator of an aircraft with a tail fin. The pair of flaps (6) is used for lift increase during takeoff and landing, since the flap neutral axis is almost in the centre of gravity and therefore no tilting moment arises around the transverse axis at flap deflection.

"Adjusted in the opposite direction, the flaps (6) can also be used for trimming around the longitudinal and vertical axes. The outer pair of flaps (7) serve primarily as horizontal stabilisers, also in the same direction adjustment for trimming about the transverse axis. The flap arrangement is thus adapted to the aircraft's layout, which allows the achievement of high lift coefficients at takeoff and landing."

The fifth drawing is of a design "basically similar" to the fourth drawing "but here the trailing edge of the wing centre section is placed perpendicular to the direction of flight and equipped with a single continuous horizontal

stabiliser (10), while the rudder (11) is divided and relocated to the kinks in the wing".

The formal version of this patent application, filed on November 14, 1941, received PA number 817312 of November 20, 1941. Filed on the same day, evidently having been drafted at the same time, but seemingly dealt with sooner was patent number PA 811167 of November 18, 1941.

This is entitled 'Höhenleitwerk für flugzeug' or 'Tailplanes for aircraft' and effectively incorporates four different ideas into a single package. The patent description states: "The invention consists of attaching an additional retractable tailplane unit, which is spatially separated in the operative position from the wing, on an aircraft with horizontal stabilisers which are mounted on the wing itself, and which can be used for altitude control. This should be retracted during the high-speed flight and deployed at take-off and landing, expediently together with the lift flaps or with the landing gear. This tailplane may consist of a fin with an invariable angle of incidence, of a controllable rudder alone or, ultimately, a combination of both.

"One might ask why one does not build this tailplane on the aircraft and use it all the time. Consider not only the additional harmful drag of the separate tailplane but

also its unfavourable location for high speed flight in the area of the fuselage flow, where it is greatly affected by changes in the airflow. These flow disturbances often cause dangerous rudder vibrations, which have often led to severe accidents. In high-speed flight, therefore, the conventional control of tailless aircraft by means of wing flaps is much more advantageous since they lie in undisturbed flow."

The patent states that there are a number of different possibilities for the inclusion of tailplanes – the first illustration shows "an embodiment of the invention in a perspective view, Figure 2 shows a horizontal section through the tail fin, Figures 3 and 4 show the planes in extended and retracted positions, Figure 5 shows a tailless aircraft with another embodiment of the invention in plan, Figures 6 and 7 show the extendable tailplane section as part of the wing in the extended and retracted position, Figures 8 and 9 show a third embodiment in the extended and retracted position, Figure 10 is a side view, Figures 11 and 12 a fourth embodiment in the extended and retracted position".

While the first means of introducing retractable tail surfaces for landings and takeoffs is straightforward enough – tailplanes that pop out of the fin or retract back into it as needed – the second consists of surfaces that extend backwards from the

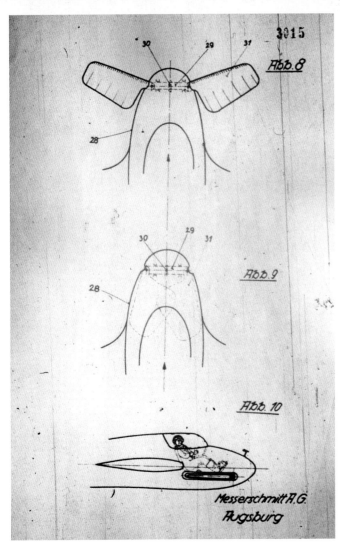

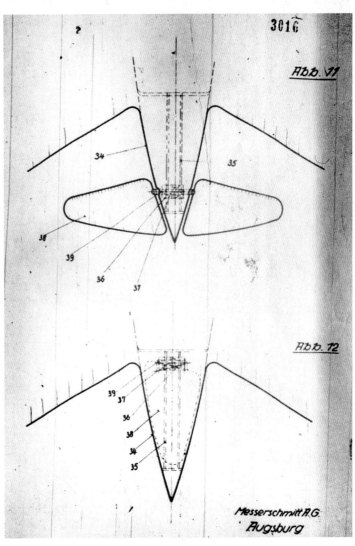

ABOVE: The formal submission of Lippisch's idea for pop-out canards.

ABOVE: Patent drawing showing the mechanism employed by Lippisch for his flip-out tail planes.

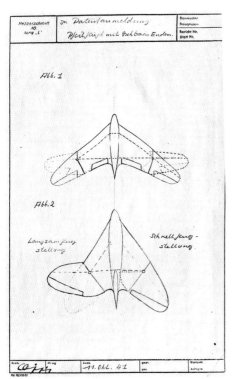

ABOVE: Lippisch's patent drawing of October 11, 1941, for a tailless swept wing aircraft with rotatable wingtips. The tips would be swivelled forwards for low speed flight, then swivelled back for a sharply swept form at high speed.

wings of a tailless aircraft, the third is a set of pop-out canards at the front of the aircraft and the fourth is a set of tailplanes that slide horizontally out of the aircraft's fuselage rather than from the fin. All were intended to achieve the same effect.

The third and last known patent from this fertile interlude in Lippisch's career has the title 'Pfeilflügel mit drehbaren Enden' or 'Swept wings with rotatable ends'. Unlike the other two patents, it is unknown whether this one was actually filed by Messerschmitt. The only known copy comes from Lippisch's own collection of papers and is both handwritten and signed by him.

The description says: "The sensitivity of the wingtips of a swept wing is based on the fact that the slipstream flows outwards and the boundary layer is accumulated on the outer wing. As a result, the swept wing has the property of tilting at maximum lift. The idea of the invention eliminates this property in that e.g. when taking off and landing the wing ends are pivoted forward about a substantially vertical axis, so that these wing sections are approximately perpendicular to the direction of flight.

"The build-up of air coming from the inner wing will then flow backwards at the bend, so that the flow on the outer wing remains healthy. The axis can be placed by slight inclination to the flight level so that rotation simultaneously generates a small

pitch change in the sense of a twisting of the outer wing.

"The rotation of the outer wings can also be used during the flight for trimming. The outer wings carry the ailerons, which can serve as rudders at the same time. The control cable goes through the axis of rotation. In a known manner also slats can be attached to the outer wing. In particular, the inventive concept is suitable for high-speed aircraft with a very strong arrow shape.

"With these aircraft, which have a very high speed range, it is necessary to achieve the high-speed flight by nose-heavy trimming and the slow flight by tail-heavy trimming. The forward pivoting of the outer wing provides besides the tipping safety the desired trim change for slow and fast flight."

In short, the large outer sections of the aircraft's wings could be rotated to provide straight leading edges and therefore additional lift for takeoffs and landings and when flying slowly. Perhaps the Messerschmitt company felt that this was the least plausible of Lippisch's three radical proposals for improving the performance of tailless aircraft at low speeds and therefore left it out when putting forward the latest round of patent applications.

The idea deemed most likely to succeed appears to have been the retractable canards, since wind tunnel models with this arrangement were tested by Junkers later in the war. ●

Messerschmitt W-wing concept

Artwork by Luca Landino

COMMENTS

Alexander Lippisch's patents of October/
November 1941 show a range of unusual
ideas for improving the low speed
handling characteristics of tailless aircraft
in general but several of the illustrations
he offers by way of explanation have a
familiar look to them. Just as the pop-
out canard concept was tested using a
modified model of the Me 163 B, it would
make sense for the same basic fuselage
to be used in testing Lippisch's W-wing
arrangement – which is how the design is
portrayed here.

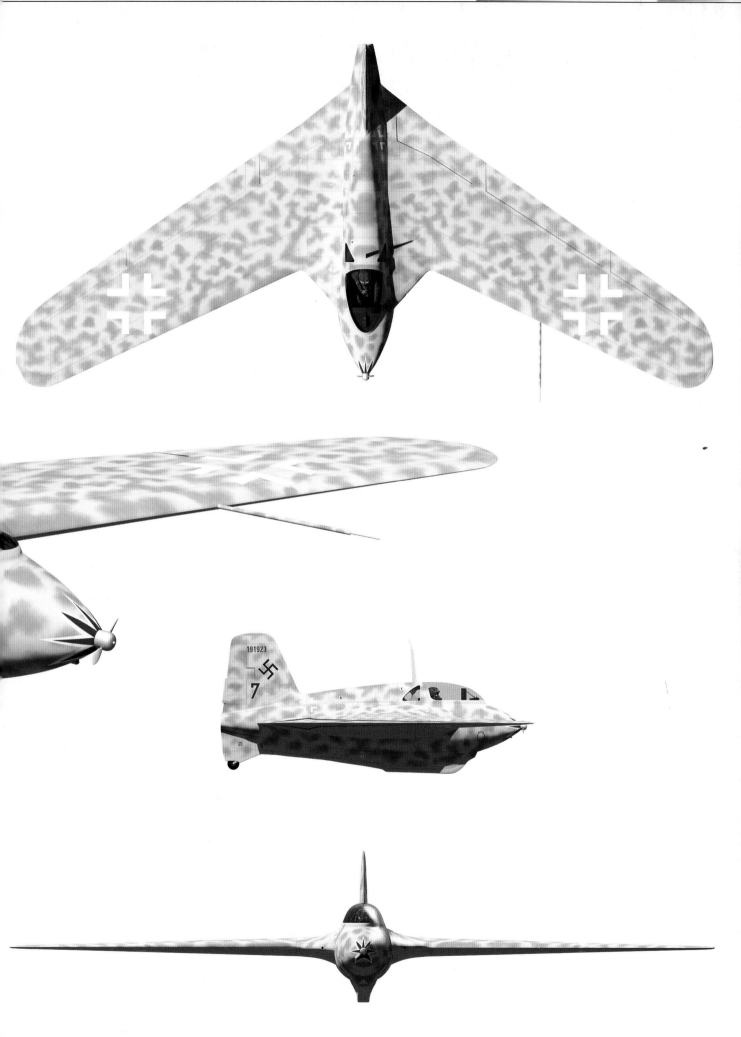

Speed racer

Messerschmitt Me 262 with delta wing

Work on testing the Me 262 as a fighter was all but complete by March 1944 so Messerschmitt decided to modify it for high speed research too. A huge number of different configurations were considered – among them the delta wing form.

During a meeting held on January 5, 1944, Willy Messerschmitt proposed that his company should design and develop a new twin-jet aircraft to explore the potential for flight near the speed of sound and on January 31 the designer of the Me 328, Rudolf Seitz, was appointed to oversee the project.

Theoretical work was carried out during February comparing the potential performance of the 'Höchstgeschwindigkeiten Me 262' when fitted with Jumo 004 C or HeS 011 engines and models were designed for a programme by aerodynamics tests by the DFS. Though based on the Me 262, the test vehicle was to be an

almost completely new aircraft. On February 17, 1944, a drawing was produced showing an Me 262 fuselage with completely new short, sharply swept wings of very thick chord – effectively a notched delta wing. The engines remained in their original positions.

A meeting was held on February 25 and Seitz proposed developing the existing Me 262 rather than beginning with the test vehicle originally proposed. Willy Messerschmitt approved this idea and also approved static tests on an Me 262 airframe. Seitz's project diary then offers a blow-by-blow account of the progress made.

The company's construction office for tails

– Kobü-Leitwerk – started preliminary work on a swept tailplane on March 10. Four days later, Messerschmitt was presented with a schedule for progress on the project. Step one would involved wider chord inner wings, swept tail and streamlined 'rennkabine' cockpit canopy.

BELOW : This detail from a drawing dated February 17, 1944, shows an Me 262 fuselage and tail with a notched delta wing. The engines appear to be installed in exactly the same position, relative to the fuselage, as those of the standard Me 262. The overall drawing is much larger but only shows a larger view of the same wing arrangement.

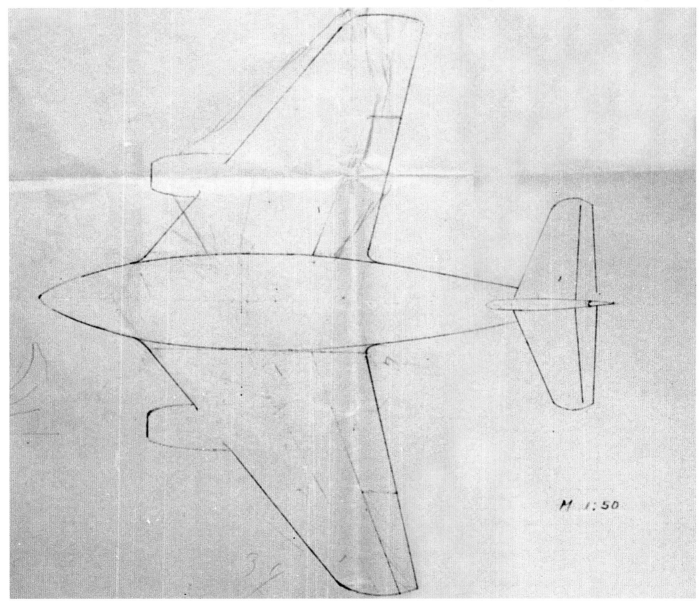

M 1:50

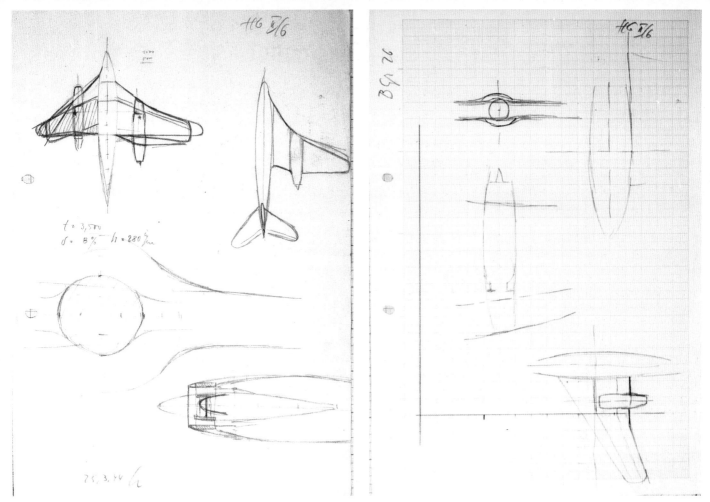

ABOVE: Two pages of sketches from March 25, 1944, showing potential options for delta or other wing forms on future developments of the Me 262 HG series. The note at the top right of each page 'HG II/6' appears to have been added later in a different hand.

Step two involved wider chord outer wings, improved engine nacelles and reprofiled fuselage. Step three was new wings with built-in engines.

Only the first of these steps was reasonably well defined by this point – the other two steps existed primarily as concepts. It is unclear whether the three steps became known as the Me 262 HG I, II and III immediately or whether these designations were applied later.

Kobü-Leitwerk and the construction office for wings, Kobü-Tragwerk, received project documents for the swept tail and wider chord wings respectively on March 17. Head office for wings, Stabü-Tragwerk, began working on the calculations for the aircraft's inner wings the following day.

Kobü-Rumpf, the fuselage office, began work on the 'rennkabine' on March 20, based on sketches provided by the design department. The next eight days were spent preparing project documents for the modified fuselage and inner wings.

During this time, a number of sketches were made showing possible layouts for the wings of the second and third stages of development. Two pages of designs from March

25, 1944, show variations on the earlier thick wing but this time also include some designs for wings with built-in engines. Two days later, Willy Messerschmitt himself drew a sketch showing how the Me 262's engines could be repositioned to the trailing edge of the wing.

On March 31, Kobü-Rumpf reported that it would be possible to lower the height of the Me 262's cockpit structure by 150mm, allowing a corresponding lowering of the canopy. Work on the inner wings was halted on April 1 and the staff responsible were switched to carrying out urgent work on the Me 109 K instead, as were the staff of Kobü-Leitwerk.

April 3, 1944, saw a report being written on the preparations already under way entitled 'Me 262 Projektübergabe V (Hochgeschwindigkeitsentwicklung)' or 'Me 262 Project Delivery V (High-speed development)' – even though only two men were now working on the '262 HG' including Seitz. This began: "The changes currently mentioned in Project Delivery V relate exclusively to measures that are to be carried out and tested on a Me 262 airframe to improve the performance.

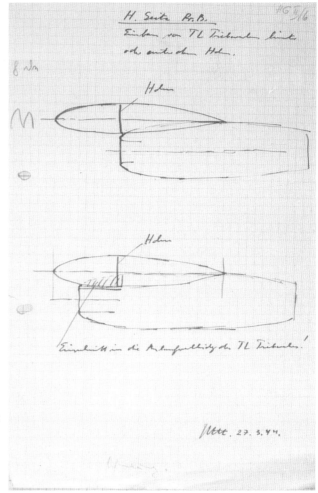

RIGHT: Sketch of March 27, 1944, signed by Willy Messerschmitt and addressed to Herr Seitz, which shows how the HG series could have its engines set back beneath the trailing edge of its wings.

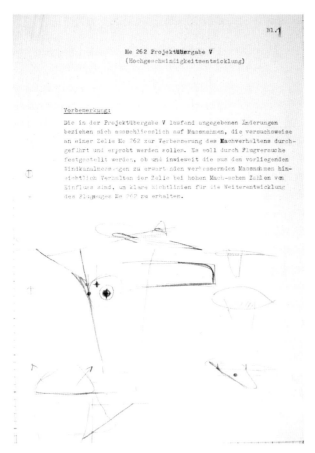
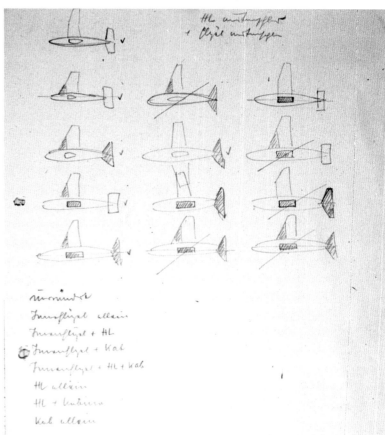

ABOVE: Two pages from the April 3, 1944, draft report showing numerous different potential wing, engine and tail arrangements for future HG series models.

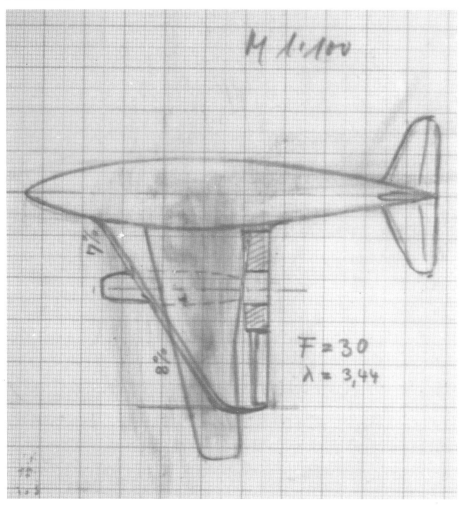

ABOVE: This sketch, apparently produced during the first few days of April 1944, shows both a delta wing and swept wing form. Beyond this point the delta would be dropped in favour of the slender swept wing form.

"It is to be determined through flight tests whether and to what extent the improvement measures to be expected from the present wind tunnel measurements are influential with respect to behaviour of the airframe at high Mach numbers in order to obtain clear guidelines for the further development of the aircraft Me 262."

There were three changes to be made: "The inner wing is deepened by attaching a new nosepiece while retaining the wing piece behind the main spar", the tailplane was to be swept back by 40° and the tail fin deepened, and "in order to improve the Mach behaviour of the cabin, its structure is to be reduced to the lowest possible level". There were three stipulations for the latter – the pilot had to be able to open the canopy while in flight, the cockpit seat had to be height adjustable so that the pilot could raise himself up to the position he had in the unmodified Me 262, and a hinged windscreen had to be positioned in front of the pilot.

It was expected that these three changes, which for safety's sake would be made without worrying about adding extra weight, would "shift the critical Mach number of the entire airframe to about 0.83. Furthermore, all three changes would be made at once "and then the improvements are gradually reversed" so it would be possible to work out what worked and what didn't by a process of elimination.

Appended to this report were several pages of sketches showing further alternative layouts for future Me 262 HG wing configurations. One page shows 13 different arrangements of different wings, tails and cockpits – among them a number of them with near-triangular delta wings.

Another undated drawing, apparently produced around this time, shows an Me 262

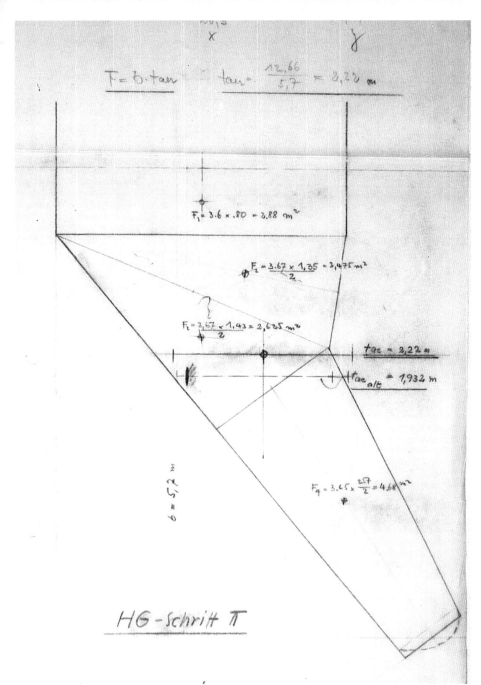

$F = b \cdot \tan \quad \tan = \frac{12,66}{5,7} = 8,22 \text{ m}$

$X \qquad Y$

$F_1 = 3.6 \times .80 = 2.88 \text{ m}^2$

$F_2 = \frac{3.67 \times 1.35}{2} = 2.475 \text{ m}^2$

$F_3 = \frac{3.67 \times 1.43}{2} = 2.625 \text{ m}^2$

$t_{ac} = 8,22 \text{ m}$

$t_{ac \, alt} = 1,932$

$b = 5,2 \text{ m}$

$F_4 = 3.65 \times \frac{257}{2} = 4.68 \text{ m}^2$

HG-Schritt II

ABOVE: Numerous different swept wing forms appear in the Me 262 HG files after April 6, 1944, indicating that although the company had not yet firmly decided on the wing shape of the HG II and III the delta was no longer under consideration.

fuselage and wing arrangement similar to that shown in the February 17 drawing but this time with a sharply swept leading edge and a straight trailing edge – the delta form – but overlaid with a more complex swept wing form.

One again, on April 5 the 262 HG group was reduced to just two men – Seitz and his colleague Brutscher. April 6 saw another series of drawings produced showing complex swept wing designs. The delta wing now disappears from the HG project records and does not seem to have been reconsidered.

The HG project continued throughout the remainder of 1944, with the designs for the HG I, II and III becoming more concrete as time went on. The three were more or less firmly decided by September. In ADI(K) Report No. 1/1946, dated January 7, 1946, an account is given of Woldemar Voigt's interrogation in which he discusses the Me 262 HG series. The Me 262 HG II "was to be a high speed version of the Me 262. It had the same fuselage as the Me 262, the same wing (or same main parts of the wing), and the same kind of power plant installation. Wing and horizontal tail surface were arranged to have a large sweep back angle. The prototype was completed, but it was destroyed by some other aircraft crashing into it.

"The HG III was similar to the HG II but with a sweep back of 45°. The power plant was installed in the wing roots aft of the main spar, and faired into wing and fuselage. The air intakes were in the wing root leading edge with ducts to the engine. The calculated speed of this machine was 1000km/h. A wind tunnel model was completed, but it was lost and destroyed during the occupation of Oberammergau."

A speculative design drawn up in modern times may be found elsewhere showing an Me 262 with a delta wing and a rear-set cockpit similar to that of the P 1106 single-jet fighter. While such a cockpit arrangement does not seem to have been considered for the 262, the delta wing actually was – although its appearance in the HG project's design files is relatively fleeting and the concept seems to have been dismissed after little more than a month. ●

BELOW: AVA wind tunnel model of the ultimate Me 262 development – the HG III. After the delta wing designs were dropped, efforts were concentrated on sharply swept wings and burying the engines in the wing roots.

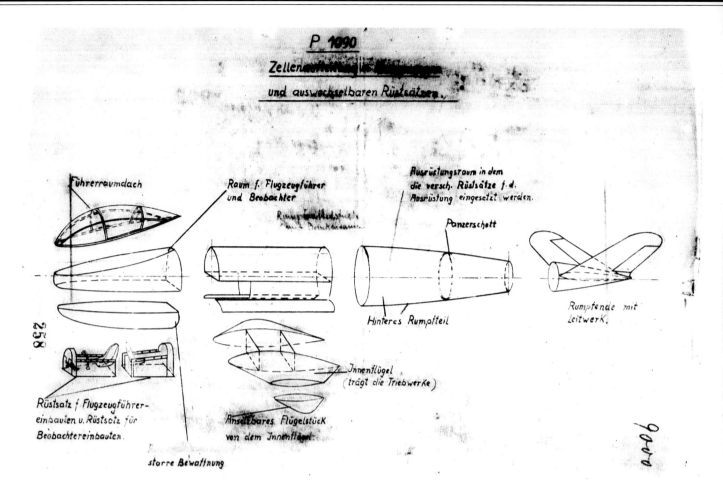

One last stab at Dornier

Messerschmitt P 1090

During the autumn of 1942 Willy Messerschmitt came to believe that the way forward for aircraft design was modular – mixing and matching standardised components to create aircraft for different tasks. While the idea was dealt a serious blow by Dornier's P 231 in January 1943, Messerschmitt persisted into February with another new modular project – the P 1090.

The Messerschmitt entry for the Schnellstbomber competition – the Me 109 Z – was an expression of Willy Messerschmitt's latest design obsession.

He saw a need to make the best possible use of Germany's limited manufacturing capacity by dramatically reducing the number of different aircraft types in production, instead creating new types by combining existing components in new ways.

For example, why build separate and incompatible day fighters, night fighters, fast bombers, torpedo bombers and reconnaissance aircraft when all of them could be built around the same proven fuselage, a selection of just three engines and a standard set of wings? The required aircraft could be made a single seater or two seater with the addition of a fuselage insert, longer wings could be fitted for high-altitude operations and a pair of fuselages

could even be combined in parallel to create a set of twin-engine aircraft.

This approach was outlined in an undated and untitled draft document. It outlined the aircraft shortages facing German and pointed to the fact that 53 different and incompatible aircraft types were in production at that time. It then suggests combining just a few standard Messerschmitt components to create 32 different modular aircraft patterns, 21 of which involve double fuselages.

The Me 109 Z, known initially as the Me 109 Zw or Zwilling 'Twin', was an attempt to create a twin-engine fast bomber almost entirely out of existing Me 109 components – thereby preventing any significant disruption to production lines and dramatically reducing the usual development time. Yet despite the simplicity of its design and the ease with which it could have been built, it was defeated

ABOVE: Messerschmitt's modular P 1090 design. Its stated aim was to replace most other German twin-engine aircraft types then in production – but in reality it was a swipe at Dornier's Do 335, which had just defeated the Me 109 Z in the Schnellstbomber competition.

by Dornier's P 231 – soon to be the Do 335 – at the Schellstbomber designs presentation meeting on January 19, 1943.

Nevertheless just 18 days later, on February 6, Messerschmitt tried again with a slightly different slant on the modular idea in a document entitled Denkschrift ueber die Vereinheitlichung der zur Fertigung zusulassenden Flugzeug-Frontmuster or 'Memorandum on the standardisation of the front-pattern aircraft to be added for production'.

The document begins by examining the options for creating generic single and twin-engine aircraft using various existing Messerschmitt components, then goes into more detail on the twin engine designs.

It says: "As an example of the feasibility of this unification of the warplanes, the basic 'twin-engine two-seater aircraft' has been singled out and examined in series as the Me 410, as well as the project P 1090, which was already designed under these provisions, then examined in detail in the following paper. Further investigation of how far the Me 109 can be used in the twin fuselage arrangement as a basic pattern for the twin-engine aircraft is not yet completed."

The P 1090 itself was loosely based on project work already carried out around the Me 210/410, such as fitting it with a V-tail, and its modular nature was supposed to allow it to be configured for a wide variety of roles including night fighter, ground-attack, single seat and two-seat heavy fighter, high altitude fighter, fast bomber, three-seat bomber, torpedo bomber and reconnaissance aircraft. For most of these roles it would be powered by a pair of Daimler-Benz DB 603 G piston engines – the engines favoured for the Schnellstbomber – but for the high-altitude fighter it would use two DB 628s. Future development, it was suggested, would allow it to become a twin-jet aircraft with Jumo 004s capable of being altered to suit the same wide variety of roles.

The P 1090's construction description explicitly states that its performance will be "approximately equal to the twin-hull aircraft (e.g., Me 109 Z with DB 603G) and the single-fuselage aircraft with the two engines in the fuselage" but with the added advantages of "better visibility for the crew and good usability as a basic starting pattern for many aircraft variations with different military tasks".

It was to have a wing area of 28m^2 that could be expanded to 31m^2 or 36m^2 through the use of inserts if necessary and the fuselage was made up of compatible components which could be swapped to provide single seat or two-seat options, with the former providing an additional fuel tank in place of the second seat. Inside the fuselage there was space for two

armoured fuel tanks and a bomb bay capable of holding a 500kg bomb load.

The V-tail could also be enlarged with inserts and the main landing gear consisted of double wheels retracting backwards into the engine nacelles. In addition "for higher flight weight interchangeability with larger wheels is taken into account".

As a two-seat night fighter the P 1090 would have two DB 603 Gs, four fixed forward-firing MK 108s and two upwards firing MK 108s with limited adjustment possible, 250kg of armour protection for the crew and two fuel tanks with 1400 litres and 800 litres. Equipment was Fu G 16 ZE, Fu G 10 KK and Fu G 25 a plus night fighter equipment. Maximum takeoff weight was 11 tons. Wing area was 36m^2.

As a two-seat ground attack aircraft, the P 1090 would have the same engines and basic equipment but the two fuel tanks would only contain 1400 litres between them. Fixed forward armament was four MK 108s and two MK 103s plus "4-5 Giesskannen". The Giesskanne was an external gun pod containing six MG 81s linked in pairs. Fixed rearward firing were two MG 151s and bombs could be carried under the wings in place of the 'Giesskannen', or 500kg of bombs could be carried internally.

Crew and engine armour amounted to 450kg and overall maximum starting weight was 11 tons. Wing area was 31m^2.

The two-seat or single seat heavy fighter version had the same engines and equipment, except for a Fu G 26a in place of the 25a. Fuel tankage was the same as the ground attack version, except with the option of an additional tank if fitted out for single seat operation, while forward and rearward armament was also the same except with the option of carrying two MK 103s or four MK 108s as a forward-firing gun pack in place of the bomb bay.

If the belly pack wasn't fitted, the bomb bay could be retained to carry a single 500kg bomb, two 250kg bombs or containers for fragmentation bombs. Armour was 250kg. Max takeoff weight was the same but wing area was just 28m^2.

In addition to its two DB 628s, the single-

seat high-altitude fighter P 1090 would be equipped with a Fu G 16 ZB and Fu G 25a. The two fuel tanks contained the usual 1400 litres but another tank could also be fitted in the bomb bay. Forward-firing weaponry was four MK 108s and rearward one MG 151. Armour was 250kg and overall weight remained 11 tons. As a single or two-seat fast bomber, armament was stripped back to just one forward-firing and one rearward-firing MG 151. Internal bomb load remained 500kg but heavier loads were 'possible', as were external fuel tanks. Wing area was 28m^2.

Other potential uses for the piston-engined P 1090 included high altitude fast bomber, torpedo bomber and reconnaissance aircraft.

A more extreme conversion saw the P 1090 become a three-seater medium bomber. The engines would be "two piston engines with up to 2000 PS", fuel tankage was 1400 litres with the possibility of external tanks or putting a tank in the bomb bay. The bomb load of up to four 500kg bombs could be carried on four wing hard points. There would be upper and lower defensive turrets each mounting an MG 151 Z and a single forward-firing MK 108. Overall weight was 14 tons with a wing area of 36m^2.

Another conversion would see the P 1090 become a single seat light jet fighter or two-seat heavy fighter with a pair of Jumo 004s. Three fuselage fuel tanks would carry a total of 2000 litres or 2500 litres in 'heavy' form and forward-firing armament was four MK 108s and two MK 103s. The jet version could also become a fighter-bomber, long-range reconnaissance aircraft, ground-attack aircraft, high altitude fighter, night fighter or torpedo bomber with various alterations of armament and wing area.

It would appear that the P 1090 went no further than this technical description, since the Do 335 had already been chosen as the Luftwaffe's new twin-engine fast bomber. In addition, there appears to have been insufficient support for Messerschmitt's grand plan of standardisation – which would have meant a dramatic re-ordering of Germany's aircraft industry from top to bottom. He seems to have dropped the concept at this point. ●

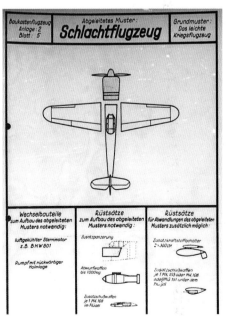
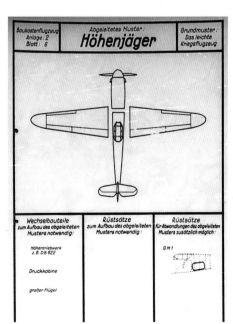
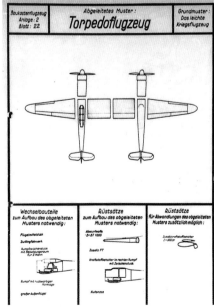

ABOVE: Three examples of modular aircraft designs from a 1942 Messerschmitt report. The BMW 801-powered attack aircraft becomes a high-altitude fighter with the addition of longer wings, a DB 622 engine and some new equipment. Or it can become a torpedo bomber with the addition of a fuselage insert, a second fuselage, longer wings, intermediate wing sections and various other alterations.

The test subject

Messerschmitt P 01-114 / Me 263

The legacy of the infamous Messerschmitt Me 163 B rocket-powered interceptor has long since overshadowed that of its experimental forebear, the Me 163 A, but in 1941, the type's designer Alexander Lippisch thought that the direct successor to the experimental Me 163 (only to become the Me 163 A when the Me 163 B arrived) would be the equally experimental Me 263...

When Lippisch and his team from the DFS arrived at Messerschmitt on January 2, 1939, and became Abteilung L or 'Department L' their first tasks were to rework their drawings of 'Project X' – what would become the Me 163 – convert the DFS 194 into a rocket-powered test vehicle and design a single engined jet fighter under the designation P 01.

Messerschmitt received the jet fighter specification from the RLM on January 4 and Lippisch began by mapping out nine concepts for different engines, weapons and other features – numbering these P 01-111 to P 01-119. Having done this, he decided to start with his concept for P 01-116.

Drawn up on April 12 and 13, 1939, the tiny P 01-116 had a 5.48m long cylindrical fuselage

and thick-chord near-rectangular wings with a span of 6m. Work on the P 01 seems to have stalled here while Abteilung L worked on an Me 210 alternative called the P 04, readied the DFS 194 for its rocket engine and engaged in other work for the company.

When work finally recommenced on the P 01, Lippisch went back to the beginning of the sequence and the P 01-111 was designed in November 1939. This was another single jet fighter though slightly larger than the P 01-116. And the P 01-112, of February 1940, was a twin jet competitor for the Messerschmitt P 65 (later Me 262) but with both engines built into its fuselage.

Work on P 01 stopped again at this point, with only three designs produced, and did not recommence until July 1940. Now two more designs joined the series: the P 01-113 was a

ABOVE: A 1:2.5 scale model of the Me 263 being tested by the AVA during the autumn of 1941.

mixed propulsion fighter with both turbojet and rocket propulsion and the P 01-114 was a rocket-propelled testbed for the aerodynamics of Lippisch's fighters. Here the sequence stopped again with five designs produced.

But the P 01-114 seems to have shown particular promise – more so than the other four P 01s – and Messerschmitt as a company decided to pursue its ongoing development.

First the P 01-114 drawing was finalised on July 19, 1940, and it was then made the subject of a full brochure, dated August 1940. The introduction to this states: "The type P 01-114 is a single-seat tailless aircraft which is used to test the design at very high speeds and high climb performances with respect to the patterns P 01-112 and 113. The structure perfectly corresponds to the wing provided for the heavily armed designs, while the fuselage was simplified with regard to easy and fast manufacture. The HWK engine, which is provided for the drive, permits a step-by-step test with different thrusts, so that the properties can be flown out at very high speeds."

The aircraft was also to embody a highly novel feature – variable geometry wings. The brochure states: "In order to make possible a far-reaching change in trimming around the lateral axis, there was provided, along with the arrangements used so far, a possibility to shift the centre of gravity while in flight, i.e. a change by shifting the wings.

"Thus the wing is shifted in the direction of flight in relation to the fuselage in such a way that the aircraft may be flown either at low speeds with the centre of gravity shifted backward and with large angle of attack at

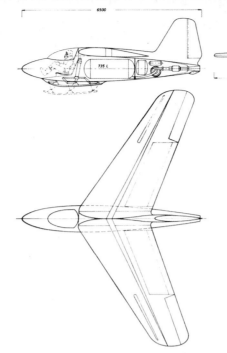
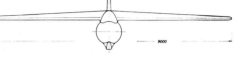

ABOVE: The original P 01-114 from July 19, 1940. This experimental design was the subject of a full brochure in August 1940.

the fuselage (landing) or at high speeds with a maximum shift forward of the centre of gravity and with a small angle of attack, at the fuselage (high speed flight).

"This arrangement, along with the sensitivity adjustment provided at the controls proper, permits far-reaching changes of the elevator sensitivity, thus making it possible to securely control the aircraft at very high speeds.

"The fuselage was constructed as a rotationally symmetrical body in order to provide simplest construction of parts that may be 'developed', thus very little machinery is needed to produce the fuselage shell. The cockpit is of pressure-tight construction. A standard landing gear was not deemed essential. An undercarriage that can be jettisoned is used for take-off; and a retractable skid and spur for landing. Experiments with a caterpillar landing gear are planned."

The P 01-114 was to be experimental in many respects – from its tilting wings, which would be jacked up at the front for landing and lowered back down for high speed, to its caterpillar landing gear. Even a pressurised cockpit in such a small aircraft would be unusual in 1940.

A little more detail is given on the landing gear later in the brochure: "The aircraft is not equipped with a landing gear of standard construction, since the big wheels do not permit economic utilisation of space and since there are no means available in the power plant to operate the retracting mechanism. For these reasons, and anticipating landings outside of an aerodrome involving the danger of turning over, a central spring type caterpillar skid, retractable by hand, was installed.

"The caterpillar track link has a braking gear and thus locomotion on the ground is made possible. A retractable skid is located beneath the vertical fin."

It is unclear what this caterpillar track skid would have looked like since no drawings of it are known to survive.

With regard to the control surfaces: "Elevator and aileron are combined, as is customary in tailless aircraft, and are located at the trailing edge of the outer wing. The vertical control surfaces are located in the middle and in the rear of the fuselage, and are detachable. The control system is standard, manual control for operating elevator and aileron had been installed. Deflection of stick and control surfaces is

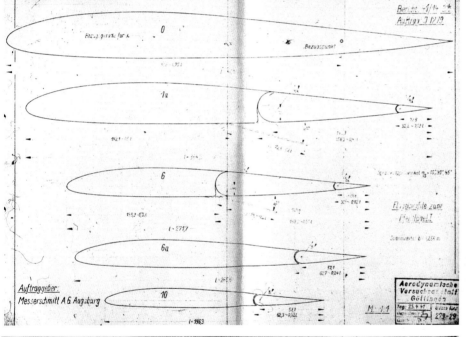
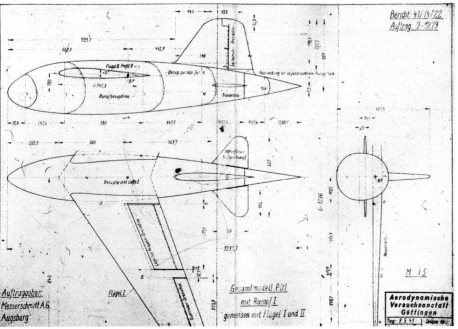

ABOVE LEFT: Wing profiles for the P 01 as tested by the AVA on April 25, 1941.
LEFT: Early model of the Messerschmitt P 01 from May 9, 1941. The fuselage is the basic 'Rumpf I' and the swept wings are 'Flügel I'.

LEFT: A sequence of photos from an AVA report on wind tunnel testing the P 01 from May 1941. The model is made up of the teardrop-shaped 'Rumpf I' and the 'Flügel I' wings.

variable by reduction gearing through a multistage switch. Foot control is adjustable, built to function as pedal control."

The P 01-114's rocket motor was to be somewhat experimental in nature: "As propulsion unit an HWK jet unit is used, proportioned in such a way that by minor substitutions of certain parts, thrusts of 750kg to 3000kg can be attained. There is no separate engine mounting; the parts are attached to the walls of the fuselage and bulkheads.

"For an engine casing the stern of the fuselage is utilised, where hand-holes are provided for servicing and maintenance. Regulation of the engine is effected by a standard throttle lever. There is no starter, instead a compressed air bottle and valve are provided."

The 735 litre fuel tank was elastically mounted behind the pressure cabin and "in order to avoid high temperatures in the stressed skin of the fuselage air-cooling gills are inserted into the side of the stern of the fuselage. Circulation is effected by a circular slot around the jet nozzle (suction). The exhaust of the turbo pump is located at the lower side of the stern of the fuselage. The pilot will not be inconvenienced by exhaust gas because the cockpit is pressure tight".

At this stage, the P 01-114 measured 6.5m long with a wingspan of 9m. It's single piece wing structure was mounted on the top of the fuselage to facilitate the mechanism which would allow the wings to tilt up and down.

In his book Ein Dreieck Fliegt, published posthumously in 1976, Lippisch states that the P 01-114 was exactly identical to the P 01-113 "except that it was equipped with a rocket engine". The August 1940 brochure suggests that this is not true. He then states: "After a lapse of almost a year which was filled with intensive work on the DFS 194 and the Me 163, we renewed our project design work. In the spring of 1941 we conceived a version of the Me 163 with greatly improved aerodynamic properties, the P 03-Me 263. This project was designed as a test aircraft for higher velocities. The angle of sweepback was 32.1° (compared to 23.4° of the Me 163). The wind tunnel model of this design was tested at the AVA in Göttingen and the measurements showed an extremely low friction coefficient). However, work on the project was stopped when the Me 163 passed the 1000km/h mark."

This was the P 01-114. By April 1941, the P 01-114 was being tested in the wind tunnels of the AVA at Göttingen, known simply as the 'P 01'. In May, a model was tested with wings set further forward than those of the original design, a lower fin and a small set of tailplanes. The near-cylindrical fuselage was labelled 'Rumpf I'. In June another model was tried with the same high wing layout and tailplanes but with a shorter nose and thinner chord wings. This one had 'Rumpf IIa'.

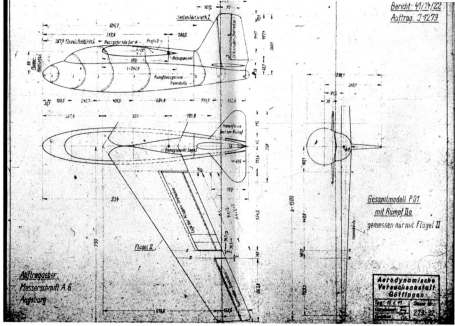

LEFT: Another drawing of an AVA wind tunnel model, this time composed of 'Rumpf IIa' and 'Flügel II'. It is dated June 13, 1941.

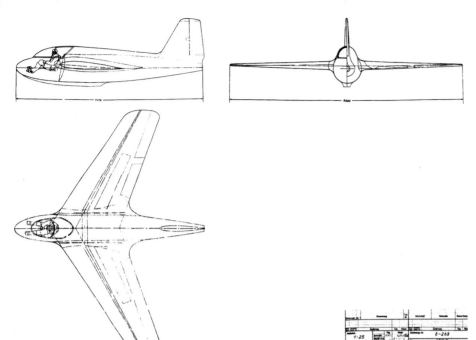

ABOVE: This drawing of the Messerschmitt 8-263, dated August 5, 1941, was inserted into year-old copies of the P 01-114 brochure, reflecting both the change in designation and the change in design.

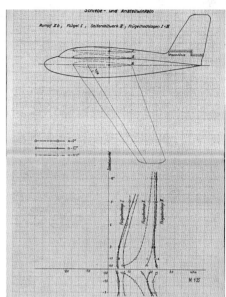

ABOVE: Undated AVA P 01 (Me 263) drawing showing 'Rumpf IIb', 'Flügel I', 'Seitenleitwerk II' (fin) and 'Flügelhochlagen I+III' (wing positions).

And in August 1941, a third model was tested with 'Rumpf IIb' and three different wing positions – the usual shoulder wing setting and two lower settings. The little tailplanes remained.

At some point between the commencement of the tests in April and July 7, 1941, what had been the P 01-114 was given the official RLM designation Me 263 and copies of the original P 01-114 report dated August 1940 had '263' retrospectively added to them. The original P 01-114 drawing was removed and a drawing of the '8-263' dated

August 5, 1941, was added. This aircraft was the contemporary 'Rumpf IIb' design with the mid-wing position and at 7.475m it was nearly a metre longer than the original.

As mentioned, Lippisch himself refers to this design as the P 03-Me 263, although the AVA reports go from being marked simply 'P 01' briefly to 'Me 263 (P 01)' then finally to 'Me 263' without P 03 appearing. The only known surviving evidence of the P 03 is a set of 12 handwritten sheets on graph paper in Lippisch's personal collection of papers at Iowa State University, which offer few clues

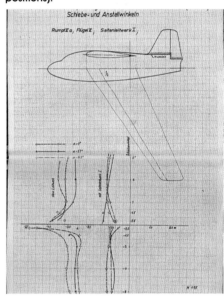

ABOVE: The stubbier 'Rumpf IIa' fitted with the lengthy 'Flügel II' wings and tail fin version I.

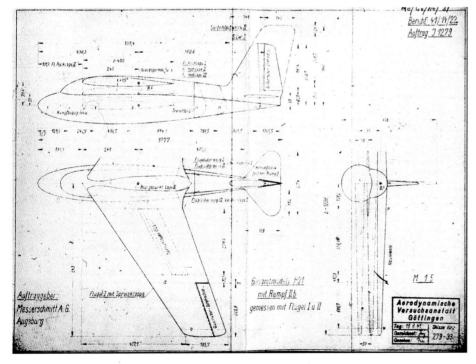

LEFT: AVA wind tunnel model of the P 01 now being referred to elsewhere as the P 01 (Me 263) or simply the Me 263, from August 19, 1941. This model has the definitive 'Rumpf IIb' fuselage and modified 'Flügel I' wings, though three different options are offered for their positioning. An alternative tail fin form is also ghosted in.

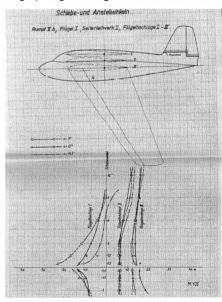

ABOVE: The ubiquitous 'Rumpf IIb' with 'Flügel I', 'Seitenleitwerk I' and 'Flügelhochlagen I+III' (wing positions).

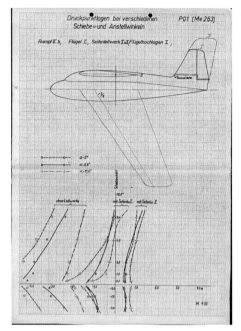

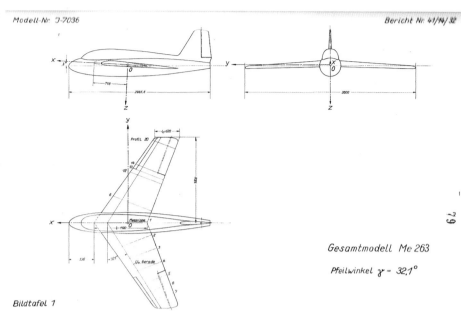

Gesamtmodell Me 263

Pfeilwinkel γ = 32,1°

Bildtafel 1

ABOVE: A three-view drawing of the Me 263 in its final form from the February 1942 report. The wings now have a slight anhedral.

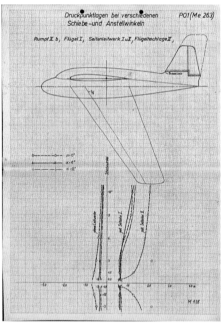

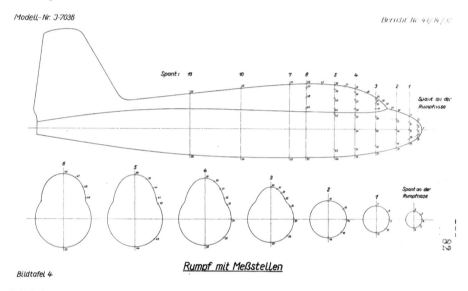

Rumpf mit Meßstellen

Bildtafel 4

ABOVE: Side view of the Me 263 fuselage from the February 1942 report.

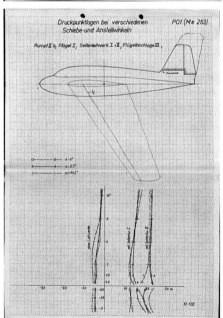

ABOVE: 'Rumpf IIb' again with 'Flügel I' and both fin versions. The wings are set high in position I, in the centre in position II and low in position III.

about the actual design. A very faint sketch on one sheet shows a design with tailplanes similar to those appearing on the AVA wind tunnel model drawings.

It is worth pointing out here too that the aircraft which eventually bore the designation Me 263 in 1944 – itself originally designated Ju 248 – was unrelated to the P 01-derived 1941 design.

On August 13, 1941, eight days after the '8-263' drawing was drafted, Heini Dittmar made the first powered flight in a Messerschmitt Me 163. The outcome of this and further tests seems to have been twofold – firstly it demonstrated to any doubters that the concept of a highly manoeuvrable rocket-powered aircraft was sound and an avenue worth pursuing. Secondly, the start of practical testing freed up Abteilung L's design staff to concentrate on whatever might come after the purely experimental Me 163.

Lippisch then seems to have turned his attention away from the Me 263 and on August 27, 1941, unveiled his first proposal for a military design based on Me 163 flight

experience – the armed P 05 Interceptor drafted by Rudolf Rentel. The P 05's fuselage was not dissimilar in length to that of the Me 263 but it was deeper and the aircraft had a wingspan of 12.8m compared to the 263's 9m.

Messerschmitt's main projects office, which operated in parallel to Abteilung L, now proposed the P 1079 fighter as a rival to the P 05 and Lippisch began to insist that the Me 163 be called the 'Li 163' instead, since he was its designer rather than Willy Messerschmitt. Messerschmitt himself opposed this change in designation and the relationship between the two men began to sour. A rift opened which would ultimately see Lippisch leaving the company in 1943.

During September 1941, however, the P 05 Interceptor project appears to have been split in two. The big rocket interceptor was replaced by succession of large long-range jet fighters and by a much smaller short-range rocket interceptor which Lippisch called the Li 163 S, the 'S' standing for 'series production'. The first drawing of the Li 163 S was dated September 14, 1941. Between then

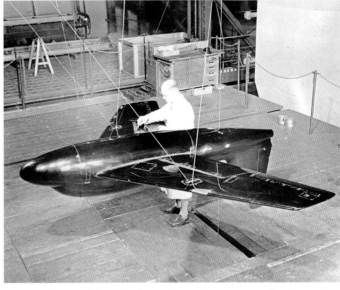

RIGHT, ABOVE & BELOW: The large Me 263 model is readied for tests at the AVA.

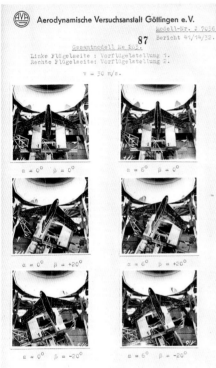

ABOVE & BELOW : Views of the Me 263 model in the AVA wind tunnel from the February 1942 report.

and the end of October, the Me 163 B was designed. And in the meantime, on October 2, 1941, Heini Dittmar became the first man to fly faster than 1000km/h in the Me 163.

Yet while all this was going on, work continued on the Me 263's aerodynamic form at the AVA. A report published on February 28, 1942, shows a 1:2.5 scale model of the design undergoing wind tunnel tests at the AVA.

It is uncertain whether the AVA continued to carry out testing on the

Me 263 beyond this point but the work they had done appears to have been highly regarded and influential. In a bundle of notes on flying wing design from Arado's projects office is a graph dated December 13, 1944, which shows details of the P 01's aerodynamics with 'Flügel I' being studied. Lippisch himself thought enough of the design to include all the drawings from the February 1942 report in his posthumously published 1976 book Ein Dreieck Fliegt. ●

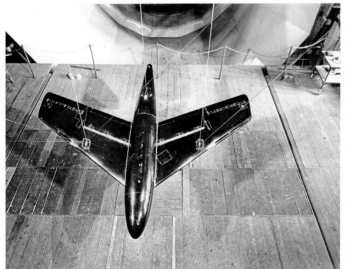

The piston-engined Me 163

Messerschmitt P 07

Lippisch never seems to have discussed his Messerschmitt P 07 design but recent discoveries provide a clearer picture of this mysterious piston-engined version of the 163.

The design sequence established by Abteilung L at Messerschmitt tended to follow a roughly chronological pattern – but with sufficient exceptions to cause real problems for anyone attempting to establish a timeline for the team's work.

P 01 is a case in point. As mentioned in the previous chapter, the P 01-XXX sequence begins counterintuitively with the P 01-116 in April 1939, progresses slowly to the P 01-111 in October 1939 and eventually ends with the P 01-119 in August 1941 but not before adding two more very different P 01-116s along the way.

P 02 is entirely unknown; P 03 appears to have been a stepping stone between the P 01-114 in August 1940 and the Me 263 in July 1941, P 04 initially runs from August to December 1939 but returns in a much refined form in May 1941. P 05 appears in August 1941 but P 06 appears to have preceded it by nine months, being outlined in January 1941. The P 08 dates from September 1941 and P 09 October 1941. P 010 was November 1941 and P 10 was May 1942. P 11 and P 12 were both September 1942 and P 13 – almost Lippisch's last design for Messerschmitt was November 1942.

It therefore makes very little sense that the three surviving drawings of the P 07 are dated November 20, 1942 (P 07-101), November 30, 1942 (P 07-102) and December 17, 1942 (P 07-103). The only explanation that makes any sense is Lippisch's habit of pre-planning designs. With the P 01, he mapped out nine concepts at the outset then worked through them non-sequentially.

By this logic, the P 07 concept could be dated back to somewhere between January and September 1941. In fact, it could be that when Lippisch designed the P 06, a piston-engined trainer version of the Me 163, he simultaneously envisioned a piston-engined fighter version to go alongside it – but then didn't get around to completing it as a project until more than two years later. Precisely why Lippisch revived the piston-engined Me 163 at this point is unclear, although the company was about to work on a turbojet version of the aircraft, the P 20 (see p100-103), so perhaps it was natural to also look at piston engine propulsion at this time.

The P 07-101 drawing shows an unarmed aircraft 6.8m long with a wingspan of 9.3m. The mainwheels of the tricycle undercarriage are 3.2m apart and the aircraft stands 3.3m tall. The aircraft's DB 601 engine is in its nose, with a nose-mounted radiator, driving a pusher prop to the rear via a long shaft which runs beneath the cockpit. P 07-102 shows a version of the aircraft that is 7.68m long with a wingspan of

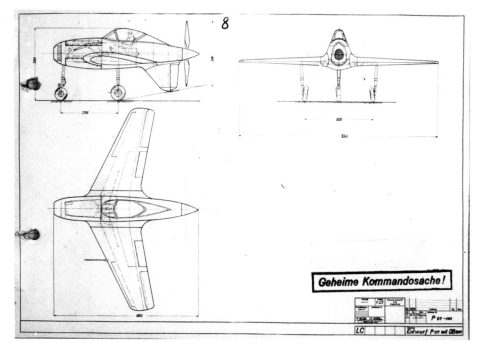

ABOVE: The Messerschmitt P 07-101, dated November 20, 1942. The aircraft was to be powered by a single DB 601 in the nose.

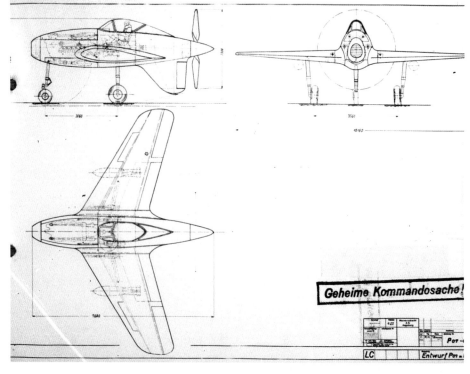

ABOVE: The DB 603-powered P 07-102 fighter-bomber, dated November 30, 1942.

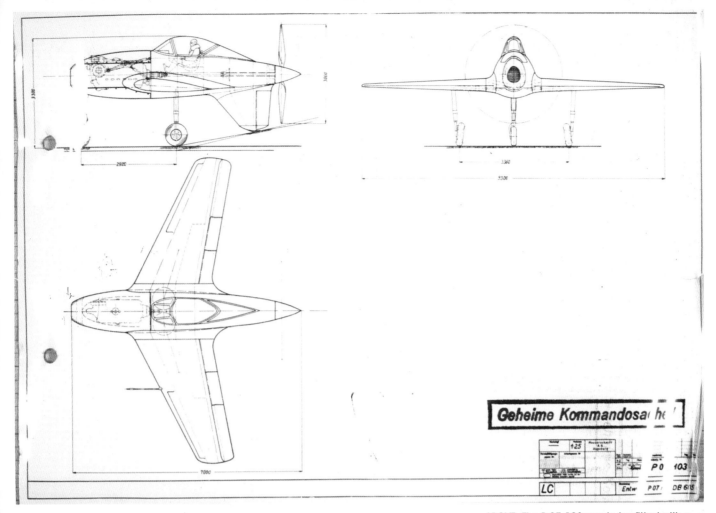

Geheime Kommandosache

P 0 103

LC | Entw | P 07 | DB 605

10.16m. Its mainwheels are 3.56m apart and it is 3.3m tall. The DB 603 engine is mounted in the same way as the DB 601 was in P 07-101 but this time two guns are fitted above it – possibly MG 131s or MG 151s. There are also two wing root cannon that appear shorter – perhaps MK 108s. What appears to be an SC250 bomb is attached to the underside of each wing outboard of the inwards-retracting undercarriage. It would seem that while P 07-101 depicts a trainer or experimental version of the design, P 07-102 is a fighter-bomber.

The DB 605-powered P 07-103 is similar to the P 07-101, measuring only slightly longer at 7m and with a slightly wider track undercarriage of 3.36m. Wingspan and height are the same at 9.3m and 3.3m respectively.

It has been suggested that the Messerschmitt P 07 and Me 334 are the same

thing and the evidence does seem to bear this out. Willy Messerschmitt wrote a note on February 19, 1943, which discusses the Me 334. It says: "I ask you to clarify in the office how the order of the 163 with Otto engines was intended. (Me 334). The new designs result in a completely new aircraft. Thus, the work will be a multiple of what was originally estimated. I can not answer for the work on this bird. I ask you to take steps in office to discuss the matter with Mr Seiler."

The timing appears to fit – the P 07 designs were worked on from November to December 1942. It would then take a short while to present them to the RLM and get them an official designation – in this case 8-334. Messerschmitt had previously been allocated 8-329 for another tailless project in September 1942 and Dornier would be allocated 8-335 in January 1943 so the sequencing seems about right.

ABOVE: The P 07-103 was to be fitted with a single DB 605 in its nose and was similar in its dimensions to the P 07-101. The drawing is dated December 17, 1942.

However, as Messerschmitt's note makes clear, conditions at the Messerschmitt company did not favour the P 07/Me 334 in February 1943. The simmering tension and antagonism between Messerschmitt and Lippisch was coming to a head and on March 26, 1943, Lippisch was told that his department Abteilung L was being dissolved. He resigned and left the company on April 28, 1943 – but not before Abteilung L had created yet another version of the Me 163 – this time powered by a single turbojet and designated the P 20, completing the piston engine/rocket motor/turbojet 163 propulsion trio. ●

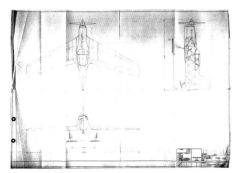

ABOVE: The piston-engined P 06 trainer of January 1941. The P 07 may have been conceived at around the same time but not formally drawn up until two years later.

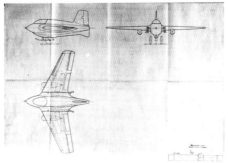

ABOVE: The classic Messerschmitt Me 163 B included here for comparison purposes. This particular drawing shows it fitted with booster rockets and extra fuel in under-wing drop tanks.

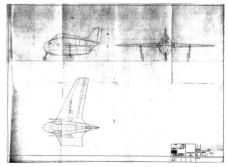

ABOVE: The P 20 was Lippisch's very last design while working at Messerschmitt. It is essentially a turbojet-powered version of the Me 163 and is included here so it can be compared against the other designs.

Messerschmitt P 07-102

December 1942

Artwork by Luca Landino

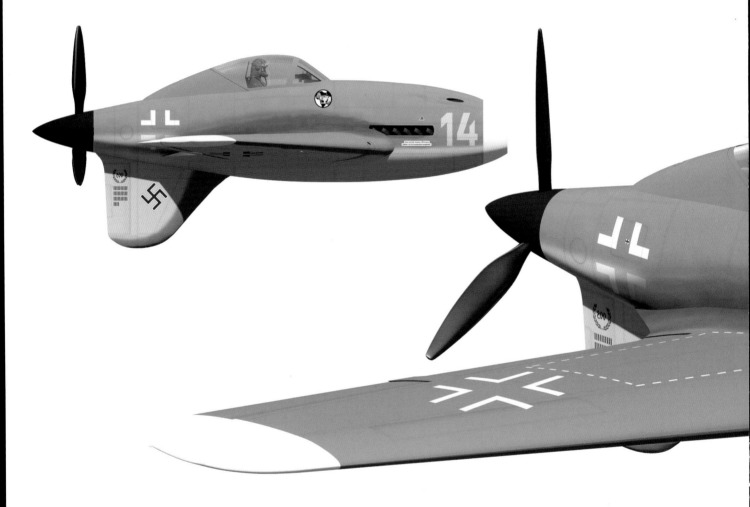

COMMENTS

The only armed version of the P 07 was the Daimler-Benz DB 603-powered design designated P 07-102. It is depicted here in the desert colours of JG 27's Bf 109s when serving in the Libyan desert during November 1942 – when the design was drafted. The P 07's big bubble canopy, short nose, swept wings and inverted tail fin would have combined to offer pilots an unrivalled view of their surroundings.

The ramjet Me 163

Lippisch P 12

The immediate predecessor to Alexander Lippisch's arrowhead-shaped ramjet-propelled P 13a rammer, the P 12, appears to have started out as yet another attempt to utilise the aerodynamics of the Me 163.

Upon leaving Messerschmitt in April 1943, designer Alexander Lippisch was put in charge of the Luftfahrt-forschungsanstalt Wien(LFW) or 'Aeronautical Research Institute Vienna' and focused his efforts on developing his twin-jet fast bomber – the P 11, aka Delta VI.

Work progressed slowly until he met with Reichsmarschall Hermann Goering on September 28, 1943, and secured half a million Reichsmarks to fund the type's development. However, as often seems to have happened, with the aircraft now approved for prototype construction Lippisch began to lose interest in it and switched his attention to what he saw as another promising field of research – this time ramjet propulsion.

In his memoir, Erinnerungen, he wrote: "Together with some competent thermodynamicists at the Vienna Institute, I succeeded in starting some basic work on the ramjet engine and also to carry out some fundamental and promising experiments. The engine, already invented by Lorin in 1912, but which can only operate economically at very high velocities, was moved into the interior of a thicker delta wing of small span, the jet emerging along the trailing edge being simultaneously used by appropriate deflection to control it.

"Such a combination is called a 'power wing'. The tests for the corresponding burners, which were originally to be operated with liquid fuel, later with solid

fuel (carbon dust or paraffin-impregnated brown coal), were carried out by Dr Schwabl in Vienna and by Dr Sänger at the DFS.

"In March 1944, a corresponding design was created for a piloted aircraft, P 12, which would be brought to the required initial speed using a Mistel combination (on the back of another aircraft) or with the aid of a launching sled with rocket

BELOW: The final form of the P 12 as sketched by its designer Alexander Lippisch for his Allied interrogators immediately after the Second World War. The drawing appears to show the aircraft looking flatter and more aerodynamically clean than wartime models and drawings show it to have been.
IOWA STATE UNIVERSITY LIBRARY SPECIAL COLLECTIONS AND UNIVERSITY ARCHIVE

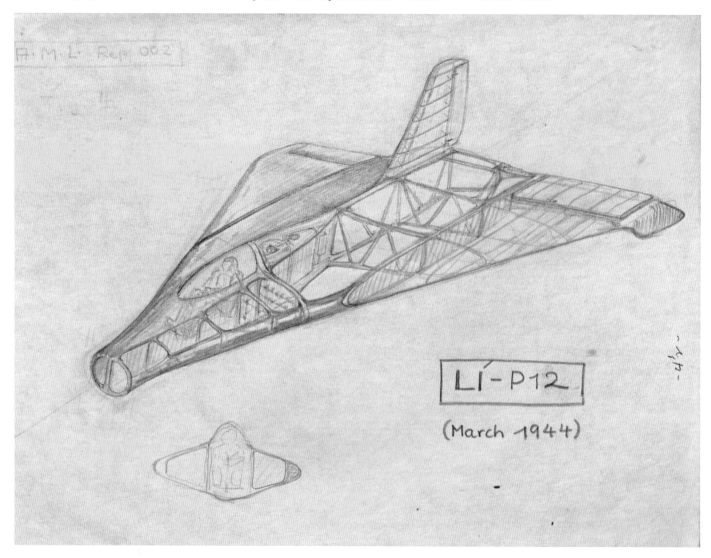

A·M·L· Rep 002

LI-P12

(March 1944)

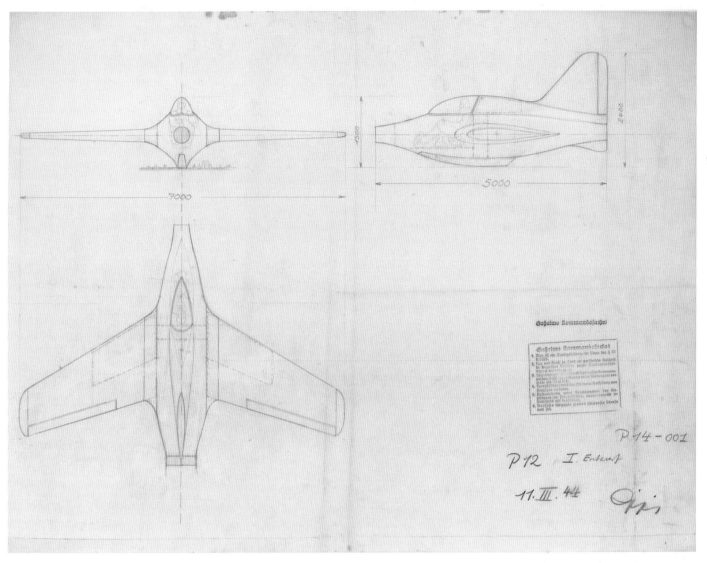

ABOVE: Lippisch's first attempt at designing a ramjet fighter – the P 12 I. Entwurf, dated March 11, 1944 – appears to have been based on the rough outline of the Me 163. Note the apparently circular exhaust nozzle. IOWA STATE UNIVERSITY LIBRARY SPECIAL COLLECTIONS AND UNIVERSITY ARCHIVE

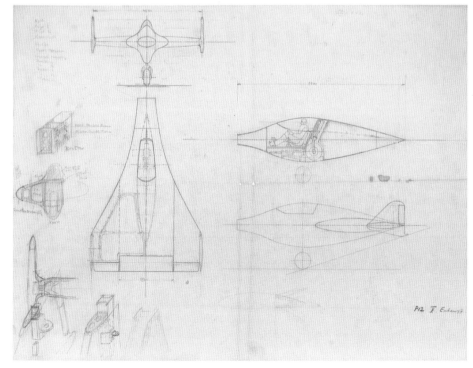

ABOVE: The P 12 II. Entwurf marks a radical departure in design from the I. Entwurf. However, it still has a split intake for its ramjet motor and the pilot, landing gear and armament are all crammed in together between the intake tubes.

IOWA STATE UNIVERSITY LIBRARY SPECIAL COLLECTIONS AND UNIVERSITY ARCHIVE

propulsion. After finding a more favourable form of the air intake, we had successfully let fly a corresponding model of the engine in May 1944 at the Spitzerberg in Vienna.

"This led to an improved draft, P 13, which was very much promoted by the Ministry of Defence."

Lippisch would go on to work on the P 13 until around late November 1944 when he renamed it the P 13a and switched his attention to another ramjet design which he called the P 13b. This lasted until February 1945 whereupon Lippisch switched back to working on turbojet designs.

So the P 13a lasted for around seven months, the P 13b less than four months and the P 12 less than three months – making the latter the shortest lived of the three. Yet as the inaugural part of the trilogy and Lippisch's first foray into the design of ramjet-powered aircraft it is perhaps the most interesting of all.

Until now, the exact design of the P 12 has been uncertain. Several photos of a P 12 model are well known - showing views from the front, top and rear. The model in question has a delta wing form with drooping tips similar to those later seen on the He 162. The cockpit is positioned centrally with the pilot sitting in the wing itself with a single swept tailfin directly

▶

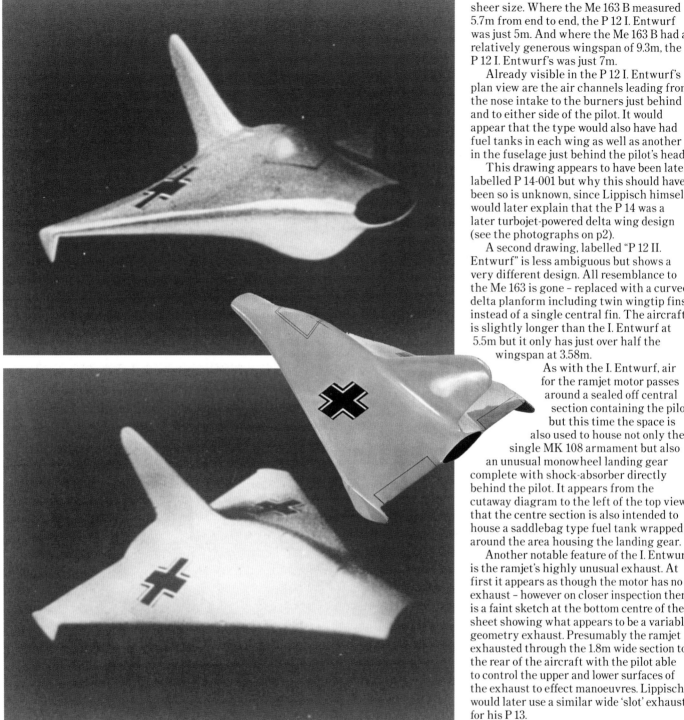

ABOVE: Three views of a wartime model of the P 12 in its final form. These images appeared in numerous Allied reports immediately after the war.

sheer size. Where the Me 163 B measured 5.7m from end to end, the P 12 I. Entwurf was just 5m. And where the Me 163 B had a relatively generous wingspan of 9.3m, the P 12 I. Entwurf's was just 7m.

Already visible in the P 12 I. Entwurf's plan view are the air channels leading from the nose intake to the burners just behind and to either side of the pilot. It would appear that the type would also have had fuel tanks in each wing as well as another in the fuselage just behind the pilot's head.

This drawing appears to have been later labelled P 14-001 but why this should have been so is unknown, since Lippisch himself would later explain that the P 14 was a later turbojet-powered delta wing design (see the photographs on p2).

A second drawing, labelled "P 12 II. Entwurf" is less ambiguous but shows a very different design. All resemblance to the Me 163 is gone – replaced with a curved delta planform including twin wingtip fins instead of a single central fin. The aircraft is slightly longer than the I. Entwurf at 5.5m but it only has just over half the wingspan at 3.58m.

As with the I. Entwurf, air for the ramjet motor passes around a sealed off central section containing the pilot but this time the space is also used to house not only the single MK 108 armament but also an unusual monowheel landing gear complete with shock-absorber directly behind the pilot. It appears from the cutaway diagram to the left of the top view that the centre section is also intended to house a saddlebag type fuel tank wrapped around the area housing the landing gear.

Another notable feature of the I. Entwurf is the ramjet's highly unusual exhaust. At first it appears as though the motor has no exhaust – however on closer inspection there is a faint sketch at the bottom centre of the sheet showing what appears to be a variable geometry exhaust. Presumably the ramjet exhausted through the 1.8m wide section to the rear of the aircraft with the pilot able to control the upper and lower surfaces of the exhaust to effect manoeuvres. Lippisch would later use a similar wide 'slot' exhaust for his P 13.

Neither of these two designs appears to be what Lippisch drew for his Allied interrogators in 1945, however. It must therefore be concluded that the P 12's final form before attention switched to the P 13 was what was previously speculated to be the 'Entwurf III'. Whether it was ever given that particular name, or whether there were further intermediate designs, may never be known.

The final design combines elements of both the I. Entwurf – the central fin and belly skid – and the II. Entwurf with its wingtip surfaces, delta planform and slot exhaust with controllable flap. However it also adds new design features such as the bifurcated nose intake and the reduction of the wingtip surfaces to what would later become known as 'Lippisch ears'.

The P 12 offers an interesting insight into Lippisch's design process. Despite

behind the bulge of his cockpit. At the front of the aircraft is a split oval-shaped intake and on its belly is another bulge presumably denoting a landing skid.

A postwar three-view drawing shows this same aircraft and after the war Lippisch himself sketched a flatter and more aerodynamically clean version of the design to show his Allied interrogators what the P 12 looked like. Confusingly, drawings later emerged showing what was evidently a wind tunnel model of the P 13 labelled 'P 12'. This led some to speculate that this was in fact the 'P 12 Entwurf I' or 'P 12 Draft I'. They further speculated that Lippisch's postwar sketch was the 'P 12 Entwurf II' and that the model from the photographs

represented the 'P 12 Entwurf III'.

However, drawings held as part of Alexander Lippisch's personal collection of papers at Iowa State University tell a different story. Some have speculated that Lippisch first created the P 12 in 1943 but a drawing labelled 'P 12 I. Entwurf' dated March 11, 1944, and signed by Lippisch himself seems to be the first iteration of the design.

The aircraft shown bears a marked resemblance to the Me 163 B, with a similar swept wing plan form, one-piece bubble canopy and landing skid. It differs from the Me 163 B, however, in having a circular intake directly in front of the pilot's legs rather than a rounded snub nose and in its

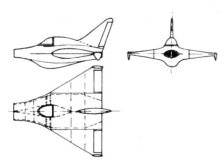

ABOVE: A postwar drawing showing the P 12's final form. Having been chosen by Lippisch himself to represent the P 12 in his own books, and corresponding to the shape of the wartime model, it is presumed that this image is a fairly accurate representation of the wartime design.

having left Messerschmitt almost a year earlier and having spent the intervening time working on twin-jet fast bombers, when it came to designing a ramjet fighter Lippisch went back to what he knew – the familiar form of the Me 163, albeit with a few necessary adjustments. The further development of the P 12 was then necessitated by the needs of its propulsion system – with all of the aircraft's other necessary parts being crammed together in the only apparent space available: sandwiched between the spit intakes.

It is easy, now, to see how the P 13 went on to solve this problem by simply lifting all these parts out of wing entirely and depositing them in a huge central cockpit/ fin that sat on top of, rather than within, the ramjet intake.

Neither the P 12 nor the P 13 would play any role in the Second World War but their unusual forms certainly epitomise the free-thinking attitude of their designer when it came to solving the problems of aircraft design. ●

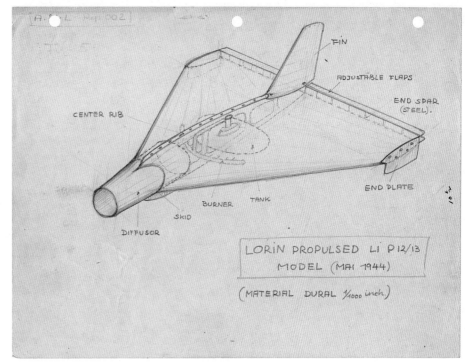

RIGHT: By May 1944 Lippisch was already considering how to free up more space for his ramjet's combustion chamber, as shown by this postwar sketch Lippisch made of a proposed flight test model. IOWA STATE UNIVERSITY LIBRARY SPECIAL COLLECTIONS

BELOW: In profile Lippisch's P 12 I. Entwurf strongly resembles the type's final form, although in planform they were quite different. Artwork by Zoltán Csombó ARTWORK BY ZOLTÁN CSOMBÓ

BOTTOM: The downright weird-looking P 12 II was primarily intended as a solution to an engineering problem – as were many German wartime 'secret projects'. If you need the ramjet's intakes to be as straight and clean as possible, where do you put the cockpit, the guns and the undercarriage? ARTWORK BY ZOLTÁN CSOMBÓ

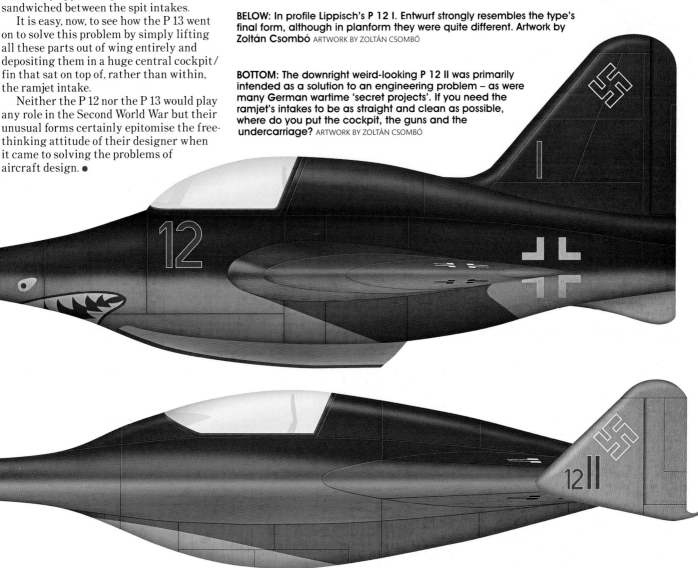

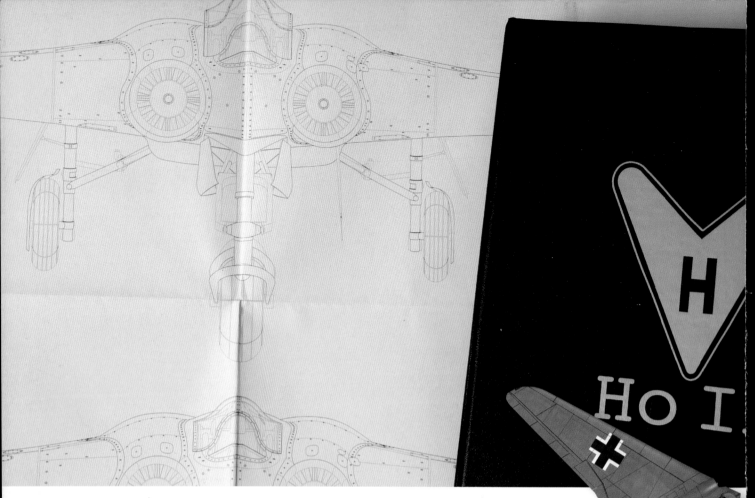